THE CITY

THE CITY

ITS GROWTH

ITS DECAY

ITS FUTURE

ELIEL SAARINEN

THE M. I. T. PRESS

MASSACHUSETTS INSTITUTE OF TECHNOLOGY
CAMBRIDGE, MASSACHUSETTS

FIRST M.I.T. PRESS PAPERBACK EDITION, AUGUST 1965
SECOND PAPERBACK PRINTING, JANUARY 1966

PRINTED IN THE UNITED STATES OF AMERICA

TO MY WIFE

FOREWORD TO FOREWORD

IT might seem almost paradoxical to deal with cultural problems at a time when all of humanity is involved in a struggle of such gigantic proportions as mankind never before has experienced. And no one knows when all this is going to end. On the other hand, there has been put into man's heart an impetus of optimism which even in the darkest of times keeps man dreaming about brighter days to come.

So even now.

In the present endeavor to design a perfect blueprint for the post-war world—and as this endeavor, to a great extent, concerns man's accommodations—there has been much discussion as to what the post-war dwelling must be.

The post-war problem of architectural design, however, is not as simple as the designing of a mere dwelling. Primarily, the post-war problem of architectural design must be the designing of such community environment as could make of the community, and of the dwelling alike, a culturally healthy place in which to live. And due to the fact that, already long before the war-clouds gathered themselves, **one third,** perhaps, of the population of the United States was forced to live in the substandard conditions of more or less decayed communities, the designing of a livable environment for one's dwelling place is by no means a post-war problem, caused by the war situation, but a problem of a fundamental importance, war or no war. This war—once over—however, might help one to realize the obligation of the post-war period to make good the indifference of the pre-war period. Indeed, this is an essential obligation which, in fact, must be a war in itself, and a serious one, too. It must be a war against slums and urban decay. It must be a war against those obsolete and obviously inadequate pre-war methods of town-building which caused the growth of these slums and the urban decay. It must be a "revolution" in order to bring better methods, and better results. But as urban growth is a slow process, this revolution, at best, can and must be turned toward a constructive "evolution": evolution based on the fundamental principles of all town-building, no matter whether in war or peace.

Consequently, in the following analysis of civic problems, I will not consider these problems from the points of view of war or post-war times in particular. That is, I will not consider the problems from a mere emergency angle with temporarily palliative solutions. I will consider them in the light of such principles as can secure results that are both constructive and lasting.

CRANBROOK, 1943

ELIEL SAARINEN

FOREWORD

"TELL me who your friends are, and I will tell you what you are." The implication of this old truth was probably felt long before it became crystallized into a popular proverb. If this truth be carried further, the proverb could be interpreted, thus: "Show me your city, and I will tell you what are the cultural aims of its population." Indeed, the latter saying is equally true with the former.

The city is an open book in which to read aims and ambitions. When it is built in a disorderly manner and the inhabitants are indifferent to its appearance, they automatically reveal this attitude. They are like the unwashed, unshaven, and untidy person who enters a social gathering and makes a poor exhibition of himself. On the other hand, that ambition which produces order in the town will always be honored because of that order.

The population of a city consists of a multitude of individuals, each of whom has an equal obligation to keep the community in order. For this reason it is the duty of everyone to make himself familiar with the problems involved so as to enable him to do his share and also to bring enlightenment to fellow citizens in order that mutual actions could be strengthened and positive results obtained for the benefit of the city. The subject at hand, therefore, concerns not only professional planners and civic authorities, but every dweller in the community. This latter thought must be strongly emphasized because of the fact that in the following analysis we have arrived at the conviction that only little can be accomplished in civic improvement, unless the people of towns and cities themselves, individually and collectively, contribute their positive support.

In the hope that I may be able to contribute toward such public enlightenment, I have written this book. Considering the fact, however, that there exists much published material concerned with professional problems and practical technicalities in town-building, but that there exists almost nothing of such material as would deal with the subject from the layman's standpoint, I have deemed it wise to write this book in a manner understandable even to the non-professional. Accordingly I have endeavored to present the subject as an analytical story of the urban community; how this community during historic times has been born, has grown, has aged, and then decayed; and why all this has happened. I have furthermore endeavored to find the proper remedies so as to be able to both restore and preserve health in the diseased urban body. In other words, **I have endeavored to explain the physical order of the urban community much in the same manner as one understands organic order in any living organism.**

My primary aim has been to discover the fundamentals of all town-building, in order that these fundamentals may be adapted to existing conditions and a strong foundation may be built for days to come. For this reason, past experiences in town-building have been explained only insofar as they clarify these fundamentals.

I have tried to visualize the city's gradual evolution toward the city to come, always retaining the human and livable side of the problem as the leading theme. That is, I have endeavored to picture the city of the future as the home city of the population in the same spirit as a house must be made the home of the family, if it is to be livable and socially constructive.

Because the problems of a modern city—due to a rapid

evolution of conditions—are in a state of transition, it is impossible to answer all questions in a mode that would meet general approval. The following pages, consequently, must be regarded as a personal analysis, digested through direct experience during a long period of time, and concerning just that period of time which has brought forth revolutionary changes, changes which in many respects still are nebulous. For this reason, much opposition to many of the thoughts expressed in this analysis can be expected. Yet, this opposition might cause discussion, perhaps growing interest, and enlightenment.

If such be the case, my efforts then have not been in vain.

CRANBROOK, 1942

ELIEL SAARINEN

CONTENTS

ILLUSTRATIONS

INTRODUCTION

INTRODUCTION

IT IS an acknowledged fact that the civilized world is now passing through a time of vivid transition. Intense efforts are being made in every country to bring the shattered social structure into order. Something new and constructive must be born to save our culture from destruction. But no lasting results can be had unless one particular problem, fundamental indeed, is properly solved: that people be provided with both satisfactory accommodations and healthful environments in which to live and work. It must be borne in mind that the family and its home are the corner-stones of society, and that man's physical and mental development depend largely upon the character of the environment in which he is nurtured as a child, where he spends his manhood, and where he does his work. The more home and environment elevate man—individually and collectively—to candor of living and sincerity of work, the better can society be prepared for a social order that will be lasting.

Because a large percentage of the nation dwells in urban communities, these communities must be formed or reformed into homes and healthy environments, both physically and spiritually. This means that planning of towns is concerned with problems of supreme importance in the life of the urban population—nay, in the life of the whole nation—for, inasmuch as even the rural dweller is in frequent direct or indirect contact with towns and cities, civic problems involve not only those living in urban communities, but everyone, no matter where his habitat may be. The character of towns and cities is for this reason bound to have significant effects on the general condition of the whole country.

1

As matters are today, these effects are both positive and negative. On which side the balance will tilt in the weighing of opposite effects one against the other depends on respective conditions, more or less different in each individual case. Most cities have slums and blighted sections, actual or doomed areas of dilapidation and obsolescence, where crime and vice of all kinds flourish. It is obvious that things are not as they should be, and that the social and physical organization of the cities has been unsatisfactorily conducted. This is particularly the case in the large cities. Alas, in these large cities the case is true to such a degree that a gradual decentralization of the overgrown cities must be regarded as a problem of vital importance. Real need for improvements therefore exists, and an investigation of all pertinent matters is urgent.

The usual halfway remedies, however, do not suffice for civic improvements. The civic disease must be examined to its deepest roots, for only in this manner can lasting results be had. To begin with, we must accept an old and obvious maxim: "The primary purpose of the city is to provide adequate living and working accommodations for its population." The more efficiently this is accomplished, and the more each inhabitant personally derives maximum benefit from these provisions to raise his material and cultural standard, the better does the city meet its primary purpose.

Fundamentally, as we see, the civic problems are of humanitarian nature. Therefore, it is clear that the city's improvement and further development must be started with the problems of homes and their environments, and not—as is usually the case—with plazas, boulevards, monumental lay-outs, and other showy things. In other words, we are not confronted with problems where superficial embellishment is the deciding factor, but with problems where the paramount issue must be the city's inner organization so as to create homes for the population. In these homes the seeds of satisfactory living and healthy environment must be planted, and must grow to transform the whole city's physical organization

2

into a like spirit of satisfactory living and healthy environment.

The chief concern of the following analysis is to learn how such a comprehensive task can be accomplished. To that end we must first of all have a clear conception of this task, so that we may be able to select such methods and means as could bring about the desired result.

A. THE SOCIOLOGICAL PROBLEM

Because the city must be formed into an appropriate place in which to live, human considerations have a dominant position in this formation. Physical dispositions must be adjusted accordingly. Man is the master: physical dispositions are to serve him.

The first step, therefore, must be to undertake an inclusive social research according to which the physical organization of the city can be developed. This social research must not only precede the physical organization, it must also continue to function parallel and together with this organization; which means that the said social research must constitute a permanent institution in connection with the planning work. Yet, because it has to deal with social conditions primarily in urban communities and for a special purpose, this kind of social research is a special social science in itself which must therefore be conducted by corresponding authorities, and, of course, in a workable co-operation with the physical organization.

One point which closely concerns the physical organization of the city must be emphasized in connection with this social problem. It must namely be borne in mind that whatever is considered to be best for man, from the point of view of inner cultural growth, must be established as the governing principle in the shaping of a healthy urban environment. Therefore, when speaking about adequate living and working conditions in the city, adequate conditions must be understood to be of both material and spiritual nature; where the material, being the necessary means of physical life, must support the spiritual. Both require adequate consideration. In order to be able to direct the city's development according to these considerations, it is necessary to eliminate those circumstances which in one way or another are likely to make of the city an anti-cultural rather than a cultural achievement. These circumstances, whether unethical, non-esthetic, or speculative by nature, must be fought with full vigor.

The city's social problem is a delicate one insofar as fully satisfactory results are uncertain. No matter how carefully the road is paved for cultural possibilities, anti-cultural tendencies always will creep in. History testifies that whenever people have been brought together and communities have been formed, both the positive and negative qualities of human nature have found their pasture grounds in these communities. This is a logical consequence of the dual characteristics of human nature. In view of this fact, it is even more essential that the city's physical form-order be developed into such a quality as can foster culturally constructive aspirations. With regard to this it must be observed—and so we will learn later on—that honest and creative architecture, just as much as honest and creative art in general, has a culturally constructive influence upon the human mind. This, then, means that **the city's "form-order" and "social order" cannot be separated: they must be developed hand-in-hand, reciprocally inspiring one another.**

In this spirit of reciprocal inspiration between the physical order and the social order must civic problems be solved, and so must be the leading thought throughout the whole urban development. Accordingly, the more an honest and creative form of modest simplicity is given the chance to permeate homes and their environments, the more will the planning of towns be animated by this leading thought. Indeed, the housing problems must be solved with this in mind.

Generally speaking, the housing problems are mass-problems in the sense that they concern a large number of people as equal individuals. This does not mean that the population must or should be regarded as a mere mass of people, and treated accordingly. On the contrary, the population must be conceived as a group of individuals, and with this in mind it is important to emphasize the fact that good individuals form good masses. Individuality does not mean, as is believed in many circles, that an individual should necessarily be disposed toward egotistic independence—toward rugged individualism—and that satisfactory co-operation is therefore difficult. Individuality means, and must mean, that the individual should realize the value of co-operation, and intelligently support those actions which result from constructive thought.

Civilization produces mass actions. Cultural movements originate from individual mental growth. **The greater the number of those having opportunity to become culturally influenced in the city's atmosphere, the stronger and the more lasting the social order in the city will be.**

B. THE PHYSICAL PROBLEM

The city's physical problem is for the city to be developed and maintained in a good physical order. Particularly in circumstances where the city has strayed from an orderly course and decay has entered—and such circumstances are our main concern—the physical problem is a gigantic task which cannot be accomplished in a short time. For sure, it must be a long and continuous process of rehabilitation work, for this reason calling for an immediate start. But, important as this immediate start may be, it is equally important to direct the work into the right channels from the first inception.

Now, it seems to be a matter of opinion what these right channels should be. Adequate organization has evidently not been sufficiently experienced in the cities, for most of the results reflect inadequacy of methods and means. As these methods and means have been many and different, it indicates that there exists a wide divergence of opinion. In fact, as matters stand, a unanimous decision cannot be had, for we are confronted with a multiplicity of ideas, conservative and progressive, stylistic and coldly technical. Obviously, it is difficult to arrive at an agreement on the right course.

Considering that we are not facing merely occasional demands for civic development or rehabilitation, but that the demand is widespread, it is of great importance that a basic thought be found according to which order really could be brought into towns and cities. This does not mean, however, that our ambition is to discover something of our own. We are not going to discover something of our own: on the contrary—as will be made clear during the course of this analysis —whatever the accepted approach to new methods may be, it must be founded on that same basic thought through which olden times—the classical and mediaeval, for example— achieved physical order in their towns. During the course of our analysis it will be furthermore demonstrated that the fundamental principles of the classical and mediaeval eras must be accepted even by our time; and it will be demonstrated that **just the fact that these principles have been discarded or forgotten is the real cause of the present day disorder in towns and cities.**

Although it is not our intention at this moment to go deeper into the matter of old methods and their principles, we will mention that, generally speaking, the chief difference between the methods of olden times and the prevailing method of yesterday and today is that the former—the classical and mediaeval—resulted in expressive design and coherent physical order, whereas the urban developments of yesterday and today have mostly been dealing with matters of practical and technical nature.

Really, as things have been to a great extent, the physical

development of towns and cities has been in the hands of the purely technically-minded town-planner. Evidently the problem has been beyond him, for town-planning, as we have found, has been far from satisfactorily conducted. Were we to go into the subject more deeply, we would find that the logical relationship between cause and effect is true even in the planner's case. No outcome could have been expected other than the general disorganization of the growing cities of today, for town-planning has been too narrowly limited to foster better results. In many quarters, town-planning has been regarded as a mere technical problem, to be solved by bringing practical issues into the foreground and by neglecting those that are spiritually important. Because town-planning has so often been degraded to superficial practice, with time it has become surrounded by an aureole of insipidity. Consequently, this kind of practical town-planning cannot satisfactorily answer the question, "How should the physical problems of towns and cities be solved." More thorough-going must the aim be, considering all the civic problems involved.

It is necessary to draw a distinct border line between the superficial understanding of town-planning and the thorough-going organization of civic problems at large. This is necessary, not because we need be particular about appellations, but rather because during the course of this analysis we will often have reason to compare the mentioned two modes of procedure: on the one hand, the two-dimensional planning of towns; on the other, the three-dimensional building of towns. More briefly, town-planning versus town-building. Now, town-planning considers—as generally has become its matter-of-course practice—street lay-outs, traffic and sanitary problems, land-use with more or less generalized zoning, and so on; and, as said, all this has been instituted from a mere practical and technical point of view. Proper town-building, on the other hand, must consider all the problems of the urban community—physical, social, cultural, and esthetic—

and bring them gradually and during a long period of time into coherent physical order. Such a gradual organization of the town must happen in accordance with a continuous, flexible, and dynamic design-process, so as to keep the formation of the physical town always on an up-to-date level with the changing conditions of life. This continuous, flexible, and dynamic design-process we may call "town-design," "civic design," "urban design," or whatever your preference may be —it does not matter, for the main thing is that during our analysis a clear distinction is maintained between this kind of comprehensive design toward organic and three-dimensional town-building, and the usual and superficial two-dimensional planning.

The following investigation, therefore, will consider the characteristics and problems of town-building, in contrast with those of the usual conception of town-planning. The first step toward such an investigation is to discover those principles on which town-building must be founded.

C. PRINCIPLES OF TOWN-BUILDING

In the search for principles, we should not be satisfied with such principles as have only local and limited bearing, or are mere man-made doctrines and theories. Our endeavor must be to discern those principles which are inherent in the nature of things from time immemorial, and are valid in any circumstance. Therefore, in order to approach our problem from the right angle, it is important to go down to the mother of things, to nature, so that we may find there such processes as can be considered analogous to the process of town-building. Now, the process of town-building—by means of town-design—must be to bring organic order into the urban communities, and to keep this organic order continuously vital during the growth of these communities. Fundamentally, also, this process is analogous to the growth of any living organism in nature, and, inasmuch as there is no difference of underlying principles between one living organism and any other, we would do well to study these principles in organic life in general. In doing so, we find ourselves in much the same position as a doctor, who, to be able to maintain organic functioning in the human body, must be familiar with organic processes in general. Analogously, we must learn to understand these general organic processes so that we may be able to maintain order in the city's physical organism. For sure, we must learn a lesson of basic consequence.

Therefore, let's for a moment dwell in the realm of nature, and see what the microscope is able to reveal. Not much manipulation, however, is needed with the microscope to discern in organic life two phenomena; **the existence of individual cells, and the correlation of these cells into cellular tissue.** In itself, this relevation might seem an insignificant matter, yet it is amazing to learn that the whole universe, from the most microscopic to the utmost macroscopic, is constituted along this dual thought of individuals as such and of the correlation of these individuals into the whole. Furthermore one learns that vitality in all life manifestation depends, first, on **the quality of the individual** and, second, on **the quality of correlation.** Consequently, there must exist two fundamental principles according to which these two mentioned qualities are constituted so as to foster and maintain vitality in the course of things. In fact, by a closer study of natural processes we will perceive two fundamental principles, "Expression" and "Correlation," **of which the former principle brings individual form-shapings into true expression of the meaning behind these forms, and of which the latter brings the individual forms into organic correlation.**

1. The Principle of Expression:

Supposing one could follow the seed's gradual growth into a tree, and that this could be done every moment in every part

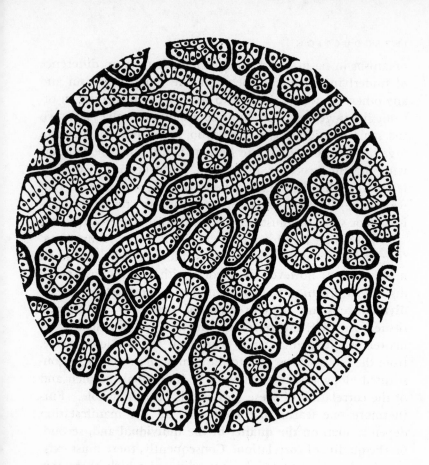

Fig. 1.

Healthy Cell Tissue: Microscopic
"community planning."

of the organism. One then would observe billions and again billions of ever-new patterns of cell-tissue; all emerging from one another according to inherent potentiality, all tuned in a key that is characteristic of the species concerned, and all organized into symbolic design representing that very species. Furthermore, supposing one were to follow the above processes along two different lines—say, along the growths of an elm and an oak, respectively—one then would discern two different worlds of form-pattern, respectively characterizing the two tree-species, and running throughout the two modes of growth, in the inner cell-structures as well as in the design of trunks, branches, and foliages. In other words, one would discover two different rhythm-worlds; one of the elm and only of the elm, the other of the oak and only of the oak. And so evident is the difference of these two rhythm-worlds, that already at a distance one is able to differentiate between elms and oaks, because of expressive rhythm characters.

It is fully obvious that these expressive rhythm characters are innate potentialities already in the respective seeds of elms and oaks, and that from these latter the said potentialities are conveyed to every single cell throughout the respective organisms. In this manner, every single cell throughout these organisms becomes an expressive exponent of the species it belongs to. Speaking in general terms, this is a statement which does not concern only elms and oaks or any other species of organic life, but nature's form-manifestations at large. That is, **any form-manifestation in nature is a true expression of the meaning behind this form-manifestation; and this is a rule from which there is no exception in all the universe. It is a principle: the said principle of expression.**

Man belongs to the realm of creation and is subject to the principle of expression. Therefore, whatever forms man brings forth through his endeavor and work, if honest, must be true expressions of his life, emotions, thoughts, and aspirations. Man's art, at best, is a significant testimony in this respect, for, by studying the various form-worlds of the great cultural epochs of the past, we do find that each of these great epochs had its own form characteristics through which the best characteristics of its time and people came into expression. This expressiveness, however, did not concern only these great epochs as such, but it concerned even each individual form-detail that was created within the framework of these epochs. Accordingly, even the most inconspicuous objects—the "cells" so to speak—can tell their true story through the expressiveness of their shapes. Take for instance the story of that humble chair. During thousands of years there have been made millions and more millions of chairs, yet you may select one of these quite at random—except for those that stupid and pernicious imitation has brought forth —and you can trace its origin to time and people. The truer this chair expresses the best of its time and people, the more it possesses those qualities that could further the growth of that cultural tree of its epoch. And the more there were of those forms which possessed similar expressive qualities, the stronger the expressive formation of that cultural tree was able to grow.

What is true about chairs and other minor objects must be so much the more true about more important features such as, for example, individual buildings. Now, individual buildings are just those "cells" which constitute the major material through which towns and cities are built. Therefore, bringing now our original question as to the quality of the individual—in this case, the individual building—to an issue, the answer is close at hand; namely, that in urban communities the quality of the individual building, no matter how humble, must be a true expression of the best of its people and time. This is an answer which is based on the principle of expression. The demand of this principle is a directive from which there can be no exemption if the aim is to achieve positive results. For, in case the principle of expression is disregarded—as it so often is by those who erect all kinds of trashy buildings—**the consequences in the city's case are** bound to be as devitalizing as they would be in the case of the tree, if false cells were brought into its cellular tissue.

2. The Principle of Correlation:

Turning now our attention to the matter of correlation as it appears in nature's manifestations, we will find an enlightening example in the landscape, when looking through micro-analytical lenses.

There are myriads of cells which capriciously, though in reciprocal action, shape the tree into a manifest species. Thousands of these species, because of an enigmatic leaning to coherence, are formed into the concerted unity of the forest. There are myriads of molecules which, although of millions of varieties, constitute, in mutual co-operation, mountains, cliffs, valleys and lakes. There are myriads of particles which, independent of one another yet in instinctive unison, form congruous mass-effects of clouds. There are myriads of molecules which individually, yet in constant adherence, break the rays of the dawning sun into light and shadow and into the brilliancy of a rich variety of color. All these myriads of molecular particles in trees, mountains, cliffs, lakes, and skies—and in countless other things—are brought into a single picture of rhythmic order: into the landscape.

Now, is there anything supernatural in all this?

Certainly not. It is just as natural a thing as it could be, because we are used to such manifestations, and because we do not seem to harbor for a single moment the thought that, if nature in her actions were not governed by the principle of correlation, cosmos would dissolve into chaos. This kind of harmonious condition in nature has come to us as a heavenly gift in such a direct manner that we scarcely have felt our own obligation to keep our environment in order in a like harmonious manner. But we must learn to understand our obligations in this respect. Particularly in the building of cities, we must learn to understand that, **it would prove just as disastrous to the city, if the principle of correlation did not exist, as it would prove to the landscape—to the "city of nature"—if the same principle should cease to function.**

Many are scarcely conscious of the significative meaning of correlation, although subconsciously they might act in accordance with its command. Take, for example, just such a little detail from everyday life as the arranging of a few flowers in one's room. One might pick a number of these flowers in order to have a greater effect, yet automatically one assorts the flowers into a rhythmic bouquet, and into a pleasing correlation with the miscellaneous features of the room. How well this is done depends on one's subconscious sensitiveness to the principle of correlation.

In cases where sensitiveness to the principle of correlation is alert, the correlative effects are carried throughout the whole field of action, from the room to streets and plazas and to the towns and cities at large. Such was the case in olden times when the creative impetus was still strong and principles were in command. Whoever, if he were sensitive, has traveled in those countries where towns were built in ancient times has no doubt felt that correlation is not an empty esthetic theory. He has felt that any group of buildings, in the country or in the town, was conceived as a rhythmic ensemble of forms of man and forms of nature. He has felt that any street or plaza was made a correlative product of many artists in accord. He has felt that any town, with all its various and varying units, was made an organism of masses and proportions where the rhythmic characteristics of building groups and skyline sprang from the characteristics of the time and the people. He has felt that the proper correlation of forms was consistently carried through the whole organism, beginning with the minor things in the rooms and residences and ending with the highest pinnacles of towers and turrets. He has felt that all this happened "once upon a time."

All this happened until man thought he was intelligent enough to get along with his practical reasoning only. Proud of his expedient practicality, he accumulated forms upon forms without proper correlation of forms. And his towns and cities became often a heterogeneous accumulation of forms. The principle of correlation was entirely forgotten.

3. The Principle of Organic Order:

When speaking about expressive and correlative tendencies in nature's form-shaping, it is obvious that these tendencies are not independent trends, but two phases of the same process; namely, of the process toward organic order. In other words, the principles of expression and correlation are not independently functioning principles, but rather daughter-principles of that all-governing mother-principle of "organic order"—which, in fact, is the very principle of architecture in the universe. According to this principle of architecture, nature's manifestations are carried out and kept in function. As long as this is the case, and the expressive and correlative faculties are potent enough to maintain organic order, there is life and progress of life. Again, as soon as this ceases to be the case, and the expressive and correlative faculties are impotent to prevent disintegration of organic order, decline and death enters. **This is true, no matter whether it happens in the microscopic tissues of cell-structure where cancer causes disintegration, or in the hearts of the large cities of today where compactness and confusion cause slums to spread.**

These facts are open to all eyes and minds to see and to comprehend. Only a short glance through the microscope is enough to convince that organic cell-tissue means life and health, whereas disintegration of cell-tissue means sickness and death. Really, our normal senses, if not actual reasoning, have accustomed us to this simple truth. We understand organic life in nature as a manifestation of rhythmic order, and whenever we find exceptions from that order—in plants,

15

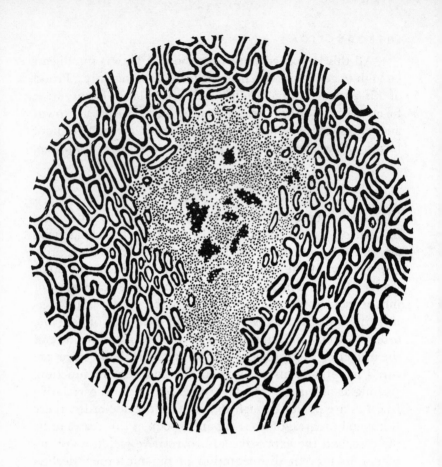

Fig. 2.

Disintegrating cell tissue: Microscopic "slum growth."

in trees, in animal bodies, and in man—we realize that sickness has crept into the organism. And we are conscious of the fact that this sickness is contagious and tends to spread itself, if preventive provisions have not been made.

In spite of this simple truth—open to all eyes and comprehensible to all minds—its consequences, insofar as civic development is concerned, are astonishingly much disregarded. Not only are slums spreading themselves because of previous thoughtless planning, but even new cities, towns, suburbs, and satellite communities are planned in the same slum-breeding manner. This kind of procedure brings conditions from bad to worse, for, instead of decreasing the evils of poor planning, continuous poor planning increases the evils. It is not too early, therefore, to take these matters seriously into consideration, in order to learn what to do, how to do, and how not to do. With regard to this, the understanding of fundamental principles as they have been described is of supreme importance.

In the light of these fundamental principles one can follow the development of towns and cities during the past, and one is able to understand the basic reasons why these developments were successful or unsuccessful. Successful results sprang from an instinctive awareness of these principles, whereas unsuccessful outcomes were due to a lack of this sense. For this reason, when the question arises as to why the towns and cities of today are so frequently heterogeneous and discordant, the answer can be found in the fact that these principles have been forgotten, or unperceived. Again, when it is asked how the growth of towns and cities can be conducted toward greater expressiveness and better unity, the answer is, and must be, **that this can be achieved only when the town designers**—and all the co-operating designers and architects for that matter—**have absorbed the meaning of these principles into the very blood of their veins.**

D. THE ARCHITECTURAL MOMENT

Because the principle of organic order is the underlying law of nature's architecture, the same principle must be recognized as the underlying law of man's architecture as well. Such is the case when the art of building is correctly understood. Architecture is not—as many have believed during the long period of its gradual decline—a stylistic decoration which can be arbitrarily pasted on the surface of a structure. Architecture must be definitely understood as an organic and social art-form with the mission of creating about man a culturally healthy atmosphere by means of proportion, rhythm, material, and color. As such, architecture embraces the whole form-world of man's physical accommodations, from the intimacy of his room to the comprehensive labyrinth of the large metropolis. Within this broad field of creative activities, the architect's ambition must be to develop a form language expressing the **best** aims of **his time**—and of no other time—and to cement the various features of his expressive forms into a good interrelation, and ultimately into the rhythmic coherence of the multiformed organism of the city.

When the architects are corporately sincere in their profession and are acting in accordance with the thoughts outlined above, then—and only then—can town and city be made a healthy place in which to live. **Just as any living organism can be healthy only when that organism is a product of nature's art in accordance with the basic principles of nature's architecture, exactly for the same reason town or city can be healthy**—physically, spiritually, and culturally—**only when it is developed into a product of man's art in accordance with the basic principles of man's architecture.** Surely, this must be accepted as the fundamental secret of all town-building.

Although the architectural nature of all town building is fully logical and scarcely disputable, there is, as things stand at present, much reason for stressing this fact. In earlier days when senses were alert and principles were in the blood, town-building matters were automatically solved along architectural lines. Later on when a divorce took place between architecture and town-planning—which deplorable episode will be described in the course of the following analysis—the architectural profession became involved in stylistic escapades, whereas the development of towns was left to the mercy of the surveyor. Since then, generally speaking, town-building has been regarded as a practical matter-of-course in terms of two-dimensional planning—and so long has this mode of procedure already lasted that it has become a rigid tradition.

It is against this rigid tradition—because of its dissatisfactory results—that we must fight. Although this fight will not be openly declared, the undertone of the whole analysis to follow will breathe the spirit of this fight.

E. SYNOPSIS

This introduction aims to explain the nature of our subject. It aims, furthermore, to stress those points as are essential in the solution of town building problems. It is highly important to have these points clear in our minds, before we attempt anything constructive for civic improvement and development. Let us therefore recapitulate these points, and by doing so, still more emphasize their significance.

First, we stressed the importance of adequate town-building from the point of view of the whole nation's welfare, material and cultural.

Second, we made it clear that social research is a necessary background for civic improvement and development. This social research, it was said, must constitute a permanent institution so as to fertilize the city's continuous development in a socially constructive spirit. The cultural phase of this social problem was particularly stressed. It was said that whatever is considered the best for man, from the point of view of inner cultural growth, must be established as the governing principle in the shaping of a healthy environment.

Third, we emphasized that any civic improvement and development must happen in accordance with appropriate means and methods. With regard to this, superficial town-planning was found lacking, because neither has it the right approach nor can it show satisfactory results: more thorough-going and dynamic town-building—by means of town-design —had best take its place.

Fourth, we found it mandatory that fundamental principles should be followed in all town-building, for only this guarantees satisfactory solutions and lasting results. These fundamental principles, we found, are the principles of expression, correlation, and organic order; of which the last is the all-governing mother principle and the fundamental principle of architecture in all creation.

Fifth, the architectural nature of town-building was emphasized, particularly stressing the fact that only when town or city is a product of human art can it be physically, spiritually, and culturally healthy. In other words, the architectural aspect of town or city inevitably mirrors the social status within that town or city as well as the cultural ambitions of the population. Consequently, any investigation of town-building matters, to be accurate and significant, must be essentially an investigation of architectural standards.

These mentioned points have a universal application, no matter whether one considers the past, the present, or the trend toward the future. In the past—in the classical and mediaeval days for example—these points were subconsciously applied in the building of towns. Later on, on the other hand, such subconscious sensing has not been sufficiently alert and it is therefore necessary to make these points consciously clear. This is important in our case in particular, as we are concerned with the city of today and with its further development toward the future in a constructive manner.

The past is not our concern. Nevertheless, if thoughts and actions of our forefathers occupy us in the following analysis for some length of time, it is only because of their important educational value for present and future thoughts and actions. Consequently, the course of our analysis will follow two different directions, one of the past for educational purposes, and the other toward the future for applicatory purposes. Accordingly, this analysis will be divided into two main parts: "The Past," and "Toward the Future."

In the first part—The Past—our analysis will deal with town-building problems during those times when principles still guided in the development of towns. Inasmuch as the mediaeval age is more or less our direct ancestor in town formation—and because our intention is not to present a comprehensive historical account of town-building matters in general—we deem it unnecessary to go farther back in time than to the mediaeval case. In the study of this mediaeval case, our main aim will be to search for those causes which brought strength to the mediaeval town, in order that we may learn from these causes **how to conduct contemporary civic processes toward strength, and how to prevent decline.**

Our further investigations—in this first part—will concern the general civic decline which took place during the course of the nineteenth century. Through this investigation we will learn that those properties which in the mediaeval case brought strength to the town had gradually, during the intervening centuries, lost their vitality until they were ultimately unable to maintain organic coherence in the town's physical formation. Decline was the logical consequence of this. This decline had two phases which reciprocally influenced one another: first, **the former creative impetus of architecture waned to noncreative imitation;** and second, **public interest in town-building matters changed into indolence and poor taste.** Because of this dual decline, the art of town-building ceased to exist as an art-form worth the name, and prosaic town-planning took its place.

In due time this fatal situation was understood in some circles, and certain movements for urban improvement appeared. These movements followed two different directions of thought, the "stylistic" and the "organic," and they will be analyzed separately as to their respective characteristics and merits. The former of these movements will be found too superficial to constitute a foundation for satisfactory town-building. The latter movement, on the other hand—because it endeavored to discern fundamental principles—will be found constructive in its influence and, therefore, it will be recommended as a proper foundation for all future town-building. With this recommendation the first part of our analysis will come to an end.

The most important harvest from this first part of our analysis will be the essential fact that the fundamental reason for success or failure in all town-building depends on **whether or not town formation is based on the architectural principle of organic order. This,** we will find, **is not only an essential fact, but also an imperative one.** Consequently, when we—in the second part of our analysis—come to investigate contemporary and future town-building problems exclusively, we are going to do it with the presupposition that, behold: **any problem must be solved so as to bring the physical formation of the town into accord with this architectural principle of organic order.**

Yet, behold even the following:

While studying contemporary and future town-building problems, we will soon discover that the imperativeness of this architectural principle of organic order is **almost the only lesson that past experiences in town building can teach us. In almost all the other phases of town-building we are confronted with problems so entirely new, so completely reversed, and so utterly absent from the experience of any previous** era as to make a thoroughly new orientation most urgent. Indeed, as radical a change in the means of transportation as we have witnessed during these days of technical progress calls for a correspondingly radical change in the mode of approach to town-planning problems. And this changed mode of approach can be found **"only in and through" present and future conditions of life.**

As for this changed mode of approach, we can already now discern a strong tendency from the present concentration toward a decentralization to come. There is much evidence that the wave of the cities' rapid growth and increased concentration has been met by a counter-wave of decentralization, bringing into existence suburbs, satellite towns, neighbor communities, and all sorts of miscellaneous settlements about the core of the original concentration.

Concentration and decentralization are two opposite poles. Opposite are even their reasons for existence. This means that, once the reasons for concentration are known, it is a matter of simple logic to draw one's conclusions as to the reasons for decentralization. Consequently, our analysis in this second part will deal with the problems of concentration before we undertake to investigate those forces which make decentralization a logical necessity. Through this analysis we will learn that concentration in the overgrown cities has caused compactness and disorder and, through these, deterioration and the spread of slums. Furthermore, we will learn that the only remedy in such circumstances is a decisive surgery which can bring openness into the compact urban situation, and which—if executed gradually according to an organically comprehensive scheme—is the surest road toward decentralization, or rather, toward "organic decentralization."

"Organic decentralization" must be the key-word, and it must be the leading theme throughout our whole analysis of modern problems. So it must be, **for only through an organic solution of the problems of decentralization can organic order be brought into the city and made lastingly effective.** This procedure toward organic decentralization, however, has too many angles to be fully explained in this short synopsis. We will mention only a few essential points of view.

The endeavor of organic decentralization must be to achieve those aims that were found fundamental in all good town-building. Accordingly, organic decentralization must first of all satisfy the old and obvious maxim that "the primary purpose of the city is to provide adequate living and working accommodations for its population," and this must happen to such an extent and in such a spirit as was set at the beginning of this introduction. However, to metamorphose the overgrown, compact, and disorderly city, with its dilapidated areas and slums, into this kind of idealistic state, cannot be done in short order. It calls for vision. It calls for openminded decision. And it calls for a long period of time, during which the compact urban body must be transformed, through a gradual evolution, into a group of individual communities separated from one another by a protective belt-system of green land. During this gradual evolution, the mission of organic decentralization must be to produce new values by changing rural land into urban land, to rehabilitate decayed values by proper replanning, to bring all values to normal level and to protect all values, old and new, for times to come. How all this should best happen will be described in our analysis of organic decentralization.

It is obvious that during this analysis of organic decentralization many new problems will arise. Many of these are perhaps of such a radical character as to make their solution seem impossible. This is true particularly concerning those problems that are of economic and legislative nature—which is nothing exceptional, for, in all town-planning, economic values and legislative stipulations constitute the chief obstacles in the progress of civic improvement. On the other hand, organic decentralization is not concerned particularly with matters of today, but with the progress of matters toward the future. Accordingly, organic decentralization recognizes the fact that those economic values and legislative stipulations which are of today are not necessarily the same as will be those of a few decades hence. To be sure, things are bound to change during as vivid a time of transition as the present time really is. In other words, organic decentralization does not consider the land values and civic legislation of that old order of static concentration: it considers revaluation of existing urban values and necessary legislative changes according to its own dynamic order. And the new values and legislative stipulations must emerge from this organic decentralization itself, during its progress.

The economic and legislative issue will be scrutinized in the chapters "Revaluation" and "Relegislation," respectively. In the former case, we will suggest a system of transference of property rights, and thus transference of land-use values. In the latter case, we will recommend certain changes in the existing civic legislation.

Furthermore, in the closing chapter of this second part of our analysis, we are going to investigate to what extent the urban population influences the development and character of towns and cities. We will find through this investigation that in olden times there was an intimate although perhaps subconscious understanding between the people of the town and those who built the town; whereas the present-day urban population, generally speaking, is rather indifferent to town-building problems and must therefore be enlightened. This enlightening, we will maintain, is the problem of the architectural profession, for the architects have in their hands the means and methods to show how towns and cities must be built. It is up to architectural education, we conclude, to educate architects toward such an end and, therefore, first of all to investigate whether or not the prevailing educational methods are appropriate in this respect.

And finally, in the "Epilogue," we are going to examine that driving motor which originates organic decentralization and directs the course of its motion: town-design—or civic design, if you please. It goes without saying that, during the transition process from static concentration to dynamic decentralization, the mode of town-design has been greatly altered as to both approach and technique. This makes it necessary to investigate the characteristics of town-design in general. Moreover, this makes it necessary to investigate the qualifications of those behind the design work, **for we consider it of supreme importance that organic decentralization be conducted by such minds as have vision, and are able to bring things into such order as is in accord with the fundamental principles of architecture.**

This, in short, will be the content of the following analysis. We thought it wise to present, so to speak, a "preview of our performance," so that the reader may get in advance a logical conception of the course of our reasoning. It will, perhaps, enable him better to follow the direction of our thought, when he has in advance a certain knowledge of where it is going to lead. Perhaps in this manner he will find it easier to build up a critical opinion of his own during the progress of his reading.

As the reader will learn, the following analysis is not going to be so complete as to cover all the phases of town-building. Our ambition will be only **to stress the present unhappy situation in urban conditions, to emphasize the urgent demand for remedies, to explain what these remedies are, and to advise how these remedies must be used.** We have done this to our best knowledge of these matters—and **in concert with our conviction.**

PART ONE:

THE PAST

1. THE MEDIAEVAL CASE

THE following study of the past is not going to be comprehensive. Nor will it consider historical dates or technical facts of town-building matters from bygone times. It will constitute no more than a short search for the causes of civic strength and decline during the course of time, in order that we shall learn from these causes how to conduct contemporary civic processes toward strength, and how to prevent decline. This was already indicated in the foregoing Synopsis.

In this Synopsis it was furthermore indicated that there is no need for going farther back in time than to the Middle Ages, as the mediaeval town is a direct ancestor of the present-day city. In the intervening centuries, the mediaeval town-type has gone through many alterations. It has been formed and reformed to meet changing conditions. During this process, the typical make-up of the mediaeval town—adequate to the demands of its time—has given rise to many preconceived ideas which have lingered on, much to the harm of sound development. By contrast, many of the virtues of the towns of the past, fundamentally significant of any age, have been slighted, or forgotten.

Considering town problems of the past, it is of weight to bear in mind that, from the days of the Middle Ages up to the beginning of the past century—and even much beyond that time—the process of town development was a slow process. Excluding exceptional developments such as palaces, parks, and monumental lay-outs for one purpose or another, the main body of the town grew in a very gradual tempo and in the same spirit of concentration as was the case in earlier days. This lasting concentrated state of things has created in many minds the preconceived idea that a town, already by its nature of being a town, must be a compact body, no matter what the circumstances of life may be. Although we now, due to changed conditions of life, have freed ourselves to a great extent from this idea of extreme concentration, its shadow still haunts us as a hampering thought—a thought which seems difficult to subdue.

This hampering thought of concentration is perhaps the only inheritance from the mediaeval era which still influences town-building of today. In all other respects, we look upon the mediaeval town as something extremely antiquated. Its labyrinth of narrow streets and dark dwellings, so it is understood, has nothing in common with present day demands for comfortable living. When the town of that period sometimes is referred to as a good example of physical order from which to learn, then this reaction is rather common: "What, should we step down from our sunny chambers and airy quarters into that dark and damp atmosphere? Certainly not!" And it is generally believed, particularly in technically minded circles, that this type of town has nothing to teach the present-day town-builder.

Superficially looking upon things, this belief is understandable: for surely, a direct adoption of the mediaeval mode of building towns were utterly unfortunate and unfitting for our age. But going deeper into the matter—into the inner meaning behind the outer forms—the situation is quite different. In the preceding introductory chapter it was mentioned that the mediaeval town—the classical as well—was built according to such principles as must be considered fundamental of all town-building and of all time. And it was emphasized that, just because our age has discarded or forgotten these principles, there is much of disorder in present day towns and cities. Considering a statement of such momentous consequences, we cannot leave the mediaeval case just by a shrug of the shoulders. We must examine the mediaeval status as to its qualities so that we may find which of these qualities have come down to us as mere preconceived ideas, and which are virtues from time immemorial. For indeed, it is necessary to free the modern city from the hindering load of preconceived ideas, and to bring into light the fundamental virtues of town-building. With this in mind we must undertake an investigation of the mediaeval town.

It goes without saying that the mediaeval town was not fully an ideal place in which to live, and, to prove this, many and perfectly valid objections could be mentioned. But inasmuch as the following investigation does not intend to be an all-sided analysis of the mediaeval case, there is no need for bringing all such points, negative or otherwise unacceptable, into our discussion. We will touch only such phases as can bring light into the civic problems of today.

On the other hand, there were many circumstances in the mediaeval town which were not only fully adequate to the conditions of life in those days, but even most functional and expressive of that time. Yet our time is ready to discover, even in these cases, insufficiencies and inefficiencies of one kind or another.

Matters being so, we must—curiously enough—start with the remark that the town of the Middle Ages sprang from contemporary conditions, and not from the demands of today. Obvious as this is, it must be stressed, for many critics, particularly those undiscriminating admirers of this machine age of ours, seem to judge problems of any time from their own close horizon only. In so doing, they are unwilling to give the architects of the Middle Ages credit for having been good town-builders.

"The mediaeval town was lacking even in the most elementary sanitary provisions," the critics say. These critics seem to forget that the mediaeval era was conditioned by demands very different from those of our time, and that these demands were satisfied by few and primitive provisions.

"The street pattern of the mediaeval town is too confusing," is another criticism. The fact that the streets of those days served a very different purpose than those of a modern city is overlooked. Actually, we will learn that the mediaeval street pattern was made confusing—if that expression is your pleasure—largely for practical reasons.

"The mediaeval town had a random growth without any tendency to orderly design whatsoever," so the critics go on. There, critics do not seem to realize that the town of the Middle Ages has an expressive design-order of its own; and just this fact is ample reason to consider the mediaeval town a particularly good example of that creative sensitiveness of form in the spirit of which towns and cities should be designed—and not as mere products of cold matters-of-fact, as our towns so often are.

Here we have three distinct points where the criticism is hard on the mediaeval town.

In the following, therefore, we will investigate these three distinct points—sanitary demands, street pattern, and expressive design—in order to discover why the towns of the Middle Ages took shape as they did. Through this investigation we will discover the creative strength of the mediaeval era; we will understand that in the formation of the town, the best of the mediaeval mentality was genuinely expressed; and we will realize that the town-builders of that era were town-builders of distinction—men from whom we today can learn much.

A.   MEDIAEVAL SANITARY DEMANDS

A present-day visitor to the mediaeval town—when studying the buildings, quarters, and chambers—will undoubtedly arrive at the conclusion that the sanitary provisions of those days were far from satisfactory. However, the same visitor would have much reason for a similar conclusion when passing through the slum quarters of today; and as there exists a horrifying abundance of such slum quarters, in and about our cities, large and small, it is evident that the lack of sanitary provisions was not limited to the towns of the Middle Ages.

Yet, there is a basic difference between the bygone mediaeval case and the present day slum conditions. In the latter case, in the slums, there is danger for both body and soul, for, besides unsatisfactory sanitary provisions, one is doomed to dwell in an atmosphere of physical ugliness and dilapidation. In the mediaeval case, on the other hand, the citizens had the opportunity to live in an art-atmosphere of superb architectural order and good taste, which was culturally constructive, no matter to what an extent the lack of sanitary provisions might have affected one's bodily health. By no means should one overlook the significance of the distinction between these two cases. For, notwithstanding the fact that these two cases were and are lacking in sanitary respects, the mediaeval case exhibits a culturally creative standard, whereas the slum case of today has wide-bearing and momentous anticultural tendencies. The ever-growing crimes, vices, and particularly that perilous juvenile delinquency within these slum districts, speak a clear language.

The sense moral then is that those eager to criticize the mediaeval conditions—conditions where progress in the field of sanitation scarcely had reached even its embryonic stage—should first of all take care of the utterly insanitary slum conditions of the present time—of a time when sanitary possibilities have been brought almost into perfection. In this criticism, to be just, the mediaeval case deserves much credit for its expressive and coherent form order. In spite of this, many are indiscriminative as to good and bad in the mediaeval case: mediaeval is mediaeval, so that's that. They seem unable to escape from that labyrinth of preconceived ideas.

It is perhaps difficult for many, living in the midst of a comprehensive network of plumbing, pipes, sewers and the like, to understand how those ancient times could get along without such facilities. This, however, exhibits the lack of that imagination which could free one from one's own living conditions to look upon things through a broader lens. On the other hand, those who take pleasure in reading history have soon found that man's life has been and is rich of inclinations, habits, circumstances, and—as it might seem—of curiosities. They have found that in the light of history things must be analyzed and weighed.

In the light of history, even man's sanitary circumstances must be studied, for sure. This phase of history—of man's concern about his physical well-being, and about manners in maintaining cleanliness about himself—is most illustrative and often surprising.

Here is a short story in these respects:

We know that the origin of the Turkish bath goes far back in time, perhaps as far as to the Egyptian, Phoenician and Chaldean eras. We have read much about the habits of the Greeks in keeping their bodies in perfect condition by means of fresh-air exercises, sports, and athletics. Likewise we have read about the Roman Thermae, those famous institutions in which the Romans—at least their upper classes— were in a daily contact with air and water, cold and hot. All these examples show that man, already thousands of years ago, was concerned with his bodily health; and that the great epochs of ancient times were interested in culture that was both spiritual and physical.

The annals of the mediaeval era, on the other hand, have nothing to mention about such endeavors for bodily well-being. Nor can we find any signs in the mediaeval town of such provisions as could indicate a desire for intimate bodily contact with air, water, and soap. On the contrary, all we can read, learn, understand, and imagine about their time is that the cleanliness of their immortal soul was their main concern, and that the earthly body had to take care of itself as well as this was possible in thick clothes and muddy quarters. And when diseases became dangerous, as often indeed happened in those conditions, things then were cured through heavenly help, or by witchcraft. Also, generally speaking, it was characteristic of the Middle Ages that the efforts were small in keeping the body clean and healthy, and so were even the efforts as regards clothes, rooms, and surroundings. Obviously this was true in private life and in public, concerning common people and upper classes as well. And so goes the story —not authentic but anyhow significant—that King Mathias of Hungary was widely famous because of his good table manners, for he got greasy up to his elbows only.

It would seem that later times—such as the Renaissance time for example—were advanced in the above respect. Yet, even in those days, desire for cleanliness was often regarded as a strange hobby having nothing in common with normal everyday life. With regard to this, one is surprised to learn that Michael Angelo, while in Rome, received a fatherly warning that for his health's sake he never wash himself with water; that Diane de Poitiers became famous because of her extraordinarily whimsical habit of taking a cold bath every morning; and that midst the splendor of Versailles the first ladies and even the king himself relied, not on soap and water, but on an extensive use of perfumes to preserve about themselves an endurable atmosphere. Certainly these random examples indicate that the progress toward desire for bodily cleanliness and sanitary provisions was slow. There is a rich literature about similar examples which shows that, although the demand for a grandiose architectural atmosphere was steadily growing, the desire for keeping oneself free from dirt and smear in this grandiose atmosphere did not grow parallel with this.

Real sanitary demands are of a rather recent date. Indeed, it is amazing to note how late the general consciousness in this respect is. First as late as in the past century has public health become a common concern and sanitary provisions become understood as important civic problems from the point of view of citizens' welfare. Yet, the practical application of such an understanding has been still slower. Look at the buildings erected during the days of our grandfathers and you will realize that sanitation in terms of plumbing and pipes was considered an exorbitant luxury. We may mention—just as an illustration—that as magnificent a palace as the Schoenbrunn in Vienna, with its elaborate lay-outs of gardens, parks, and fountains, did not have a single bathroom or water-closet —not even in the days of that last of the great Hapsburgs, Emperor Francis Joseph I. In fact, the Emperor did not allow such things to be installed there.

So much about sanitary conditions in the past.

Notwithstanding the fact that extensive areas of the most dreadful slums constitute the crying civic problems of today —in which slums we scarcely can speak of sanitary demands, but of insanitary satisfaction—we have made great advances, at least insofar as a conscious necessity of improvements is concerned. We are sure that, whenever civic improvements from now on are undertaken, sanitary provisions will be the leading issue. We have been educated in the spirit of cleanliness and toward desire for air, light, and openness about our abodes. And the more we become accustomed to such conditions, the less can we understand how earlier times could get along without a comprehensive network of plumbing, pipes, sewers, and the like. Hence the sharp criticism of the mediaeval era.

By no means should it be considered a virtue that the mediaeval town was wanting in sanitary provisions. But the important point is that, granted the conception of cleanliness in those days was so completely different from that of today, it is understandable that their physical accommodations were established accordingly. Therefore, far from blaming the mediaeval town-builder for negligence in sanitary matters, we must acknowledge his ability in other fields of town-building.

The fact that our age has made great progress in sanitary fields is, of course, to our credit. On the other hand, another fact remains that this same age of ours has to a great extent lost its sensitiveness in the creation of satisfactory unity in the city's architectural order. This, again, is a negative factor in our account. Hence it is to be regretted that the creation and appreciation of architectural order in our days—so distinctly apparent in the mediaeval time—has declined rather than paralleled the desire for cleanliness—so distinctly lacking in the mediaeval time—and that conditions have changed during later centuries from "orderly dirt" to "clean discord."

B. MEDIAEVAL STREET PATTERN

To begin with, let's take it for granted that the mediaeval street pattern is confusing. It seems so to a stranger, at least, for he has difficulties in finding places in the elaborate canyons of winding streets, alleys, and irregular plaza widenings. It is much easier to get along in the modern city, he thinks— particularly when the lay-out of streets is right-angular and regular, as in New York or Philadelphia. This is a rather popular observation, and it might therefore easily give the impression that the art of town-building has in the course of time developed from romantic whims into intelligent straight-forwardness. In other words, one discerns here a distinct and gradual progress toward better scheming.

History of town-building does not agree with such an assumption. History of town-building rather shows that progress of time was not a decisive factor in planning characteristics, and that lay-outs equally regular as those of today can be found way back in a distant past. Furthermore, history of town-building shows that the character of town formation depended mainly on two factors: on the **tempo in which towns grew,** and on **changing conditions of life.**

When the town community was built for a certain immediate purpose and its construction was brought into com-

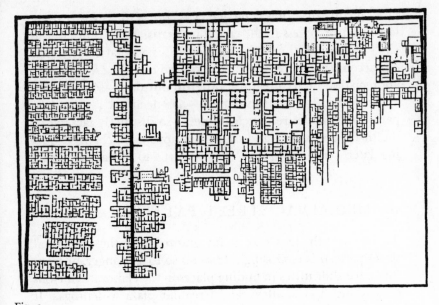

Fig. 3.
Kahun, Egypt.

Fig. 4.
Roman Castrum.

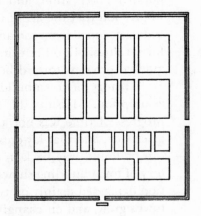

pletion within a short period of time, it was quite natural that the scheming of such a community was more or less regularly conceived. When the Egyptian Pharaoh built the town of Kahun—about 3000 B.C.—to house those workmen engaged in the erection of the Illahun pyramid, the town was completed in a short time. Similarly, when the Romans instituted their military camps—Castrums—which at the same time served as fortifications against both regular enemies and the surrounding aggressive population, the process was quick and concise. In these two cases, Kahun and Castrum, there were no reasons for romantic whims in the planning work, but the schemes were laid out in a straightforward manner, functionally, practically, and regularly. The same was more or less true in any town development where the planning program was clear and the erection immediate. On the other hand, where the planning program was uncertain and the growth covered centuries to come, it was to be expected that in such circumstances the character of the lay-out with its deviations from regularity was bound to reflect the uncertainty of the planning program and the slow actualization. For here was time enough for the other mentioned factor in town development—"changing conditions of life"—to exert its influence.

Examining, in the light of these changing conditions of life, the rich material of planning forms which has been accomplished by various epochs, races, and countries—such as the Egyptian, the Assyrian, the Mycenaean, the Greek, the Roman, and the Middle Ages—we will find a complex situation of all character varieties between the extreme irregular and the strictly regular. We will get a distinct impression that all this was not just a haphazard play with forms, but that there always was a deeper meaning behind these forms. No doubt, in all this, the psychological leaning of the respective peoples played an important rôle in producing these design varieties. But, as any sensible design must follow functional demands, so must one presuppose, even in the planning of all these towns, that clearly conceived functional demands led to

the various and varying plan patterns. This must be true even in the mediaeval case. From this angle of "functional demands" we must now examine the mediaeval street pattern.

Any street is a route of intercommunication for those transportation means available. Because in the mediaeval days, generally speaking, the only means of travel was by foot, the streets were laid out in an informal and intimate manner into a system of roads such as were fitted primarily for pedestrian purpose. These roads—or rather walks—had a varying width and shape so as to make the slow movement of masses easy and natural. At certain important corners, these roads were broadened in order to introduce more openness in the street panorama and to allow occasional gatherings of people without disturbing traffic. About the City Hall, the Cathedral, and other public buildings, still broader areas were left open, and these were formed into squares and plazas of informal, yet of impressive character. As such, they constituted the nuclei of the town where public meetings and ceremonies were held. Functionally, they therefore had to serve the same purpose as the Roman Forum of the ancient time, and civic auditoriums and convention halls in communities of to-day.

The town was surrounded by protective walls where towers and similar features at certain intervals constituted central points of protection. Only a few entrances to the town existed and these were formed into imposing gateways of architectural significance through which the entrance roads led to the various centers of the town.

Such was the mediaeval town-plan as a truly functional organism.

On the whole, as we see, the lay-out of the mediaeval town was well thought out, logical, and expressed excellently the conditions of contemporary life. Every street, every path, every corner, and every plaza was a well-known feature to the citizens of the community. The whole lay-out, therefore, was not at all confusing to them: on the contrary, to them it was functional, practical, familiar, and above all, intimately pleasing as their beloved home town should be. Others did not count, for in those days there were no such things as pleasure travelers and international conventions. And if a stranger occasionally visited the place, he met with utmost hopitality.

Strangers in large numbers seldom entered the town: and if they did, obviously they entered with intentions that were far from friendly. The mediaeval time was cruel and full of dangers, and during the frequent enemy invasions the streets of the town were the battleground of attacks and counter-attacks. Matters being so, why should the enemy have straight and convenient roads along which to enter? Straight and convenient roads would have facilitated the entering and spreading of enemy troops, whereas fighting in a street labyrinth which was designed for hiding and surprising, was usually successful against an enemy unfamiliar with the confusing plan scheme. Accordingly, the mediaeval plan scheme was made "confusing" for protective reasons.

This idea of protection, however, was not an original invention of the Middle Age planner. Any age previous to the mediaeval had designed street systems and town lay-outs to serve necessary military functions. Even the Greeks, who, so it would seem, had a strong inclination toward regular order, made their community schemes irregular and confusing for the same reason as did the mediaeval time. Aristotle, when writing about the towns of his time, makes the significant statement that a straight-lined plan might have added to the beauty of the place, "but," said he, "it would have been impractical from the standpoint of defense." Xenophon makes remarks to the same effect, and very probably many others shared the same thought, for the necessity of protection goes back in time to the cliff-dwellers and the origin of the first hut.

Methods of warfare, as described, decided for their part the character of the mediaeval street pattern. As long as these methods were the old ones, where hand to hand fighting was

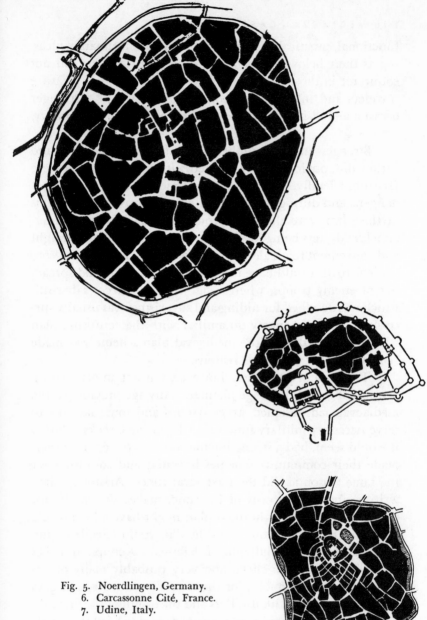

Fig. 5. Noerdlingen, Germany.
  6. Carcassonne Cité, France.
  7. Udine, Italy.

the prevailing mode, the confusing labyrinth of streets was most appropriate. The discovery of gunpowder changed much in this respect and, particularly when artillery was introduced into the battle, the change was rather radical. Napoleon III, for example, was soon aware of this fact, for he had much trouble with the frequent uprisings in Paris. In the mediaeval street system of that city his cannons were of little effect, and for this reason he had to cut straight streets in the urban body, producing in this manner a new type of protective street pattern for those means of warfare that he had at hand.

Today's methods of warfare have little in common with the laying out of streets and, therefore, if the problem of protection after all enters into the planning of modern communities, it does not do it very much insofar as street pattern is concerned. Because such is the case, people but seldom notice the protective point in the street lay-outs of olden times, particularly now in the lay-outs of the Middle Age towns. They simply consider those lay-outs confusing—in a degrading sense.

By no means should the mediaeval street pattern be considered confusing in a degrading sense. Such a statement would only disclose a surprising lack of sensitiveness to form, for sensitiveness to form can easily discern the rhythmic qualities of the mediaeval street pattern. Sensitiveness to form can furthermore discern that these rhythmic qualities have characteristics of their own, and that these characteristics are expressive of the mediaeval era—and of no other era. This holds true no matter whether one considers mediaeval town-building at large or individual town developments.

Considering first the mediaeval town-building at large, we will find here in main two phases. First, we will find those towns which had their origins as small settlements under the protection of fortified castles. The slow growth of these settlements happened about the castles in much the same manner as the stem of the tree grows thicker by producing its year rings. The respective plan patterns characterize this kind of gradual growth by circularly curved streets. Second, we will find those towns which constituted strategic points as military, commercial, and communicative centers and, therefore, were expected to grow to a considerable degree. This kind of town type was often of a later date, and its plan pattern shows a certain leaning toward regularity. Of the former group—the ring-formed—we may mention as typical examples, Noerdlingen in Germany, Carcassonne Cité in France, and Udine in Italy; the latter with its Castello, a fort in the focus of the town, on a hill—which latter, as the story goes, was built by Attila in order to watch from there the burning of Aquileja. Of the latter group, with its leanings toward regularity, we may from the rich material of examples mention at random, Rostock, Aigues-Mortes, and Verona, respectively in Germany, France, and Italy.

As much as the mediaeval town development at large expressed through its plan conception the characteristics of the Middle Ages, so much was the plan character of the individual town an expression of its own individuality in mediaeval terms. No preconceived design pattern was imposed upon the town, but its formation emerged indigenously from local conditions of life and from topographical circumstances. This was perfectly in accord with the laws of nature, for, as we have learned, any species has its own characteristics of form through which its inner nature comes into expression. Even the mediaeval town builder, just as life manifestations in nature, sensed intuitively the fundamental principles that govern things in all creation. To prove the above statement, one needs only to compare, with a perceiving eye, mediaeval town plans with cell-fabrics of organic life. Through this comparison one can easily discover much similarity of character between these two manifestations—the one an accomplishment by man, the other by nature. One can discover particularly a distinct rhythmic design in these two manifestations. Those

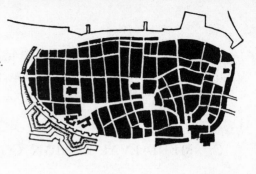

Fig. 8. Rostock, Germany.
  9. Aigues-Mortes, France.
  10. Verona, Italy.

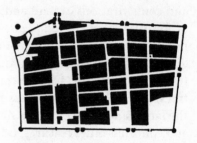

who, offhand, deem the mediaeval plan pattern disorderly for the mere reason that it is not regular, should have another and closer look at this matter.

C.   MEDIAEVAL DESIGN CONCEPTION

It is always fascinating to look at maps, with their contours and configurations of land and water, of hills and valleys, and of forests and cultivated areas: and yet, it is impossible to detect the beauty of a landscape from a mere map. One must grasp the landscape's real value as a three-dimensional manifestation of all the features embodied. Now, inasmuch as trees, bushes, and many other natural objects are essential to the landscape's charm, so too must buildings, building groups, and countless other features, be taken into consideration when judging the physical aspect of the town. For, in reality, the town is **never** a two-dimensional flat plan, but a three-dimensional embodiment of architectural proportions and masses.

In the foregoing, we have dealt with the mediaeval street pattern as a mere plan formation of two horizontal dimensions. As such, we learned, this street pattern is not only indicative of intercommunication and defense, but even rhythmically expressive of mediaeval psychology. From the viewpoint of design, however, the plan's two-dimensionality is incomplete, unless even the third dimension, the vertical, has been taken into consideration. In other words, a plan as such is of little value, unless it is an integral part of design. In this close interrelation between plan and design, the characteristics of the plan pattern must reflect the characteristics of the town's architectural formation. This means that the horizontal plan formation and the vertical formation of building masses cannot be separately conceived, but must be developed in organic unity. This development in organic unity is: **design.**

Considering now particularly mediaeval design, one significant point must be observed; namely, that design was de-

Fig. 11.

Malines, Belgium.

Fig. 12.

Cross section through the "sartorius" muscle of man.

Fig. 13.

Frankfort-on-the-Main,
Germany.

Fig. 14.

William Penn's plan
for Philadelphia.

veloped in the mind, and not on paper. Obviously, the mediaeval master-builder possessed both a vivid imagination to
see things three-dimensionally in his mind, and the ability to
form and conform his buildings into an expressive and coherent organism. All this he did with only little aid of graphi-
cal plans, sections, elevations, and like things, so essential in
the procedure of today. Mediaeval design, therefore, was
basically spatial conception, and must be understood and appreciated in this spirit. Indeed, the town of the Middle Ages
did not develop from a stylistically preconceived and fixed
plan form, but from a three-dimensionally visualized picture
of that particular town organism it represented. **It was not
town-planning, as conceived today. It was town-design in the
best sense of the word.**

Comparing town patterns in the above light, it is easy to
understand why the mediaeval irregular plan produced good
form-order, whereas the present day regular plan—of that
gridiron pattern for example—results in a three-dimensional
form-disorder. Because the mediaeval town, as said, was conceived as three-dimensional design, and not as a plan configuration of mere streets, it was built into an organism of co-
ordinated mass-effects. The geometrical plan of the gridiron
pattern—or of any other preconceived pattern—on the other
hand, was drawn on paper with scarcely any organic thought.
On this flat and spiritless scheme, the third dimension was
placed at random, the result of individual independence
where form-correlation was only of slight concern.

It is a matter of common sense that these two entirely
different modes of approach were bound to foster their respective results as they did. In this respect both the mediaeval
towns and the cities of today offer much of material for observation. The mediaeval town of Frankfort-on-the-Main is a
good representative of the Middle Ages; and William Penn's
gridiron plan of Philadelphia is illustrative of the spiritless
era of town-planning. The former, Frankfort-on-the-Main,
is positively convincing of the mediaeval case. In the case of

Philadelphia, on the other hand, one can soon find that the result was doomed to be unhappy; just as much as the result were doomed to be unhappy if someone were to produce a mosaic pattern by just letting someone else—or rather many someone-elses—put stone pieces at random into this scheme, stone pieces of any size, of any color, and in any place.

The above discloses that, insofar as the method of approach is concerned, mediaeval town-design differed widely from that of today. This was because of very fundamental reasons. There is no one single universally correct design method, for methods must spring directly from conditions of life. Because there is a broad gap between mediaeval conditions of life and those of today, the difference in the respective methods of town-design must be correspondingly great.

There are, in the main, two characteristics of modern conditions of life which vitally concern modern town-design. First, the designer of today, having been for a long period of time imprisoned by imitative stylistic forms conceived on paper, has to a great extent lost his spatial imagination. Second, towns of the present era are rapidly growing into large cities, which fact calls for pre-established schemes along which building work could proceed. The mediaeval era, on the other hand, was characterized; first, by a genuine instinct in transmuting the spirit of the time into an expressive form of its own; and second, by the slow growth of the towns, offering sufficient time for prehension. From these two characteristics emerged the mediaeval method of town-design and of actual execution. It was a step by step procedure; whereby any new building was fitted into the spatially conceived scheme, and whereby any new step was controlled by the infallible instinct of proportion, rhythm, and form-coordination. The growth of the mediaeval town, therefore, was much the same as the growth of a tree: **in the seed of the tree lies hidden the potential power of the tree's growth; and from that seed the tree is formed into an expressive design of its own.**

1. Mediaeval Conception of Space:

When we say, as was said in the foregoing, that mediaeval design was basically spatial conception, it must be understood that in the mediaeval case this means particularly **"mediaeval space conception."** One must bear in mind that conditions of life and spatial conception are closely interrelated, which indicates that ages and races have their own characteristic conceptions of space. The Egyptians in the narrow valley of the Nile River had one conception of space; the Greeks, living in a hilly and colorful environment, had another; the nomads of the boundless desert sense space very differently than do the Tyroleans midst their majestic Alps; and surely, because of vital differences, the mediaeval space conception was bound to be very different from that of the Western World of today. Whereas we are striving toward openness and unlimited distances, the mind of the Middle Ages tended toward an intimate enclosure of limited space. Whereas we desire airier living conditions, the mediaeval mind preferred to dwell in dark chambers amidst narrow streets. In contrast to our "open" conception of space, that of the mediaeval was "closed."

The change from the mediaeval closed conception of space to the present open conception was a gradual development, running parallel with the gradual changes of conditions of life. As such, the development was fundamentally sound. There was, however, another point in this development which was far from sound, and which has caused much disturbance in the architectural make-ups of the cities of today. Although this point in the said development does not belong directly to the mediaeval case—being a concern of today—we will bring it into our discussion in spite of this. We will do so in order that we, through this, may still more stress the good points in the mediaeval understanding of space, as contrasted with the less good points of our time.

During the past century, changes in the understanding of architectural design brought about a state of affairs where the physical and spiritual conditions outside of the building were not considered important; but where just so much the more important were considered the outside style of the building and the space within. In other words, that space into which the building should have been formed, has been disregarded; while that space enclosed by the building—of which the latter constituted the stylistic shell—has been emphasized as the very and only space to be considered. This emphasis was brought to its climax when the theorizing esthete stamped architecture as the specific "Art of Space," limited to only that space enclosed by the building. Animated by this easy theory —a dangerous one—the architects, generally speaking, have since then designed their structures as independent units, almost entirely neglecting that function of the structures' outside formation which has to constitute satisfactory street and plaza enclosures in the city. Much space has been enclosed by these independent structures. Alas, much more has been left outside to vibrate in discordant distress.

In contrast to this space understanding, the mediaeval master-builder—not having been poisoned by the esthete's spatial misteaching—built his structures to satisfy spatial demands both within and without. Every new building was fitted into the site like a piece of stone into the mosaic pattern. In this organic manner the mediaeval town was formed into a complexity of spatial effects. There were no theories to hamper the work. Intuitive sensing was the supreme adviser, and thanks to this the mediaeval town was moulded into winding streets, into street openings, into plazas, into vistas, and into a playful labyrinth of picturesque groupings and perspective effects. From the depths of these streets and plazas, the building masses arose to form plastic skylines of gables, towers and turrets. These plastic skylines—typifying mediaeval life and psychology—reached their loftiest peak in the elaborately carved forms of the imposing Cathedral. In this playful ensemble of building masses, the Cathedral made it clear that its outside formation was just as important in the forming of street and plaza enclosures as was its inside space-embracing formation. And the setting of the fountain at the corner of the plaza was not accidental or arbitrary, but as many-sided a spatial consideration as was the grouping of buildings and the formation of the Cathedral itself.

So did the mediaeval builder design his town into narrow and shadowy enclosures of delightful intimacy and of ample protection. Dwelling in the depths of these enclosures, the mediaeval mind strove upward—just as did the masonry masses of the town—seeking heavenly light, and protection.

2. Mediaeval Sense for Correlation:

To be imbued with spatial imagination, presupposes that one's instinct for form-correlation must be alive. Consequently, because this spatial imagination was indigenously vital in the mediaeval sensing, instinct for form-correlation was a natural gift which made the Middle Age master-builder a genius in his profession. Instinctively he felt that towns could not be successfully built out of any number of beautiful buildings, unless those buildings were properly interrelated: just as in nature, where a landscape could not achieve its ultimate beauty by the mere growth of trees, bushes, and plants into exquisite specimens, unless the individual and collective parts were conformed into proper interrelation. In the mediaeval town a proper interrelation of building forms was instinctively achieved. In fact, just this proper interrelation constituted the mediaeval town—just as it constitutes the landscape.

The landscape is—as is any appearance in nature—an open book where one can read about the drift to form-correlation, and about the significance of this drift as a fundamental law. In much the same way, the mediaeval town is an open book where it is written with clear letters that man's creative instinct in those days was inspired by the same drift to correlation as in nature. If only the eyes are opened to see

Fig. 15.

The Uffizi Gallery with the Palazzo Vecchio in the background, Florence.

Fig. 16.

The Signoria Plaza Florence.

and the mind to understand, this open book of the mediaeval town contains many enlightening chapters about that form-correlation through which the architectural form of the mediaeval town became so animating.

Since the mediaeval era, the instinct for correlation has gradually waned—for reasons which will be explained later. Even the eyes have lost much of their sharpness, for oftentimes we cannot discern the significance of correlation, no matter how clearly it is manifested about ourselves. In general, people have little notion of form-correlation between the various buildings in the town. They look at buildings, as such, with little or no consideration as to whether or not these buildings are adequately interrelated one with another and correlated to the surroundings as a whole. That town which has many beautiful buildings they regard as a marvel of beauty. But only few seem to realize that if a town really is a marvel of beauty it is so because of a proper correlation of its buildings. Remove this correlation and the town becomes slovenly in appearance, regardless of the number of beautiful building units. Jumble together all the single handsome features of a well-furnished room, and the result is plain.

Were a great number of the most beautiful and famous buildings in architectural history all re-erected to form a single street, this street should be the most beautiful in the world, were beauty merely a matter of beautiful buildings. But such would most certainly not be the case, for the street would appear as a heterogeneous medley of disrelated edifices. The effect would be similar to that produced if a number of the most eminent musicians all played of the finest music at the same time—but each in a different key and melody. There would be no music, but much noise.

The above example might suggest the idea that style unity is necessary for obtaining proper form-correlation in town building. The answer to this is that form-correlation is the supreme issue, whereas those means for obtaining this form-correlation are of secondary importance, be it with style unity or style variety. Style unity, generally speaking, was the prevailing situation as long as styles were genuine—as they were prior to the Renaissance era and, consequently, during the whole mediaeval period. During the days of the Renaissance, the situation became style-complex, but, although architecture lost much of its creative vitality—which was true during the Late Renaissance when direct copying was introduced—this did not mean that form-correlation was in danger. There are countless cases where different styles were satisfactorily co-ordinated. We need only mention the superb co-ordination of the famous architectural triumvirate of the Palazzo Vecchio, the Loggia dei Lanzi, and the Uffizi Galleries, in Florence. Here, the Palazzo Vecchio is a thirteenth century fort, austere and solid; the Loggia dei Lanzi a Gothic product of almost Renaissance character, lofty and rich; and the Uffizi Galleries a Renaissance structure by Vasari, elegant and light.

When the Middle Age town development was still in its cradle, and its form conception began to emerge from the mediaeval night, the style of that period did not exist as yet. Conditions of life decided form-shaping of both buildings and towns, and unity of form—at least in spirit—was therefore a self-evident result. The more time progressed, however, the more the era became conscious of the characteristics of the mediaeval styles—the Romanesque and the Gothic—and accordingly the towns were developed in the signs of these styles. But when the mediaeval era was a completed fact, its styles were ripe, and something new was bound to come.

The Renaissance period brought new styles to the mediaeval town. On the whole, these styles were infused into the mediaeval pattern with a good sense of correlation, and this made the town formation expressively and historically richer. This richness of expressive and historical effects was still more the case in those towns which had their origin from the Classical era, and which continued to exist during the subsequent periods of various style formations. So was the situation in many a town, particularly in Italy, not to forget that eternal city of Rome. Inasmuch as these various style forms were properly interrelated, for the most part at least, this richness of style varieties was not an infringement of the principle of correlation. To use a parallel, the situation was much the same as to bring new and different instruments into the musical ensemble. As in music there is a broad graduation of instrument use between the uniformity of the string concerto and the rich orchestration of the symphony, so the development of the towns during the various style periods became a gradual process from style uniformity to a complex of styles. In those cases where the sense for form-correlation was alive, this complex of styles brought richness and charm to the place. So, for instance, is that famous San Marco Plaza in Venice a lasting symphony of architectural forms, just because of its many and well-balanced styles.

In the cities of today there is much of another situation, as we know so well. Here we find an accumulation of all kinds of style forms—not genuine, but imitative from previous epochs, irrelevant, and often fantastic. This is the unfortunate result of the nineteenth century style confusion. But, as the bulk of the buildings erected during that time, particularly during the latter part of the said century, are superficially decorative and lacking cultural significance, they might as well be made away with, at least in such cases where civic improvements would gain by such an action.

But in new communities, and in new parts of old communities, the mediaeval case can be of good advice. This advice is simple, yet fundamental, for it suggests such obvious facts as that any new building must express the demands of the contemporary life, and must be correlated into its surroundings. Style is not the essential thing. This fact, that style is not the essential thing, is important to bear in mind particularly at the present time, for we are just now about

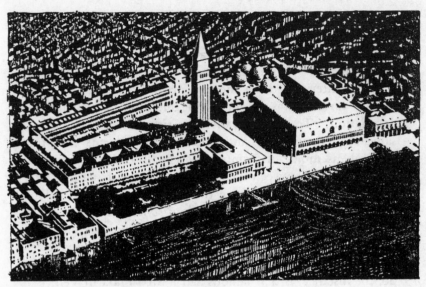

Fig. 17.
The San Marco Plaza, from the air.

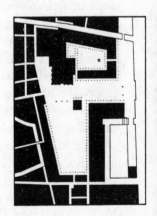

Fig. 18.
Plan of The San Marco Plaza.

to discard those imitative styles which the past century so abundantly has brought into our cities, and consequently we are in the midst of a time of vivid transition in trying to find an expressive form of our own. We do wisely, therefore, in not playing carelessly with all kinds of stray forms, tricky or otherwise, which have no lasting value and which only would bring about irreparable difficulties in the striving for sound form-coherence in the cities. The mediaeval town-builder was cautious in this respect, as the result of his work so clearly testifies.

3. Patina of Time:

As much as the mediaeval town-builder was cautious with his form-coherence, so is the sceptic of today cautious when this form-coherence of the mediaeval town is emphasized. "Patina of time," says he, "is a strong agency in keeping things together," and "this fact deceives one's judgement as to the actual mediaeval situation," he maintains. By this, the sceptic means that the Cathedrals, the Town Halls—and all the other buildings of the towns, for that matter—when they were brand new and their outside materials still had their natural color and shade, gave the towns quite another aspect than they have now. "Undoubtedly, therefore," he adds, "form-coherence was less noticeable in those days than it is at the present, when patina has had time to bring cohering harmony of color into the scenery."

We take it for granted that the original color scheme of the mediaeval town was brighter and more outstanding than it is now. But it was so only for some time after the various buildings had been completed. Only for some time, we repeat, for aging in nature is not a very slow process, and enters into action almost immediately in bringing mellowness to the exposed surface. Because of this, even the cities of a recent date have been mellowed by this aging process. This is so much more the case in industrial cities—and they are not few

—where smoke and grease in a short time have affected the building surfaces. Yet, because patina of time changes only the building surfaces and does not change the building forms, there is an excellent opportunity for a just comparison on equal basis between the towns of the past and those of the present, insofar as form-coherence is concerned.

Aging is a general process in nature. Rocks, cliffs, and stones do not appear in their material color, but their surfaces are softened to such neutral shades as melt them harmoniously into their natural surroundings. The bark of stems and branches ages parallel with the trees' growth so as to render color unity to the landscape. Buildings, naturally, are subject to the same aging process, **and therefore buildings must be so designed that aging adds to their beauty rather than making them less attractive.** This fact is a memento to those who are trying to base their design on perpetually immaculate perfection of wall surface and coloring, as is often the case when new and perfected patent materials are introduced. This is to act against the laws of nature, for indeed such perfections do not last, and soon the immaculate virtues of the design are changed to the reverse. It is already fully experienced that aging in this kind of case has made the buildings look dirty, spotty, and unpleasant. This is a danger to the general appearance of the town, for in the town any building should add to the community's beauty.

The town-builder of the mediaeval era was successful with regard to the aging of his town. The testimony of several centuries proves this to be true, for, not only has patina of time brought softness to the general color scheme in the town, but it has even effected occasional bright accents of color. Particularly the use of copper as outside building material was fortunate in the aging process. The impressive towers and pinnacles of Bremen, Hamburg, and Lübeck, for example, testify that the mediaeval town-builder was aware of nature's aging tendencies, and that good co-operation between man and nature was of great value. The mediaeval town-builder knew that nature was ready to help man in his efforts, provided man made it possible for her to be helpful.

4. The Mediaeval Town and Nature:

There is still another moment where a fortunate co-operation existed between the mediaeval town-builder and nature. The tendency to form-correlation included not only the forms of architecture, but the forms of nature as well. The natural beauty of the town-site was a decisive factor in the mode of planning so as to fit the town into its setting. The hilly site was improved with the forms of the town, by emphasizing that hill still more. The long horizontal lines of the flat landscape were made richer by a lively skyline of vertical accents. And in the valley the abundant vegetation melted together with the plastic and colorful rhythm of steep roofs, tall towers, and rich turrets.

It is true, of course, that the mediaeval town-builder did not have the pleasure of playing with nature's forms within the town in the same manner as the present day designer can do it. For no garden cities were possible in those days, and this for obvious reasons. But the beauty of the surrounding landscape was respected. The landscape lay there beyond the fortification walls and moats, green and fresh with its vine-yards, vegetable gardens, fields, and wooded lands. Or, per-haps the landscape was untouched—rocky, wild, and roman-tic. Or, whatever it was, indeed, features comparable to present-day random railroad-yards, disorderly factory-grounds, and dilapidated areas of one kind or another did not exist to make the town surroundings unpleasant.

Italy is famous for her many mediaeval hill-towns, of which we may mention Orvieto, San Gimignano, and Monte Compatri. We mention particularly these, because each of them is typical, in its own way, of fitting towns into the land-scape. Orvieto is situated on a high plateau surrounded by deep precipices, which plateau is so overpowering a feature in the landscape that the buildings, even those of large size, seem to lose in scale. It seems as if nature had been the master-builder, leaving for man only the details to deal with. San Gimignano is different from Orvieto, for here man mastered the situation by erecting the town along the gently rising contours of the hilly site. At the highest elevation, the core of the town was formed into a highly significant skyline of a group of straight towers, dominating the surrounding countryside. Because of this group of towers, one may have the impression that San Gimignano is the prototype of Lower Manhattan. Monte Compatri is an ant-heap-formed town on an ant-heap-formed lonely hill. As such it is both original and attractive. In its general shape—but not in its spirit and form-richness—it has much in common with Mont St. Michel, that architecturally romantic cathedral-island at the Bay of Mont St. Michel, between Normandy and Brittany.

Whereas the hilly site decided much of town-formation, flat land offered more freedom in this respect. Mostly the flat land towns were located by water—by a river, a delta, or open sea—and because of this the character of the towns was to a great extent dependent on the form and function of its water front. And because any town in those times of unrest had to be more or less a fortified place, an elaborate system of fortification walls and moats surrounded the town against attacks from the land side. A logical result of this was that in many cases the town was shaped like a semi-circle, where the water front constituted the diameter, the fortification system being the periphery. Of such towns we might mention, as typical examples, Frankfort-on-the-Main and Antwerp; the former having its origin already from the days of the Romans, the latter, as far as is known, from the seventh century. The three already mentioned Hansa towns—Bremen, Hamburg, and Lübeck—were much of the same type.

Speaking about water fronts, Venice should not be forgotten, for sure—for as an island-town it is sole in its category. Another island-town of the mediaeval time was Old Stock-

Fig. 19.
Orvieto.

Fig. 20.
San Gimignano.

Fig. 21.
Monte Compatri.

holm, founded in the twelfth century as a strategic point surrounded by water. Its origin, also, was similar to that of Paris, founded by the Romans on the little island of Lutetia.

In short: there were mediaeval mountain-towns midst the Alps and Apennines; there were towns on the steep slopes of mountains, and on mountain peaks; there were towns in the deep valleys between gigantic mountains; and there were those by water, and those surrounded by water. But, whatever towns there were, and whatever the differences were as to setting and formation, and no matter which of these towns we might select as a subject of closer examination, all the same there was a significant characteristic common to all—significant to the mediaeval era, and entirely unlike the conditions of today—namely, that there was a distinct borderline between town and country, a borderline which protected the town from outside attacks, and which protected the natural beauty of the surrounding landscape from the dangers within the town. **The mediaeval town was like an ornamental pattern of man's art fitted into the majestic environment of nature's art. So to speak, it was like a precious stone of the mediaeval time, in the precious setting of all time.**

5. Mediaeval Architectural Atmosphere:

Indeed, when following the gentle play with the copious forms of the mediaeval town in the varying landscape settings, one gets the distinct notion that the mediaeval town-dweller was a lover of nature. Nature lay there, outside of the town, only at a short distance from his door-step. At any time, when peace prevailed, he could enjoy nature's freshness and quietude; he could do gardening if he pleased, or occupy himself in many other ways. No doubt, he found in this a genuine pleasure. Probably, as a child of nature, his intuitive sensing was indigenously receptive to nature's beauty.

Perhaps the mediaeval town dweller was subconsciously influenced by nature's architecture and liked to linger in its atmosphere. Perhaps—by the same token—he was subconsciously influenced by man's architecture, too, and felt at home in the architectural atmosphere of his home town.

"**Subconsciously,**" we repeat, for so must it be, and this for the following reasons:

As musical impressions are received through a certain rhythm and cadence of tune and time, so are architectural impressions received through a certain proportion and rhythm of material, color, and space. The fundamental laws are the same in both cases. The reactions are related, yet different. Generally speaking, we may say that musical reactions are "conscious," whereas architectural reactions are primarily "subconscious." When one attends a musical performance, one expects a certain conscious reaction from the performance—just as much as one expects a certain conscious reaction when attending a theatrical play, when visiting an art exhibition, or something of that nature. But when one passes his life, day after day, amidst architecture—at home, in the city, or elsewhere—the reactions are primarily subconscious. So they must be, as said. For, **one should not dwell in a constant state of conscious reactions to one's architectural environment, but in a lasting state of subconscious satisfaction.** This subconscious satisfaction, induced by one's architectural environment, is just what we mean by **"living in an architectural atmosphere."**

Because of his innate sensitiveness to proportion and rhythm, the mediaeval town-builder achieved a genuine and satisfactory architectural atmosphere about his town. This is a fact which can be proven by analytical methods, if you wish. Anyone sensitive to architectural language can undertake the task, just as much as any music critic—being a priori sensitive to musical language—is able to analyze a musical composition to its merits.

Supposing now that we were to try the task ourselves. Supposing, for this reason, that we would reconstruct in our imagination a picture of the mediaeval town in its original state, and then make a tour of the town—of any of them—in order to try a **"conscious analysis of our subconscious reactions"** during the tour. To make our study a many-sided one, we might as well start from one of the less conspicuous places, and then tour toward those places of more prominence. Indeed, our first observation is that there is an entire lack of imported decorative nonsense—so abundantly accumulated in the cities of today—and that every structure along the street is not only an expression of its time, but even, because of the slow intercommunication in those days, an indigenous product of that very town. Already this fact is apt to tune our minds into harmony with the mediaeval key so as to feel the silent accord of the street's architectural ensemble—much in the same way as the mediaeval town people probably once felt it themselves, **subconsciously.** This accord, as we move along, is growing richer by occasional accents in the street picture, for we find an original gate-way here, an attractive bay-window there, and a pinnacle of some distant structure beyond the street's curvature. In fact, we are amazed to find how every new feature fits into the silent tune that vibrates in our minds. This silent tune becomes gradually rhythmic and alive; and the more we move along, the more this silent tune seems to form itself into a distinct melody, yet simple in its directness like a folk-song. It grows, we feel, from the soul of the town, as grow folksongs from the soul of the people.

Turning now around the corner, we arrive in a broader street, and we feel as if more instruments had joined our silent melody. There is a richer variety of forms and features, larger in scale, occasionally elaborate, and at certain intervals breaking the skyline with strong vertical effects. So is the new picture, and accordingly we record its vibrations; and, when the view broadens at the intersection of diverging streets, its effects broaden correspondingly into a new tempo, yet still slow and moderate—Andante.

But we proceed along, and soon we find ourselves on the main street of the town. Here the scenery is more picturesque than ever, for here windows, gates, gables, and pinnacles of a multifarious form and number enrich the panorama; and as lively and varying as once was the human movement here, just as lively and varying is still the play of form and color. Ever new motifs pass our eyes—sometimes elastic and slender, sometimes broad and plastic, but always at the right moment to form accords in the rising and sinking rhythm; and then, suddenly, a powerful accent flashes through our minds, for we get a sight of the massive contours of the Town Hall tower, that symbol of the town's strength, order, and justice. Soon we are there, at the Town Hall Square, within the framework of buildings, small in size, large in size; and then the very focus of that square, the Town Hall itself, solid and dignified—Largo.

Yet, still farther we direct our steps. We enter the deep canyon of a small alley, narrow and dark. It is quiet. Quiet is even its melody of diminuendo—then pianissimo—a long pianissimo foreboding a change, a change to a sudden crescendo, or, perhaps, to a full orchestral fortissimo—and, in fact, when the last curve of the winding alley has been passed, we get a glimpse of the imposing Cathedral: through a narrow and bright stripe at the end of the path, we feel its masses; between the sharp silhouettes of roofs and gables, we discern its lofty lines rising toward the sky; and, before long, there we stand facing the majestic edifice—the climax of the town and the ambition of the age—raising its elaborate features way over the town with its gables, pinnacles, towers, and turrets—Festivo.

With the above tour of our fancy we tried to bring into light the different phases of the mediaeval town life: the intimate moment of the silent street; the commercial moment of the main street; the official moment about the Town Hall; and the religious thoughts and sentiments in and about the Cathedral. Moreover, we tried to emphasize the different expressions of cadence and rhythm—the different symphonic movements, so to speak—of the mediaeval town-design. Although we have referred in this explanation to musical parallels, this does not intend to suggest that architectural movements are the same as musical movements or that the mediaeval town was formed according to some musical consciousness. Certainly, the mediaeval town was thoroughly an architectural achievement, conscious or subconscious from the builders' side, and subconsciously sensed by the average citizens. Architecture is not music—whether "frozen" or otherwise. Architecture is merely based on the fundamental law of organic order; which means that it is based on the same law as is music or anything else that is organically healthy. **This is the sole relationship between architecture and music; a relationship which, in fact, is significant indeed.**

Basically the mediaeval town was a modest creation. But, because protection of the people was an essential issue, the protective fortifications were built into impressive architectural features, strong and substantial. Furthermore, because the thought of eventual divine punishment—so often and eagerly stressed by the Church—lay heavily upon the people, the Cathedral was erected lofty and form-abundant so as to symbolize the fears and hopes of the immortal souls.

It is this combination of a natural tendency to bourgeois modesty, and the imposed threats, both earthly and divine, which made the mediaeval town-pattern so rich of varieties—ranging from utmost simplicity to extravagant elaboration, yet always mediaevally picturesque. In fact, one scarcely could find in any branch of all the ramifications of human art, such a rich variety of individual form-combinations as in the mediaeval town-development. In this development there were the simple street pictures of unlimited varieties—pictures which to the average eye were perhaps too inconspicuous to attract attention, but where the trained eye could find fine art qualities. There were the striking street pictures of any possible mediaeval concept, pictures which pleased both strangers and the town people themselves. There were all the thinkable plaza-formations, which constituted the nuclei of the towns, and bestowed upon these towns their peculiar individualities. Finally, there were those plaza-formations of prominence, which made the towns famous for their beauty. In short, within the organism of the mediaeval town, one could find all the form-combinations that were thinkable along the mediaeval pattern.

Now, if we were to select from this abundant form material a few typical examples for closer study, this selection, for sure, were bound to be a random one. It is not, however, our intention to go into an extensive and detailed investigation of the subject. We are satisfied with one single example among the thousands—not a random one, but one which is a significant representative of the best of the mediaeval era. It is the famous San Marco Plaza in Venice, which already in another connection was characterized as "a lasting symphony of architectural forms."

Correlation of individual buildings into a magnificent architectural ensemble—into architectural atmosphere—is perhaps nowhere better shown than in the formation of this said San Marco Plaza. Built over a period of one thousand years—from 800 A.D. to 1800 A.D.—this plaza was begun far back in the earlier part of the mediaeval age. In the course of time it slowly developed with frequent substantial changes, until it assumed final form during the Napoleonic days. But, throughout this long evolution, the retention of a harmonious correlation of forms was held sacred, for the mediaeval spirit of form-sensitiveness had originally set the course, and guided the long development.

In this sunny Venetian plaza one finds a broad variety of styles, materials, proportions, mass effects, and scales. The San Marco itself is in colorful marble and mosaic; the Doge's Palace is in sandstone and marble tile; the Library in white marble; the powerful masses of the Campanile in common brick; and close by, the little Loggetta by Sansovino in a refined architecture of delicate marble. San Marco's rich silhouette enlivens the restfulness of the plaza; and the long horizontal lines of the Procuratie contrast strikingly with the verticality of the Campanile. The general form of the plaza is irregular, but gives a distinct impression of formality. There is no symmetry, but the contours of the plaza and the grouping of building masses, varying in simplicity and richness, give to the whole an extraordinarily fine balance. And finally, each edifice tells the true story of its own era.

It is true enough that the San Marco Plaza was not wholly an achievement of the Middle Ages, for, as mentioned, many of its buildings were from a later date. For this reason its architectural atmosphere is a combination of mediaeval and Renaissance form-atmosphere. As such, this combination is a very happy one, which only shows that any time—now considering particularly our time—can be perfectly honest and contemporary in its architectural expression, even in an environment of another age, and yet achieve a harmonious form-atmosphere together with those structures representing past times. This is an important wisdom we learn from the style-combination of the San Marco Plaza. Particularly for this reason we selected this plaza as an example of study.

However, in spite of its style combination, the San Marco Plaza is fully mediaeval in its conception. Its mediaeval conception lies in the informal relationship of the San Marco, the Doge's Palace, and the Campanile. The rest of the buildings are, so to speak, only a more or less formal background of this informal relationship. Furthermore, it is just this exquisitely informal relationship of the choice forms of the mentioned buildings which gives vitality and strength to the said plaza.

Those who have visited the San Marco Plaza know of its very real emotional appeal. But few realize why mere brick and stone built into buildings of such varied type and irregular location can have so vital a power of influence. It is not because of an accidental grouping of these structures. Nor is it a result of a theoretical system, invented by human intellect. It is more than so. **It is the enigmatic impetus of something that prevails in all of creation, which "something" our intellectual ego understands to be a matter of mathematics in terms of proportion and rhythm, but for which the mediaeval creative sensitiveness needed no name.**

With this short visit to the San Marco Plaza we will conclude our analysis of the mediaeval town.

Perhaps it would be enlightening to delve still deeper in the mediaeval soul and bring into light all the psychological nuances from which sprang the mediaeval form-expression, its conception, its characteristics, and its richness of motifs, both in town-design and in the lay-outs of individual buildings. But such a delving would bring us too far from our objective. **Our objective has been to search for the causes of strength in mediaeval town-building, in order that we might learn from these causes how to conduct contemporary civic processes toward strength, and how to prevent decline.**

This program we have tried to follow; and, as we know from our introduction that strength or weakness of an organism depends on whether or not the principle of organic order—the principle of architecture—has been in command, we have studied the mediaeval town in this light. Having done this, we have found it fully manifest that the said principle has been thoroughly in command in the mediaeval case. In other words, we have found that in the mediaeval town-organism the lasting values have been achieved through honest and creative approach in building-design and through good correlation of buildings. Because of these facts it is easy to understand that the Middle Age towns are still in good shape in spite of their old age, whereas slums are spreading themselves along many of those developments which are of a rather recent date. Because of this fact, it is furthermore easy to understand that visitors to the mediaeval towns invariably terminate their visit refreshed in mind and enlivened in spirit, in spite of the cramped and dark conditions in these towns. **Although these visitors may not be aware of it, the reason for such reactions is the fact that they have been in close touch with the true and creative values of man's art and have breathed of their atmosphere.**

2. DECLINE OF THE CITY

BECAUSE the mediaeval town was formed into a genuine expression of the best aspirations of the population, there is every reason to assume that this genuine expression was subconsciously appreciated by the population as something of their own blood and soul. This subconscious appreciation, on the other hand, encouraged the development of towns along genuinely creative standards. In other words, there were two reciprocally active forces in the mediaeval town which kept the town's formation in good order. On one side there was a strong art-form, and on the other side there was a vitalizing appreciation of this art-form. The situation, also, was exactly the same as in any genuine art development, primitive or otherwise, **where art-form grows from a soil which has been fertilized by this same art-form.**

As long as conditions in town-building remained on this creative and appreciative stage of reciprocal influence, town-development was strong and healthy. But, as soon as the creative strength began to weaken and the appreciative attitude to become indolent, decline was to be expected. This process was and is quite similar to organic processes in general, **where the crop is bound to grow poor in the same ratio as both seed and soil grow poor.**

Therefore, when we now undertake to examine the reasons for civic decline, this examination must follow along the above thought of reciprocal influence, where the architectural formation—the "seed"—on one side, and the attitude of the population—the "soil"—on the other side, are both influencing and influenced. In doing so, we will arrive at the logical conclusion that civic decline, metaphorically speaking, resulted from the dual effect of both deficient seed and fallow soil, acting reciprocally.

In the following manner this decline took place:

In the first instance, architectural form-expression had developed into superficial stylistic decoration because the art of building had gradually declined to the mere imitation of obsolete style-forms from bygone days. Parallel with this downward process, a proper interrelation of building-forms became ignored. This spirit of "imitation" and "irrelation" brought about a multitude of arbitrary and irrelated style-forms into the city. Such was ultimately the case during the nineteenth century.

In the second instance, changes in social conditions had gradually caused a general lack of understanding in town-building matters. When towns began to grow and expand, the augmented population brought into the towns new viewpoints and methods which were not in harmony with the previous and prevailing form-order in these towns. These new viewpoints and methods laid on the growing towns their stamp of materialistic superficiality and indolence in civic affairs. This likewise took place during the nineteenth century and the early years of the twentieth.

To these two causes, the slow but certain decline of the city can be attributed. Indeed, when these two causes—the one a lack of creative impetus, the other a lack of cultural ambition—are contrasted with the creative spirit of the Middle Ages, so strongly stressed in the foregoing chapter, it is evident that matters were doomed to follow a downhill road.

To get a true picture of the situation, it is necessary to study these two causes more closely. Through this study we will learn that these two causes were historical inevitabilities in the floods and ebbs of cultural evolution. We will learn, furthermore, that the lowest ebb was reached in the latter part of the nineteenth century, that is, during that very period preceding ours. **Alas, we are just now living in the midst of the consequences of this lowest ebb.**

A. THE "SEED": ART-FORM

1. Decline of Form Expression:

Already long before the Middle Age wells of creative inspiration had run dry, the mediaeval soul was fertilized by impressions from the Classical Antiquity. In the form of Humanism, the discovered treasures of ancient literature and art became the spiritual food of mediaeval scholars and artists. These treasures brought new impulses into the mediaeval life, and they affected the mediaeval mode of thinking and form-conception. Two entirely different world-feelings met one another: the Classical, representing the image of man as the ideal; and the Mediaeval, representing that of God as the ideal. When time passed and the course of the Middle Ages was close to its end, these two world-feelings—the Classical and the Mediaeval—melted into one and the same world-feeling, where the dwindling spirit of mediaevalism lost ground to the ever-growing interest in the Classical world. The Early Renaissance was the result of this process.

The Early Renaissance was a logical result of the gradual change from mediaevalism into the new era, and as such it was to a great extent a creative process. The mediaeval mode of thinking was changed into the new mode of thinking, and through this change the new form conception emerged as an expression of the new world of thought. It developed into a refined style-form of its own, full of imaginative power, excellently adapted to the conditions of life and to the manifold problems of the time.

However, because the Early Renaissance form was born as a transfusion of alien blood into mediaeval veins, and because this transfused blood was taken from an old body—the long ago expired Greek form—it could not in the long run enliven. Therefore, in its further development the Renaissance form declined into a direct adoption of classical forms. During the Late Renaissance time, this adoption was methodically systematized. These classical forms were measured, scrutinized, dogmatized; they were put into doctrines, formulas and what not, and then superimposed upon conditions very different from those which they originally represented. These adopted forms, consequently, were doomed to become artificial. Worse than that: they became momentous, for the principle of expression—requiring creative genuineness of form—was disregarded, and the baneful microbe of imitation was implanted. A dangerous step had thus been taken, the effects of which were bound to appear sooner or later.

Fully to grasp the momentousness of the step toward imitation, we may suggest historical parallels:

Supposing—to begin with a rather absurd thought—that the Greeks had adopted the already ripe Egyptian form. In such a case the Greek cultural form would not have come into existence, but the Greeks would have been compelled to dwell midst an artificially superimposed style form. Supposing furthermore—to continue with another absurd thought—that the mediaeval time had not had the ambition to create its own form, but had imitated the Greek one, or any other previous style form; there then would not have been born Romanesque and Gothic art, but only a dead mediaeval decoration borrowed from somewhere else and, therefore, lacking cultural significance. Surely, in both of these instances, the Greek and the Mediaeval, such an imitative action would have been much the same as cultural suicide. This statement is plain and clear to everybody, and does not call for further comments. And even if some Greek architect had built **only a single** Egyptian portico midst the Greek form-world, or some Gothic builder had erected **only a single** Greek temple into the mediaeval town, even those incidents no doubt would be regarded, today, by everyone, as stupid doings.

Well, on the other hand, look at the towns and cities from yesterday! There one can find more than plenty of worthless imitation of Greek, Roman, Byzantine, Romanesque, and Gothic style. There one can find all the Renaissances, general and provincial. One can find all kinds of ramifications and bastards of almost any style that has been created by previous eras under this sun. Moreover, one can find that these styles have been mingled together without any logical reason whatsoever, and one can soon discover that the architects, speaking generally, have selected their styles just as easily and capriciously as one selects the pattern and color of one's shirt and tie.

Now, why is it that we are so indifferent to the imitative form-menace of our own days, when we at the same time so clearly discern how disastrous the same imitation would have been to earlier epochs? Isn't the only answer to this, that we have been accustomed to look upon the world of architecture with such spectacles as show clearly only at a distance. That is, we have been born and bred in an atmosphere of architectural fallacies which have demoralized our architectural conscience as regard our own actions, whereas we at the same time—insofar as distant epochs are concerned—do feel instinctively that **"form a priori must be a true expression of the best endeavors of contemporary life."**

Any time and race, primitive or cultural, has felt instinctively that "form a priori must be a true expression of the best endeavors of contemporary life." They have not only felt it. They have even put this feeling into practice. So things really have developed during the long journey of human culture. It was the doctrinal masters of the over-ripe Renaissance who introduced imitative methods into architecture. Since then—alas, for full four centuries—the thought has echoed about countries, towns and cities, that the Greek form is paramount to all forms that man possibly could create. It is the very foundation of all architecture. Therefore: take it, and use it. And certainly, it has been taken and used. It has been cast and carved in thousands of possible and impossible modulations. It has been moulded to suit any purpose, to cover any structure, and to decorate any wall surface, exterior and interior alike. In this manner the Greek orders have been used and overused till the last drop of expressiveness has been squeezed out of these originally so expressive orders.

This was the decline and death of indigenous expressiveness in the art of building; and the sensing of that fundamental principle of expression was a lost sense.

2. Decline of Form-correlation:

Infringement of the principle of expression was not the only momentous result of the imitative episode, for even the principle of correlation was violated. It happened, thus:

Prior to the imitative era, building-design was conceived as a fitting feature on its proper site. So to speak, the building grew like a plant from its soil, and was moulded into its surroundings as a rightly correlated member of that building family which constituted the architectural atmosphere of the town. This procedure, therefore, was not only a matter of "building-design," but even of "town-design," and thanks to this latter fact, the town became gradually shaped into its three-dimensional formation. After the introduction of imitative styles, however, the design procedure became the reverse, and reverse became even its effects. When building-design was conceived at the command of an alien and ancient style-form and independent of its location, the building was bound to be irrelevant to time, site, and surroundings. So was building-design conceived, and accordingly it was taught. Once the Classical orders were accepted as the fundamentals of architecture, almost the entire machinery of architectural education was turned to further this thought. Building-design was, from that time on, moved to the class-rooms of the schools, where design was conceived on paper with scarcely any consideration about site characteristics. In this spirit of independence, generally speaking, architectural education has been carried on, generation after generation up to our time, imbuing every student with the thought that the virtue of architectural design lies in the supremacy of style, and that site characteristics and environment are of no importance. Contemporary influences, such as the spirit of the time—not to speak of the spirit of the town—had no place in the teaching of design. Surely, this has been a faulty conception of architectural education.

This faulty conception of architectural education produced what we may call the "self-sufficient" building, meaning a building-type which leant entirely on the excellence of its stylistic treatment, and had nothing in common with connecting buildings. Such a building type became an egotistic member of the society of buildings in the town, it created discord wherever it was erected, and it made the town's form-coherence impossible. This is fully obvious, **for as there cannot be a socially healthy population consisting only of egotistic individualists having no common spirit, so there cannot be an architecturally healthy community consisting of only self-sufficient buildings.** Anyone can easily perceive the truth of this. Therefore, it could have been easily predicted what would ultimately happen to the town's architectural formation when the prevailing mode of both architectural education and building-design was carried on in this spirit of self-sufficiency. This was not predicted, however, for the time had gradually become undiscerning as to the importance of form-coherence.

This was the decline and death of three-dimensional unity in town-building; and the sensing of that fundamental principle of correlation was a lost sense—just as was that of expression.

3. Imitation and Irrelation:

When the two indispensable principles of expression and correlation were abandoned, their antipodes, imitation and irrelation, entered into action. Such was the ultimate growth of the seed that was planted by the Late Renaissance. The Late

Renaissance, however, did not realize the potential dangers of its action, for the art of building was still deeply rooted in the past, and the architects—in spite of doctrinal reasoning—were subconsciously animated with the strong form-sense from previous days. Such conditions prevailed much beyond the Renaissance period, for even the Baroque and Rococo times were characteristic in their respective form-expressions. The incubation time of the bacteria of both imitation and irrelation, as we see, was of a long duration; and it was some time before the real effects appeared in full force. The real effects appeared during the latter part of the nineteenth century, when the free play with imitative forms became proverbial, and irrelevancy between building-design and site-character became complete. This brought about divorce between plan and building, and changed "town-building" into "town-planning."

It is significant that the change from town-building into town-planning was a gradual process spanning several centuries. It indicates that the subconscious sensing of principles—innate in man—needed a long time to become subdued. Besides, the old towns still possessed an aspect of coherence from times past, and to disturb this inheritance by conspicuously irrelevant form-effects would not have been acceptable to that innate sensitiveness of form still present.

But, although these towns remained coherent in form, they were doomed to lose their former indigenous form-expression, and gradually to become dressed in new architectural garments of more or less classical origin. The sense for true form-expression weakened before the sense for good form-correlation yielded. That is, the decay of the plant commenced at the core, and not until later was the whole body affected.

But, however gradual the downward change was, and in whatever order the decay entered, all the same the direction toward decline was definite. When poison enters into the body, and there is no knowledge how to confine its effect, the body is doomed. Surely, there was no knowledge how to confine the gradual civic decline. In those days when the decline was toward its worst, nobody thought of civic problems in terms of expressiveness of form and correlation of forms. Imitation and irrelation were the stronger forces. They took the command of things into their hands.

4. The Stylistic Episode:

In order to understand the salient aspects of town-building after the Late Renaissance time, one must be familiar with the spirit of the epoch, and with its history. In the foregoing we have already outlined the development from the Middle Ages to the Late Renaissance time. Here we learned of the gradual fermentation of the mediaeval spirit through humanistic thought and classical form, till ultimately the classical form became to such a degree accepted in actual use that a direct imitation was the result. This process was primarily a matter of mind, where the **"instinctive sensing"** of the creative mediaeval form was gradually metamorphosed into the **"intellectual acceptance"** of the imitative Late Renaissance style.

This metamorphosis indicates that the Late Renaissance conception of matters was in many respects contrary to the mediaeval. The mediaeval conception was genuinely intimate with informality as the leading theme, and with great architectural achievements of common nature, such as fortresses for common protection and cathedrals for common cult. The Late Renaissance, in contrast, symbolized a striving for the stylistic magnitude of individual palaces which were to a great extent erected for families of importance and wealth. Frequently, these palaces were erected as stately mansions for local rulers, and were of such dominating significance that the adjacent areas had to subordinate. Many of the developments of the Late Renaissance time and thereafter, therefore, must be interpreted from the point of view of palatial lay-outs of distinction. Many outstanding schemes in Renaissance and Baroque were actualized in the prevailing spirit of formal architecture, and these schemes were to a large degree instrumental in keeping order alive, at least in their immediate vicinity.

We see no reason for going into a detailed study of the palatial developments during the various style-shiftings after the Renaissance era. There is the less reason for doing so just now, especially as we are going to return to this subject later on in the following chapter—where the formal trend of architecture will be more closely dealt with. There is one particular instance in these palatial developments, however, which must be mentioned in this connection. It is the case of that magnificent development of Versailles. This development must be mentioned because it externalized the highest peak in the gradual upward climb. Alas, it was not only the highest peak, but it was also a peak with a tremendous precipice concealed as in ambush.

We are not going to undertake a comprehensive explanation—not even in this Versailles case—of all the magnificent palaces with their wings and courtyards; of Le Nôtre's parks and gardens with their lakes, pools, and fountains; or of the Trianons, and of all the rest. We are going to touch only the grandiose lay-out's weak points as confronted with the conditions of life in the realm of France at large.

Surely, the rulers of France constituted an exhibition of power and magnitude in an extraordinarily magnificent manner, for themselves and their dazzling courts. But the people had to suffer. If all the money spent to satisfy royal ambitions had been used instead for satisfactory accommodation of the people, there would have been achieved a splendid cultural result. If such had been the case, it would not perhaps have been necessary for us, in our school years, to have had to remember all the many facts and excitements of the French Revolution—but rather to have studied a less agitating French evolution. This was not the case, however, for the trend of the era was directed toward magnitude of form by means of which to feather the rulers' own nests—in which feathering, the proper accommodation of people had no place. But, because there was so great an emphasis of such a narrow conception of life, and because the rulers continued to augment this overemphasis, the breaking point was destined to come. It came with a vengeance. It came as the French Revolution which changed entirely the conditions of life and the existing social order. Nay, **it changed even those presuppositions on which town-building of the time was founded.**

Those presuppositions on which town-building of the time was founded had little to do with organic town-design in the right understanding of this term. Those presuppositions, as we have seen, were mere civic embellishment by means of grandiose lay-outs and magnificent edifices. Now the situation reversed itself, for, after the many ups and downs which followed the French Revolution had been gradually normalized, the palatial problems lost their former significance and the problems of the people came into the foreground. This required entirely a new orientation. It required more than that, for it required new men to try the task. It required new educational methods to prepare these men for their new task. It required a new art-form of town design based on new principles, new social order, new physical organization, and new architectural expression. And finally, it required considerable experience—which of course was a matter of time, and of a long time, too.

Now, one would think that, when the need is urgent, the help is close at hand. After the intemperate form-gourmandises of the Baroque and Rococo, it would have seemed refreshing to revert to the real soil, and to start a new era of honest, simple, and direct form, expressing the new life. Undoubtedly this would have been the logical step to take, yet the time was not ripe for such a creative deed. Before this could have been achieved, a high wall of preconceived ideas and opinionated style conceptions should have been torn down. It must be borne in mind that, because of the adoption of alien style-forms, the matter of style had gradually become so thoroughly imprinted in the spirit of the time that the designing of buildings and towns could scarcely have been considered in any terms other than those of style. In the course of time it was forgotten that architecture—just as any other art-form—is fundamentally a creatively expressive art-form and that **style evolves gradually from the progress of creative architecture, and not architecture from style.** During this long stylistic adventure, the underlying principles had become indiscriminately lost in an ornamental jumble and, therefore, the architects had neither the knowledge nor the creative potentiality to continue in any other than the old road of historical style-forms. They had to apply earlier formal experiences to less formal demands.

These attempts were doomed to failure, naturally, because strange methods were superimposed upon conditions having little in common with these methods. This failure however was not recognized in those days, and the building of towns went on as heretofore.

This failure in town-building did not appear at first in its worst form, for most of the buildings were designed in a comparatively quiet manner. Besides, these buildings were relatively small in size, and therefore easily adaptable to a satisfactory ensemble. Consequently, large sections of the town were formed somewhat coherently.

In spite of this, form-decay went on. When the lack of architectural understanding finally led to the Neo-Romantic extravagances with their full fathom of possible and impossible style combinations, there was not much left of honest design. The unreal attitude of the Neo-Romantic movement poured unreal spirit into form-conception, form-imagination was released, and ran wild. Towers and battlements decorated the buildings according to the Romanesque recipe, not in Romanesque spirit however, for no one attacked the

miniature towers and no one shot from the Lilliputian battlements. The Gothic form was revised and given a whiff of
romanticism. Romantic spirit was infused into the forms of
Renaissance, making the style rich and exuberant. A deluge
of forms in all styles arose, and luxury of cheap ornamentation governed the degree of beauty. In this manner the Neo-
Romantic time brought into the city a super-abundance of
miscellaneous pseudo-style-forms.

At the bottom of heart and soul, the Neo-Romanticism
was an idealistic movement. It endeavored to elevate the
minds of men above the petty matters of prosaic everyday life
and for this reason its aim was to create, by means of architectural forms, a romantic environment in which to live. As
such, the movement was in direct opposition to the materialistic attitude which the growing industrialization brought
about almost simultaneously. This opposition created competition between the two movements. But as the Neo-
Romantic movement was artificially super-imposed upon the
conditions of life, and often indeed overemphasized, the wells
of its enthusiasm were soon exhausted and the materialistic
attitude—which possessed a strong practical appeal—got the
upper hand.

This materialistic attitude, on its part, had no ambitions
to create a form-world of its own. It simply adopted the ornamental scraps of the Neo-Romantic movement—in which
scraps, after the artificial romanticism evaporated, nothing
was left but an insipid smack of parvenue vulgarity.

There is an old saying: when one gives a finger to the
devil, he takes the whole hand. In the case of the city, this
saying has been proven more than true. For, when the gods
of creation were abandoned and the devil of imitation was
accepted, this unworthy gentleman took not only the individual building, but even the whole city.

The foregoing analysis of the gradual downfall of the imitative style-form shows clearly what kind of fruit that innocent

seed of the Late Renaissance imitation ultimately bred. It shows, furthermore, the hopeless state of things into which the city's development had been brought. However, the bottom of this hopeless state of things was not as yet reached by the mere style confusion in the town. This came still more into appearance when buildings of private ownership and of commercial type became big, tall, and massive. Because these buildings were erected without sufficient control so as to safeguard good correlation of form, matters progressed steadily toward increased disregard of form-unity. The city, instead of having been developed into a three-dimensional manifestation of human cultural aims, became a heterogeneous display of all kind of buildings. Ideals were abandoned. Commercialism was accepted. The materialistic attitude became predominant, causing a grim atmosphere of superficiality.

Town-design vanished from the field of architecture. It became mere two-dimensional planning. The self-sufficient building, now with full freedom for dangerous spread, pushed itself to the forefront. Made decoratively conspicuous by its own ornamental merits, it became the leader of the city's two-dimensional trend toward discord. In this manner the city became an accumulation of irrelevant building units, heterogeneously distributed, with no other influence on the population than its materialistic platitude.

B. THE SOIL: SOCIAL CONDITIONS

Considering social conditions—now particularly social conditions in the town community—it is quite natural that our preceding analysis of the gradual changes in the town's physical formation already indicate corresponding changes in the social characteristics in the town. It must be so, for, after all, form mirrors the aims and actions of that society which originated this form. This holds true, no matter whether form stands high in quality, or low.

The population of the mediaeval town was almost thoroughly a bourgeois society of the intellectual middle-class, of warriors, of merchants, and of men of trades, crafts, and the like. It was a large urban family which took care of the town affairs through its burgomaster and councilmen and through officials of one kind or another. It was an informal group of citizens who practiced their respective vocations when peace prevailed about the town, and who stuck together in mutual defense when danger was within sight.

But, as in the course of time certain families, because of wealth or strong personal qualifications, rose into power, the balance in civic affairs turned toward these families. Ultimately they became the ruling families, not only of their own town proper but even of surrounding towns and territories. As, in some instances, this power increase went on in a constant acceleration, those families which got possession of this augmented power became the rulers of important realms. This power was used differently in different cases. Sometimes, it was used to the benefit of the people. Sometimes again, the people were kept down. Often the people were kept down with hard-handedness, which hard-handedness in the Versailles case—to recall that outburst—resulted in a social uprising of momentous consequences.

But, whatever the social changes were and whatever had caused these changes, they were reflected in the town's physical order. In the mediaeval case where the maintenance of social order was a common concern, the physical order was carried throughout the whole town. In the case of the ruling families, on the other hand, the physical order of the town was concentrated primarily about the palaces of these ruling families. And the more the ruler's influence expanded into the enlarged realms, the more conspicuous grew the gap between the magnificent palatial developments and the destitute situation of the town peoples themselves.

1. Industry, Intercommunication, and Social Changes:

The above remarks concerning urban social conditions in earlier days may serve as a background against which to reflect the radical changes in urban social conditions during the nineteenth century.

In the dawning years of the said century—or perhaps somewhat later—there was an entirely new picture on the socio-historical screen. It was the picture of those changes in the social and economic life which paved the way for that tremendous civic development we have witnessed during the past decades, and which still goes on. In this picture we can discern three distinct tendencies, of which each one was, in one way or another, instrumental in the furthering of urban growth. First, we discern the rapid development in the fields of sciences and machine production which brought about the industrial situation and ultimately the present machine age. Second, we discern the development of means of transportation, which brought about a closer intercommunication between town and country and caused a townbound movement of the rural population. And third, we discern the general development toward a new social order, with its excesses and drawbacks.

These three tendencies prepared the soil for an enormous growth of cities in both number and size. Yet, at the same time, these three tendencies neglected to prepare the urban soil to raise satisfactory product during this growth. On the contrary, because of their respective materialistic inclinations, they forced things toward indolence in townbuilding matters.

Analyzing now these three tendencies separately, we have first the industrial situation and its effects upon the urban population.

Already in the middle of the eighteenth century there appeared a movement, the so called "Industrial Revolution," meaning emancipation from handi-work and turning toward machine-work in industrial production. Naturally, this movement was, in the beginning, comparatively slow, and could just as well have been characterized as "evolution," for those machines at hand were primitive in efficiency and limited almost entirely to textile manufacturing. Besides this fact, the industrial establishments were relatively small in size and generally located where water-power was available; that is, in the free country. For this reason these industrial developments had no particular effect on urban conditions. The rural population was engaged in these industrial plants and in agricultural work as well; hence there was not as yet, insofar as class distinction is concerned, much difference between agricultural and industrial workmen.

When steam-power first came into use, industry had the freedom to select its location guided by other considerations than those of driving-power. And as the towns were in many respects preferable for such a location, the industrial plants were, in most cases, moved there.

This was of great consequence in civic development.

To bring industry into the town, meant that large areas were needed for plants and workmen's housing. It meant, likewise, that the town boundaries had to be extended toward the country. It meant, furthermore—and this is most significant in our case—that an entirely new class of people was brought into the town—the industrial workers' class, which in its viewpoints and habits was of rural origin, but which now became predominantly urbanized. Town characteristics, both social and physical, were affected accordingly. The former population, having thus been blended to a considerable proportion with industrial workers, was to a corresponding degree changed in its aims and policies. And the physical aspect of the town was transformed by the erection of industrial plants and workmen's housing districts.

These workmen's housing districts—in their further development, and often, indeed, in their rapid dilapidation—

bear witness that the industrial movement had many stumbling-blocks to overcome. Instead of smooth co-operation between industrial leaders and workmen, there arose controversial interests; there arose economic differences; there arose political differences; there arose uncertainty in the earning of living; and there arose malcontentment of one kind or another.

This is a long story, but the main thing now is that the town faced social problems which were new and entirely lacking the sound support of sufficient experience. In fact, the course of events discloses that these problems got a far from satisfactory solution, generally speaking. And, as the main issues in the solution of these problems were of economic and material nature, the result was bound to be materialistic in spirit.

Second, we have the growth of means of transportation.

The new means of transportation, too, were a direct result of scientific discoveries and technical inventions. Here too, the introduction of steam-power was most effective, for it heralded the railroads to come. These railroads, in fact, came first into use when a third of the nineteenth century had already passed, and therefore their development coincided with the industrial development at a time when the latter had become industrial revolution in reality and not only in name.

Railroad traffic established a convenient intercommunication between the towns and the vast country lands. This fact caused a great change in civic development, for it animated the movement from the country to the town. A considerable portion of the rural population began to invade the towns, for the towns attracted the country dweller with their many novelties. Expecting to find more interesting work than tilling the soil, many left their quiet country homes to seek the restlessness and excitement of the town.

Just as was the case with the industrial worker's invasion of the towns, so was the case even with that of the rural population in general. This invasion brought into the towns new elements and new conditions of life. It diluted the consistency of the traditional urban population with new attitudes such as were bound to dilute even the physical coherence of the town. The harmful element in this dilution was that growing tendency to materialism.

Third, we have the growth toward a new social order.

The trend to a new social order in the Western world may have had its roots somewhere in a more or less distant past, but most certainly the French Revolution was the decisive turning point in this respect. The French Revolution brought the thought of human equality to the surface; and although this thought, in the turmoils of the revolution, was emotionally overemphasized to such an extent that inequality in a reversed form was frequently the result, the thought of equality after all was injected in the general attitude of the time. In the course of the nineteenth century, therefore, the said thought became the source of much unrest, of many social upheavals, and of a great many adjustments and compromises in the existing social order. As time passed, historical mutations so changed the social structure of former days that the heretofore repressed masses at the bottom began to move upward with insistent demands for rights in the conduct of common affairs.

Perhaps the undercurrent at the bottom of this movement was a logical trend along, say, democratic lines; a natural evolution toward human rights and civil liberties on a sound basis where each individual member of the human society demanded a reasonable place in the sun. If that had been the case, on the whole then **the trend would have been fully congruent to the endeavors of such advanced town-building as we are trying to further, where the fundamental aim must be to provide everyone in the community with a proper place in which to live.**

But, however sound this said striving for human equality might have been at the bottom, we are not now considering the movement from that angle. That is, we are not considering the movement as a long time evolutionary process growing from within and caused by inner potentialities. We are rather considering it as a circumstantial manifestation caused by outer events—historical, political, and economic—such as had little in common with human potentialities and other conditions growing from within. To be exact, we are considering now mainly the equalization movement's negative tendencies, both social and economic. It must namely be understood that the equalization movement was not a smoothly running process in cultural terms, but a social and economic struggle, often of revolutionary character, and with growing malcontentment as the leading theme. For this reason the movement was frequently of hampering consequences to the social life at large. It was perhaps more so to the social life within the town, for primarily within the town boundaries the social struggle took place. To the physical aspect of the town it was most serious, for the leveling of the urban population usually meant the leveling of the town's physical order down to a commonplace and stereotyped plane. And as the increasing struggle for livelihood, particularly in those communities of rapid growth, made the materialistic point of view predominant, the physical atmosphere of the towns was doomed to sink to one of superficial platitude of materialistic civilization.

This quality of superficial platitude of materialistic civilization was a rather general trend in the course of things. For, when now summarizing our harvest from the three above scrutinized movements—industrialization, intercommunication, and the changes toward a new social order—we find that the trend toward materialism was the prevailing characteristic in all of these.

Furthermore, we can find that these three movements coincided in many other respects. Coincidently, they caused the town-bound movement, and, because of this, the cities growth. Coincidently, they changed the urban social structure from a formerly coherent body to a heterogeneous accumulation of diversified elements and diverse interests. Coincidently—as a natural result of this—they influenced the growing city's physical aspect toward a corresponding heterogeneous accumulation of diversiformed structure elements—which heterogeneous accumulation brought into the town's architectural atmosphere the said superficial platitude of materialistic civilization.

2. Toward Materialistic Attitude of Mind:

We do not mean by the above statement that industrialization, intercommunication, or social reforms of one kind or another were necessarily in themselves of such natures as could cause decline in the manner just described; that is, toward superficial materialistic civilization. Most certainly, in themselves, these developments could as well have been turned to bear satisfactory cultural fruit, provided the aim of the time in these matters had been strong enough to foster such endeavors. But we do mean that, when these developments emerged from the progress of things and continued to form themselves into distinct movements, the time was not conscious of the fact that, besides those economic and material issues that were innate in these movements, there were even spiritual issues of manifold natures and of vital consequences. We do mean, furthermore, that, just because these spiritual issues were not taken into consideration so as to direct things along cultural channels, the materialistic point of view was brought to the surface, the towns were expanded accordingly in a haphazard manner, and ultimately into countless slums.

These slums are morally and physically most dangerous to human society, and, because the burden of their clearance is our inheritance from those times when the groundwork of the materialistic era was laid, we are fully justified in asking whether or not such pernicious consequences as these disorganized conditions in the cities of today could have been prevented by a careful survey before things drifted beyond man's control? The usual excuse that any new movement is full of unknown quantities, and that through the making of mistakes one becomes wise, does not satisfy us. Although we know perfectly well that mistakes always constitute a good lesson to remember, this does not necessarily mean that one should not at least **try** to avoid mistakes by a careful survey of the situation at hand before action is undertaken. The larger the problems at stake and the more momentous their possible effects, the more must one be concerned about the mode of their solution. Otherwise one's behavior must be stamped as unpardonable negligence.

Certainly, those problems at stake when the town boundaries had to be extended, were important and, as experience has fully shown, the consequences of their solutions were most grave. In spite of this, only occasionally can one find evidence of careful surveys preceding the solutions. The general trend to laxity and unconcern left things to develop as best they could without proper advice.

It is amazing to observe that, while the time now in question was progressively alert in many fields of cultural activities, it was dull and narrow in its conception of the arts of both building and town-building. Perhaps the answer to this lies in the fact that the psychology of the time had been lulled into the sweet-dreams of pretty decoration of windows, door-ways, cornices, and the like, and that the architectural ambitions of the time were satisfied with this. In this satisfaction the time did not bother itself with any serious search for an architectural expression of its own. The time did not seem to have realized that the development of one's own architectural expression is an essential part of man's cultural duties, and that this calls for more concern than just an indolent aping of previous achievements. The time did not seem to have realized that architecture, whether good or bad, is that art-form which with its influence everyday and everywhere—in cities, towns, villages, and homes—penetrates deep into the intimacy of human life, constituting its atmosphere, good or bad, in which to live. Indeed, **the time did not seem to have realized the cultural importance of living in an atmosphere of true, direct, and creative architecture, and of art in general.**

The time did not seem to have realized all this, for the materialistic attitude of mind was not concerned in such matters and, therefore, the instinctive sensitiveness in these respects had gradually been beclouded.

3. Debasement of Taste:

Speaking of "living in an atmosphere of true, direct, and creative art," there were, generally speaking, two circles where such living took place. First, there was the urban community—the city, the town—where art activities were concentrated, where the population had the opportunity to become acquainted with these art activities and, consequently, where proper art understanding was genuinely nursed. Second, there was the rural community—the village, the hamlet, the country-side—where indigenous folk-art was widely practised by many, and understood and appreciated by everyone. As long as art life—in town and country-side—had not as yet been influenced by that superficial platitude which the materialistic era brought about, unalloyed taste and appreciation of creative art still prevailed. But as soon as the materialistic attitude got its roots into the soil and industry began to affect art—art in general and folk-art as well—debasement of taste took place.

Way back in the Middle Ages, or perhaps particularly then, the town was a living place of men of art from all of the branches of that vocation. Almost everything of any form-value, from the modestly formed poker at the fireplace to the most elaborately carved pinnacle of the Cathedral,

was the work of artists and skilled craftsmen. In the mediaeval towns, therefore, an intense spirit of art-creation existed. Later on, when towns grew larger and the mighty
princes established there their grandiose palaces, these
princes summoned to their courts famous architects, sculp-
tors, painters, and artisans of all kinds in order to create an
atmosphere of artistic activities about themselves. In this
manner, the princely courts became the enlivening centers
of comprehensive art production, and of great inspiration
about the towns at large.

Now, whether we consider the mediaeval town or that
of the ruling prince, there is one significant thing to bear in
mind; namely, that every simple object of art work was a
hand-made unique piece, no matter what the material of
execution might have been—whether stone, metal, wood,
tile, glass, textiles, or something else. As the demand for
objects and implements was general and comprehensive,
covering all the classes and ages no matter what the circumstances of life, consequently everyone was more or less in
everyday contact with conception and production of art work
of all kinds. This everyday contact with conception and
production of art imbued the citizens with the subconscious
sense of living in an atmosphere of true, direct, and creative
art. It kept understanding and appreciation of creative art
alive, and the general taste for art values remained on the
safe foundations of this understanding and appreciation.

But when the machine was introduced into this field of
art activities and was able to produce by the thousands cheap
imitations of hand-made objects, conditions in design and
craftsmanship were entirely altered. Elated by the rapid
progress of industry, the machine was turned to manufacture
all kinds of art-objects in unlimited quantity. And as the
time had gradually become so ornament-conscious that a
surface could scarcely have been appealing to the eye unless
it was covered with decoration, there arose considerable bewilderment as to good and bad in design. This was still

more the case because the prevailing decoration was not of that indigenous quality of the past, but just ornamental medley from here and there and everywhere.

A gradual and general debasement of taste was an inevitable result. To begin with, this debasement took place primarily in the large urban centers, and particularly among people of small means who, thanks to a misdirected instinct of pride, welcomed keenly the opportunity of coming into possession of unlimited ornamental richnesses by little money. Because of the improved means of communication, however, these ornamental richnesses were soon spread throughout the land, to town and country, and even to those regions where folk-art still was untouched by the pernicious effects of materialism.

The contact with materialism was a hard blow to folk-art, for it brought a strange and harmful disposition into the formerly so clean and healthy atmosphere. This atmosphere was the reverse of materialism, for folk-art did not originate from the work for daily livelihood or for other material reasons; it grew from inner drift for inner satisfaction. As long as this was a fact, folk-art was strong. But as soon as the materialistic spirit of mercantilism affected the genuine spirit of folk-art, folk-art ceased to be an expression of inner drift for inner satisfaction, and became instead commercial production of souvenirs for tourists and gift-shops. It was not any more an art-form to live with, but the source of material profit. The art-form to live with was from now on imported from the manufacturing centers of mercantile-objects-of-art, which to a large extent consisted of the most tasteless stuff that the human brain and the machine in unholy alliance were able to produce.

In this manner poor taste penetrated all the layers of the people, in town and in country-side. It affected everyone. Even the innocent child was a victim of this fate, for behold what happened to the child. When the budding imagination of the child should have been directed by means of toys simple enough to give his imagination free play to develop, instead, from the first days that the child became conscious of all the curiosities this new world of his could bestow, glimmering and glittering trinkets were put into his hands. Thus, beginning with the nursery and the home, and ending with shops, show-windows, and market-places, this pernicious taste was exhibited in thousands of varieties and imprinted into the minds of youth and adult, of man and woman, of poor and rich, day after day, year after year. Alas, in the face of all this, how could it have been prevented **that the general taste degenerated ultimately in to a parvenu taste of a kind which the world never has seen before, and which—we are sure, and certainly hope—never can be surpassed.**

Such as above described had ultimately become the prevailing taste. This result was unavoidable as things logically and gradually developed during a long period of time from creative sensitiveness to imitative insensitiveness.

We have endeavored in the foregoing analysis to trace this down-bound development from creative sensitiveness to imitative insensitiveness along two different lines. In the first part of this analysis—pertaining to art-form—we have endeavored to trace the development along the professional line, namely, along that line where architecture in general and town-building in particular should have been maintained on a creatively high level, **but was not.** In the second part—pertaining to social conditions—we have endeavored to trace the development along the layman's line of the general public, where the creative values of architecture and town building probably would have been accepted with considerable appreciation, provided these art-forms had remained creative—**which, however, was far from the case.**

We have followed this double development all along the progress of several centuries, beginning from the mediaeval high tide of creative alertness, and ending with that lowest ebb of taste of the "Gay Nineties." During all this progress, we have recorded the step by step happenings which played their respective and decisive roles in the gradual degeneration. In this manner, we have finally arrived at the same conclusion as in the beginning was stated in metaphorical language, thus: **"civic decline has been caused by both deficient seed and fallow soil."**

C. TOWN-PLANNING

Dissolution of town-building brought town-planning into the foreground. Town-planning, however, was regarded as a rather prosaic occupation for an architect, as it did not befit him to deal with such non-artistic matters as the measuring of land and the making of maps. These were left entirely into the hands of the surveyor and the engineer, who with the aid of their instruments staked out land areas, building lots, and streets. For such routine work no more ability was required than an average technical knowledge, common sense, and considerable labor. Creative ability was considered of no consequence.

In this light was the greater part of the later nineteenth century town-planning understood, and the results surely mirror this understanding. When studying town-plans from this period of rapid urban growth, it is easy to discern how superficially planning was carried out. The prevailing street schemes were those of a monotonous gridiron pattern of straight streets and right-angled corners, no matter whether the terrain was level or otherwise. Save for Main Street and a few exceptional spots in the town where style was in command, street construction was always the same, regardless of whether this happened in the center of the town or in its outskirts.

It is obvious that the city's third dimension was almost entirely disregarded, for actual building work had little integral relation to the plan, which latter provided only a stereo-typed site for the building. On that site the architect could at any time erect his structure in any shape or style, much in the same way as a cabinet-maker sets up his products at a furniture show. Building character mattered little, for the laying out of a proper sewer system—if any—was considered more important than form-coherence of the city.

In this manner the planning of towns proceeded, wasting urban potentialities, fostering insincere cultural aims, and decreasing possibilities for later generations of bringing better conditions into the town.

D. THE ARCHITECT

While people moved into the town, while the town grew and became a crowded city, and while the surveyor measured lands and worked out his maps for further growth, the architect took but little part in these activities. The art of town-building had slipped from his hands, and this had happened so gradually that the architect scarcely was aware of the fact that the most fundamental part of his art was gone.

Where was the architect during this period? Was he designing, copying, or collecting ornaments? Was he busy with his innumerable styles in forming towers, pinnacles, crenelations, or other picturesque stage stuff for the survey-or's settings?

Evidently he was.

When passing along streets built during these decades of decay, one's eyes are met by a fanciful overflowing orna-mentation, with little or no plain surface save the ornament-free restfulness of the backyard. One wonders how all this ornamentation could come into being, and one wonders why the owner dwelling behind this outfit allowed it to remain there. Did he enjoy it? Did he desire it for cultural satis-faction? Did he intend to advertise cultural ambitions which perhaps did not exist? Or, perhaps he was boasting of his pecuniary wealth?

Emerson hits the point: "We are all physiognomists and penetrators of character, and things themselves are detective. If you follow the suburban fashion in building a sumptuous looking house for little money, it will appear to all eyes as a cheap dear house."

Surely, an obvious statement. And even if the building sometimes did cost huge sums of money, nevertheless the ornamental treatment with borrowed style-decorations brought the architectural value of the building down to the level of cheap imitation.

Why did the architects of those days lend their supreme art-form for such ends? Architecture should have been regarded with higher esteem than that! And what is the effect of this kind of a superficial procedure for times to come? Indeed, it is bound to be negative, for when every building is covered with meaningless ornamental decoration having no cultural value whatsoever, the architectural aspect of the bulk of the town is just ornamental nonsense. Midst this ornamental nonsense, we and our children alike are doomed to dwell and to suck of its depraving influence.

The only note of relief in this decorative sadness is the work of the gardener. The gardener could not go astray, for he dealt with nature's products. His form-language was truthful, for nature is truthful. With each added opportunity given to the gardener to plant, the town became more livable. And when his plantings grew into lofty trees and shadowy parks, coherence was restored in the town through nature's forms.

We owe the gardener much credit for this.

It was in the nineteenth century that the materialistic growth became dangerous for the city's organic coherence.

During this same period the sense for form-coherence reached its lowest ebb.

Isn't this significant:

Just at the time when the creative instinct for town building was most needed, it ceased to exist. The sense for the most comprehensive art of man was lost. Yet, the great loss was not understood—much less regretted.

3. CIVIC REHABILITATION

THE preceding investigation of civic decline has dealt with the average course of urban development, in particular with that of rapid urban growth which took place during the latter part of the nineteenth century. As such, this investigation does not cover the whole field, for unquestionably there were a great number of towns in which no signs of decline could be found during this said period. One may have traveled around in Western, Southern, and Central Europe, or in Scandinavia, and quite frequently and in almost every country one could have seen delightful towns with perfect form-order. One could have had the same experience in different sections of England too, and in many places of the New England States one could easily have gotten the impression that all this talk about civic decline is just exaggerated fault-finding.

We know, of course, of countless cases where civic decline was an unknown thing. So was the situation for instance when conditions were rather static, and the waves of materialism had not yet crossed the town boundaries. The situation was similar in those conditions where earlier cultural values were kept in honor, and culturally enlightened and communally influential groups of citizens took pride in the development of their home town. Any new building in such conditions was an event, and its design was often discussed from every angle before it progressed to the final stage of execution. This kind of civic development, naturally, raised a keen interest in the community's affairs, and resulted in the appreciation of good form-unity.

Such conditions must have existed in a great number of

towns, and in many countries too, although perhaps not infrequently both efforts and results have vanished into the darkness of oblivion. Perhaps much will remain unrecorded because the conduct of civic affairs might have been a sincere but quiet striving without blatant self-advertisement. Many achievements, perhaps, have been ignored because they took place in such slowly growing communities as were looked upon with disdain in a time when rapid growth was regarded by the prevailing attitude of materialism as the only acceptable sign of vitality. Perhaps, in many cases a subsequent materialistic development has destroyed the fruits of previous efforts, and these communities for this reason have become enrolled under the general banner of devolution.

But, however numerous and manifold in character these exceptional cases might have been, nevertheless our statement about civic decline stands firm. It must namely be observed, that most probably almost every one of those cases where civic decline was absent were towns at a relative standstill; whereas our analysis considers primarily those urban communities which, during the course of the past century and even much thereafter, had to face a rapid growth. It was just because of this rapid growth—and of course because of the lack of sufficient experience to meet this rapid growth—that decline took place.

Therefore, despite exceptions, the average trend in urban growth continued in a manner which was prejudicial to the organic unity of the cities. And we are fully justified in vindicating our previous statement that the art of town-building had declined to a dwindling art-form.

Yet, things could not go downhill forever. Sooner or later, the brakes had to be employed, and constructive efforts had to be undertaken to rehabilitate conditions in the blighted city.

So matters really came to pass, and these rehabilitation efforts were carried along two different movements and in two opposite directions. One of these movements essayed to superimpose upon the city formal monumentality in a stylistic sense. The other endeavored to restore forgotten but fundamental principles. Also, in short, **the former imposed outside means,** whereas **the latter tried to restore things from within.**

The former movement—essaying to superimpose formal monumentality—had its roots in that stylistic episode which was analyzed in the preceding chapter. As can be remembered, after the French Revolution there existed a prevailing leaning to keep the palatially formal architecture alive, notwithstanding the fact that the revolutionary changes in social conditions—having gradually, after many ups and downs, become normalized on a rather bourgeois level—made such a leaning unnatural. There was no escape from this leaning, however, for, as was said in the cited chapter, "the architects had neither the knowledge nor the creative potentiality to continue in any but the old road of historical style-forms. They had to apply earlier formal experiences to less formal demands." Later on, this leaning to formality developed into a conscious movement with the distinct aim to preserve the mode of formal design in the city. Considering that this movement was a continuance of the previous mode of formal design, we will designate it as the "Formal Continuance."

However, when time passed, this superficial method of stylistic civic embellishment caused much opposition in progressive circles. In the course of time, it became obvious that sooner or later something more fundamental than mere stylistic decoration had to be undertaken in order to save civic developments from their downbound trend. The latter movement—the endeavor to restore forgotten but fundamental principles—became therefore an effort to revive town-building: first, by studying the classical and mediaeval mode of informal town-building, and then by applying to contemporary town-building those fundamental principles revealed through this classical and mediaeval study. This movement, consequently, we may legitimately term the "Informal Revival."

A. FORMAL CONTINUANCE

Stylistic formality was much discussed in our previous chapter on civic decline. So far, however, the question was merely about Classical and Renaissance styles, insofar as these were used in the designing of towns and as they ultimately became the means by which to glorify ruling personalities and their environments. But, when we now are about to turn our attention to that conscious—or why not say "self-conscious"—movement of stylistic formality, the problem of formality must be analyzed from this particular angle. In order to be able to give a clear description of this said movement, we must first examine its case in historical light by going to the roots and reasons of its origin.

While events had their course and the Middle Ages came to an end, even the means and methods of warfare changed. The tightly concentrated and elaborately fortified mediaeval castle—once the symbol of power and wealth— became outmoded, and the town itself was made the protective stronghold in the heart of a widened realm.

So did conditions of life change.

But human nature does not change as rapidly as do conditions of life, and inasmuch as vanity is immortal, even power and wealth had to have their means of expression. Therefore, when the castle was no longer needed to fulfil its protective purpose, and when even its function as a symbol of power and wealth expired, the time stood in need of a new symbol. And because the town constituted the new center of military and political activities, this town then became the new symbol of power and wealth.

The town itself grew from the humble needs of the

people and its formation was nurtured by the intellectual middle-class. For this reason its architectural expression was informal. But those of power and wealth, more ambitious than the unpretentious bourgeoisie, were not satisfied with an informal manifestation of their importance. They required rigidity, discipline, and grandeur; and because the modest Greek form—as reflected in the Early Renaissance—could not offer this rigidity, discipline and grandeur, the craving for magnitude turned to the more imposing Roman pompousness. Accordingly, the Late Renaissance form—that image of Roman pompousness—was moulded to express power and wealth. It brought about the "pompous palace," that token of power and wealth.

But history continued on its course. Power and wealth faded, and appeared again in new forms and with new personifications. Old realms were conquered, and new realms arose. So the palatial "Vanity Fair" went on. New palaces were built. They had their time of importance. They lost it with the downfall of power and wealth. And new palaces were erected with the appearance of new realms.

In this manner, while time passed, towns and cities shared these days of rising and sinking tide. Almost all of them had their palaces of various sizes and grades, beginning with the famous Palazzo Pitti, and ending with that nonsurpassed magnificence of Versailles. These palaces mirrored a reciprocal emulation on the part of those with power and wealth.

During these floods and ebbs of reciprocal emulation, towns and cities were planned, replanned, and cleared of undesirable structures in order to provide necessary grounds for palaces and for those features connected with these palaces, such as plazas, gardens, and extensive parks. Influenced by these palaces, even the governmental and other public edifices were shaped in accordance with the formal mode of planning. In this process, the rulers' palaces not only constituted the main and most conspicuous features in

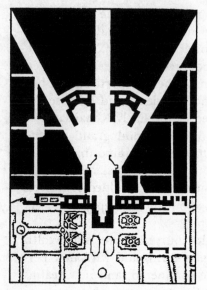

Fig. 22.
Versailles.

Fig. 23.
Mannheim.

Fig. 24.
Karlsruhe.

the towns, but even directed many other developments toward a formal solution.

Not infrequently was the whole town laid out in accordance with the palatial development. That oft-mentioned palace of Versailles, for example, decided to a large degree the street pattern of the adjacent town of the same name. Here, the three main arterial avenues of the town were designed into a formal and symmetrical unity with the palatial scheme. Another typical example in this respect is that of Mannheim in Germany. Here, the main portion of the town was laid out formally and symmetrically into a gridiron pattern within a horse-shoe-formed framework of streets, in which pattern the palace's middle axis constituted the middle axis even of the town proper. Many other examples could be referred to in order to prove our case, yet there scarcely could be found another which could more clearly stress our point than that case of Karlsruhe in Baden-Baden in Germany. Here, the tower of the palace constitutes the very focus of the whole town community. From this focus, thirty-two avenues radiate, covering with equal intervals the whole periphery. Of these thirty-two avenues, seventeen cross the broad acreage of the palatial park, whereas the remaining fifteen of these avenues impose their unnatural street pattern upon the town itself. In spite of this unnatural street pattern, Karlsruhe is a quiet and delightful town with much of refinement. Yet, the significant fact remains that the pattern of the town was inspired by palatial formality. Still more: the fact remains that the time in question could scarcely conceive town-design in other terms than those of palatial formality, just as little as the time could conceive design characteristics carried out in other terms than those of the prevailing style.

The prevailing styles during these times were, subsequently, Renaissance, Baroque, and Rococo. During the latter part of the eighteenth century, however, there began to mature a strong inclination toward a dignified simplicity along the classical order. After the ornamental excesses of the Rococo, this classical inclination reflected much of a longing for non-ornamental relaxation. Because of this longing, the eyes were turned toward plain Doric forms such as those of the Parthenon and of the temple of Paestum. Meanwhile, when ancient Pompeii was discovered—in the year 1748—this discovery unveiled a new world of form-material which seemed perfectly appropriate for adoption. And because the time was exceedingly imitative, this discovered Pompeian pattern, and the Doric form as well, were soon developed by their enthusiastic admirers into a lively Classical Revival.

This Classical Revival had a general appeal and therefore it was accepted almost everywhere. In fact, it became the prevailing style of the time. In France, it was brought to its highest peak through the strictly imperialistic developments of the Napoleonic regime. In Germany, the fine work of Schinkel brought an atmosphere of dignity about the royal center of Berlin. In many other countries, cities and towns, this Classical Revival gained ground, and so many ramifications had this trend that even as far away a country as Finland had its share of this new form-order. The Main Church Plaza in Helsinki by Karl Ludwig Engel is an exquisite example in this respect.

This, in short, is the long story of the gradual development from the informal mediaeval castle to the monumental understanding of stylistic formality. This story was told so as to explain the roots and reasons from which the continuance of town-building in terms of formality developed into a widespread movement. Besides this story, it must be furthermore borne in mind that in the above process all the forces of architectural education were most instrumental. It was particularly thanks to that famous École des Beaux-Arts in Paris that the formal understanding of the art of town-building became much of a conscious movement. Now, when all these were the conclusive and glorious facts behind the said movement, one might then have expected that this formal school of architectural thought would have been fully effective in the building of a strong dam against the flood of a general civic decline when this finally took place in the manner described in the preceding chapter. It was not so, however, **for the dam of the formal school was not of that reliable timber its glorious background might have indicated. Alas, the formal school of architectural thought was only a stylistic front, lacking that indispensable inner stamina which could take a successful leadership into its hands.** Yet, the time stood in need of leadership, and in those non-creative days the stylistic formality was the only chance. Hence the Formal Continuance.

To determine the exact time period when the Formal Continuance became a conscious movement in the service of urban development, is optional of course, and depends on from which point of view one is inclined to look upon things. As for our own point of view, we are inclined to select the most outstanding event in civic development, which particular event was rather effective in the efforts to build a dam against urban decline—at least in its own case. This event was Haussmann's plan for the reorganization of the city of Paris. It was a reorganization plan which was meant to be a "long range planning for years to come," and as such it was apt to serve as an encouraging example for many a city and in many a country. Really, it inspired a widespread movement. It might not, therefore, be out of place to mention a few further details about this Haussmannian episode.

In its earlier development, particularly during the regimes of Louis XIV, Louis XV, and Napoleon I, Paris was embellished with many monumental lay-outs of local nature. The bulk of the city's area, however—thanks to the rulers' unhappy policy of not allowing growth to expand the city's circumferential limits—was a highly concentrated, compact, and picturesque accumulation of buildings amidst narrow streets and dark quarters. The rulers only rarely considered the improvement of the living conditions of the general population, for they were too engrossed with their own ambitions. The development of Paris, therefore, was an exhibition of vanity with both remarkable results and unpardonable negligences.

Particularly expensive was the vanity of Louis XIV. Enormous sums of money were required for his regulations of Paris, yet more were required for his exorbitant undertakings in Versailles. Such expenditures were not always in agreement with the opinion in his capital, for even Voltaire—who liked splendor himself—wrote: "had Louis XIV spent in Paris only one-fifth of that money he spent in Versailles in violating nature, Paris then in its whole width were as beautiful as it is now around the Tuilleries and the Palais Royal; and it were the most beautiful city in the world."

Napoleon I, on his part, did much for Paris. Yet it was left to Napoleon III, if not to complete the embellishment of his metropolis, at least to establish his large improvement scheme, and to a great extent to bring it into actualization.

Vanity probably influenced even Napoleon III. Not completely, however, for many of his improvements were established for practical reasons. The Emperor, when deciding to go ahead with his regulations, did not consider primarily the beauty of his capital: he had more "serious" thoughts in his head. The city of Paris was frequently the battle-ground against malcontent revolutionists, and it was difficult with those means of warfare at hand to police the situation in the narrow and irregular network of streets. Because straight and broad boulevards were more suitable for an effective use of artillery, the Emperor decided to re-plan his capital accordingly. A system of straight arteries, therefore, constituted for Napoleon a practical scheme—a scheme which fortunately was in accord with the beauty of Paris; and it was fortunate indeed that the execution of this scheme was placed into the able hands of Haussmann, the great "Préfet de la Seine." In this manner, Haussmann became the leading spirit of these Paris improvements which were so enormous that they could be only begun during his lifetime.

Because the nature of Haussmann's work was predetermined by those developments as previous rulers had accomplished during their regimes, Haussmann's problem was to continue in the earlier spirit of formality. Under such circumstances Haussmann's mode of approach was logical, for the problem was not to satisfy the needs and demands of the population of Paris, but merely to carry out the Emperor's wishes. From this point of view, Haussmann's plan must be judged.

The results of Haussmann's work do not satisfy modern requirements of fast motor traffic, nor the present day demand for light and air. But Voltaire's dream of the most beautiful city has to a great extent been fulfilled.

The Haussmannian development was a natural outgrowth of Paris' earlier reconditioning, and in a true Parisian spirit. It was carried out in the manner of Classicism, to be sure; for how could it have been otherwise, with Paris the very center of Classicism and with the École des Beaux-Arts as the Classical nursery.

On the other hand, education of architects almost everywhere was carried along according to the same stylistic methods followed in that École of Paris, and almost everywhere the Classical point of view was decidedly predominant. The Haussmannian conception of civic improvement, therefore, found a well prepared soil in many a city and country. Furthermore, it was perhaps not entirely an incidental happening that the Haussmannian undertakings coincided with that time when urban communities began rapidly to grow and urban problems were pushed everywhere into the foreground. No wonder, then, that the Parisian development was followed with keen interest in those innumerable cities where similar developments were urgent.

Meanwhile, political events and nationalistic pride poured augmented stimulus into civic growth along the formal pattern. The unification of Italy under the sole sovereignty of Victor Emanuel II—in which affair that clever Cavour was the leading genius—gave impulses to many monumental features such as Piazzas, Corsos, and the like, which were named after Vittorio Emanuele, Cavour, or after victorious battles—and they were many. Almost simultaneously, the unification of the many German kingdoms and dukedoms into the Great German Reich—after the German-French war of the year 1870—offered heartily-welcomed opportunities to celebrate illustrious men and glorious events by means of bombastic urban design. Even in smaller circumstances the time was contaminated by this well-meaning but false patriotic passion of self-glorification in terms of pompous town-building.

The Columbian Exhibition of the year 1893 in Chicago brought a strong and long wave of classical enthusiasm into the United States. This enthusiasm was reflected in a vivid spell of civic embellishment along the classical thought, and many a city got its share of this spell. Daniel H. Burnham was the champion par excellence in this beautification development, of which his grandiose schemes for Chicago and San Francisco must be particularly mentioned in this connection. These schemes were great achievements in themselves, but surely they disclose undisputable Haussmannian influences.

This example set by Haussmann was considered the last word, and many cities became "haussmannized," regardless of whether it suited them or not. Through such a spiritless adoption, this new movement—the Formal Continuance—became arbitrarily planted into strange circumstances. It became mere academic superficiality. The important edifices—the City Hall, the Museum, the Library—were designed in accordance with the prevailing stylistic doctrines, and about these edifices the surroundings were regulated in an imitative French spirit—which in fact was often more French than was the origin. And the average citizens of modest habits, in the informal circles of Jones's, Smiths, and the like, felt themselves mirrored in this grandiose environment which paraded there like formal courtiers of bygone days in bygone attires. To be sure, a borrowed glory.

The Formal Continuance had a mere stylistic background, and from the standpoint of style demands its problems were solved. It had no social background insofar as the population at large was concerned: in fact, **the Formal Continuance almost forgot that there was a population in the city, and that this population stood in need of many things more vital than that classical decoration. It offered the population mere theatrical effects, instead of offering the most elementary requirements of decent living.** For this reason the Formal Continuance was not able to build that dam which could prevent the deluge of civic decline. More sincere efforts were needed to accomplish this.

B. INFORMAL REVIVAL

It was to be expected that formal expression of informal life could not be satisfactory in the long run. There was needed a properly adjusted direction in town-building, such as could be in accord with the informal everyday life of the town people. As this need grew urgent, for sure, urgent grew even the demand for some action to satisfy this need. When this action really came, it came as a new movement, constructive and refreshing. And it found its field of study in that rich material of town-building of olden times.

Town-building of olden times appeared in a multifarious variety of form. Despite this variety of form, thoughtful analysis revealed a certain general trend in the cadence of masses and outlines, and in the forming of plazas and street perspectives. This trend was present as an underlying idea in the varied instances, and was manifested through a distinct tendency to organic correlation of the whole and of the details.

It was understood, of course, that this organic correlation originated from instinctive sensing, and could not be put by later generations into theoretical formulas for practical use. Yet, when going down to the fundamentals—so it was thought—one might get an answer to the question: "why are the towns of today so unpleasant physically and spiritually, whereas the towns of olden days manifested themselves to the contrary as to both form and spirit?" In order to answer this question, there was needed an investigation. This investigation was undertaken and carried out thoroughly by Camillo Sitte, and it brought about the Informal Revival.

In the year 1889, Camillo Sitte, a Viennese architect, published his book: "Der Staedtebau nach seinen Künstlerischen Grundsaetzen" (Town-building according to its artistic principles). This book was published in the month of May, and as early as in June of the same year Sitte had to write the foreword to the second edition. In the foreword to the third edition, of the year 1900, Sitte mentioned that considerable actual building had already been accomplished as a result of his writings, and he added: "it can be stated that such a result through literary work can be achieved only when the whole problem already is, so to speak, in the air."

This was a true statement. The dissatisfactory result of the prevailing superficial mode of town-planning had been discouraging indeed. A reaction was bound to come in one way or another, for a lasting feeling of dissatisfaction is a strong promoter in the search for better methods. In such circumstances the right word at the right moment is effective. Sitte wrote the right word at the right moment, and since then this word has echoed as an awakening herald in many a country and town, inspiring a new and wholesome movement in town-building.

Sitte undertook an extensive study of Classical and Middle Age towns, aiming to discover in the organism of these towns the fundamental laws of town-building. As such, his mode of search differed from our direction of approach, for we endeavored to discover the same fundamental laws in nature's architecture. Even Sitte was keenly conscious of the relationship between man's architecture and nature's architecture, for the first remark that he made in his book was about the beauty of the Greek and Italian landscapes into which the towns were built in a manner that made the towns breathe the same beauty as breathed the landscapes themselves. "This," he wrote, "was perfectly as it should be, for fundamentally towns should inspire human senses much in the same manner as does nature's beauty. Already Aristotle," he continued, "epitomized all the principles of town-building into the guiding thought that towns must be erected so as to offer, not only protection, but even happiness. In order to accomplish this latter," Sitte wrote, "town building must be, besides a technical problem, even one of art:" and he continued by saying that "so was the case during the Classical, Mediaeval, and Renaissance eras, and during all those eras when art was professed in its fullest sense. Only in our mathematical century, town lay-outs have been mere technical concern; and for this reason it is essential to stress that a mere technical concern is only one part of town problems, the other part being the artistic concern which must be considered equally important." So wrote Sitte in his foreword, emphasizing that the main aim of his study was to further this art quality of town-building.

It is not our intention to delve lengthily into Sitte's ideas about town-building: this would only bring us too far into more or less insignificant details. There are, however, three points which must be particularly mentioned in this connection, each of them of basic importance. First, **Sitte emphasized the informal nature of the classical and mediaeval mode of town building.** Second, **he emphasized the coherent organism of these towns which was achieved through proper correlation of building units.** And third, **he stressed the formation of plazas and streets into organic spatial enclosures.** These three points formed the core of Sitte's town-building philosophy, and whatever other viewpoints he brought forth in his analysis of civic problems, whether historical or contemporary, they all grew from and about the core of these three points.

These points are rather familiar from our previous discussions of the mediaeval case. Actually, they constituted the core, even of these discussions. It then would seem unnecessary to recapitulate a theme which has been already fully digested. On the other hand, it might be illuminating to survey these problems also from Sitte's standpoint so as to show that many paths lead to the same conclusions. A closer look at these matters, therefore, seems desirable.

As for the first point—informal design—the chief observation that impressed Sitte in studying olden towns was the informal conception of these towns. This impression was so much the deeper because of the fact that Sitte—just as every architect of those days—was educated in the formal school of architectural thought. Sitte traced the causes of this informal mode of town-building to the historically gradual growth of the towns in which, as he maintained, one might be able to find, in each individual irregular case, a logical yet perhaps ceased reason; such as, for example, a former stream, a road, or some subsequently disappeared structure. "Yet," said he, "this informal irregularity is not at all unpleasant. On the contrary, it seems quite natural and makes the scenery picturesque." So impressed was Sitte by this informality, that he accepted it as the leading thought of all town-building.

This conclusion of Sitte's seems rather surprising. For, when he stated that the historically gradual growth of the towns was the reason for informal planning, his conclusion did not cover cases where growth was not historically gradual. Yet the classical and mediaeval mode of planning was always informal, no matter whether gradual or immediate. To prove this, we might as well refer to as eminent an example as the Acropolis of Athens, with its four main features—the Propylaeum, the Parthenon, the Erechteion, and the Monument of Pallas Athene. All these four features were conceived and erected during the regime of Pericles—also during a rather short period of time, historically speaking—and yet none of these features was *formally* interrelated to the others. Considering the fact that the Greek architecture of the Pericleian era had reached its climax of creative perfection, one would have expected that the lay-out of the Acropolis had been formally conceived, provided formality was considered a virtue in planning. The Greeks did not think so, however, for they sensed instinctively the demands of universal laws, of which the law of creative expression is fundamental. This law calls for freedom in creation and cannot be chained by such doctrines as call for sterile formality.

Undoubtedly Sitte sensed, instinctively, this law of creative expression, and therefore—notwithstanding his limited and one-sided reasoning—accepted informal freedom of design as the leading thought in town-building.

Considering the second of Sitte's points—interrelation of building units—here, both his mode of approach and the obtained results were thoroughly convincing. Every town, whether classical or mediaeval, had an unlimited number of examples to offer where a proper correlation of building units was present, for almost every structure in these towns was

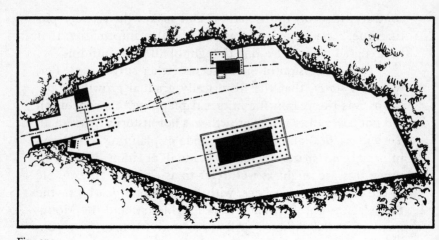

Fig. 25.
The Acropolis.

erected with a keen sense for this principle. Consequently then, Sitte was in an excellent position to draw valid conclusions from all of what he discovered and experienced.

Indeed, in this spirit of proper correlation were towns formed in olden times, and their buildings were grouped into a multitude of varieties, and of these there were not two alike. Prior to the formal mode of town-building there were no such stereotyped formulas as could hinder creative freedom in the forming of town pattern. Every town development emerged indigenously from local conditions and from the psychology of its people. Therefore, when Sitte undertook his study of the towns of the past, his study became, so to speak, a psychoanalytical examination of both the human aspect and its architectural expression.

As such, Sitte's examination is of great value. The essential harvest of this examination, however, was his indication that there must exist in all town-building a universal law of correlation, and that this law was instinctively sensed in olden times, but that its sensing, regrettably enough, was almost non-existent in contemporary town-building.

Sitte illustrated his thought of correlation with many examples. With these he proved the positive points as manifested in the towns of the past. The greater part of these examples seem to us rather obvious, once we have accepted the principle of correlation, as we did already in the introduction when fundamental laws were examined. There is one example however, an illustrative one—and rather amusing—which might be mentioned.

Michael Angelo, after having completed his famous marble colossus of David, placed it against the monumental stone wall of the Palazzo Vecchio in Florence. The interrelation of these two features—the David statue and the Palazzo, so different in form and scale—was perhaps one of the most significant examples of good relationship in art. Here the monumental masses of the Palazzo were emphasized through the statue, and the statue manifested itself in its full strength against the powerful wall of the Palazzo. So things remained from the year 1504 till the year 1873. In the latter year, however, the high dignitaries of the formal school released Michael Angelo's masterpiece from the "debasing" vicinity of that "vulgar Palazzo," and brought it into the "refined" atmosphere of the Accadémia di Belle Arti.

So goes Sitte's story. To render Michael Angelo some rehabilitation, later generations have replaced the original David with a replica. There this replica now stands in front of that Old Palace as if nothing had happened, and many admire this Michael Angelo masterpiece believing it to be the original. But Sitte's story remains intact. It testifies of the ridiculous predicament to which the champions of the formal thought sometimes subjected themselves because of their dogmatically conceived attitude. It testifies also how little these champions sensed the sublime meaning of correlation; and if they sometimes did sense this correlation, it was only superficially in symmetrical and stylistic terms.

As for the third of Sitte's points—spatial enclosures—he drew a parallel between the room of a building and the plaza of a town. "One cannot achieve a satisfactory room merely by four walls," Sitte wrote, "but the room, to be livable, must be agreeably formed and properly furnished. Similarly, one cannot achieve a satisfactory plaza by just leaving a building-block free from buildings. This would only reveal a nonchalant lack of planning. The plaza, just as the room, must be adequately proportioned, and furnished with such features as can make it spatially attractive."

This parallel of Sitte's is highly illustrative. It indicates that the planning of buildings and the planning of towns are related problems. Therefore, if one is accustomed to plan buildings in a manner which is not mere stereotyped routine procedure, but thoughtful and creative organization of all the problems of a building—technical, human, and esthetic—one then, by the same thoughtful effort and creative instinct, is able to bring all the civic problems into proper organization. And one will soon discover the fact that, although the planning of buildings and the planning of towns are two different languages, they have the same grammar, so to speak. **They both deal with organization of space to accommodate man.**

In the above spirit, Sitte analyzed plaza problems as spatial enclosures. But, as space was conceived differently during different times, so were these spatial enclosures differently planned. The Greek conception of space was rather free from enclosure, as shown by Sitte's examples of the earlier-mentioned Acropolis, and the Olympus. The Roman conception of space shows a distinct leaning toward enclosure, as can be seen in the Roman and Pompeian Forums, published by Sitte. The Mediaeval conception of space was highly enclosed, as can be seen in the mediaeval town pattern throughout the whole field of Middle Age town-building. And as this Middle Age town-building was closest to Sitte's personal inclinations, his town ideas therefore—so one might think—were much based on the mediaeval conception of space.

Now, one can imagine Sitte walking around in the olden towns and dreaming of how contemporary towns could be altered and new ones shaped in an equally harmonious manner as were shaped these towns of the past. This dreaming of future town-building in such narrow quarters seems almost paradoxical when considering the fact that, only a few decades later, these restful towns were filled with speeding automobiles, and that these automobiles required entirely other spatial considerations than Sitte was dreaming about. Facing such facts, one would easily think that Sitte's ideas about town-building matters could have no bearing in so completely changed circumstances as ours. It is far from so, however, for it must be borne in mind **that Sitte was dreaming of the future town primarily from the point of satisfactory disposition of space enclosure so as to fit both**

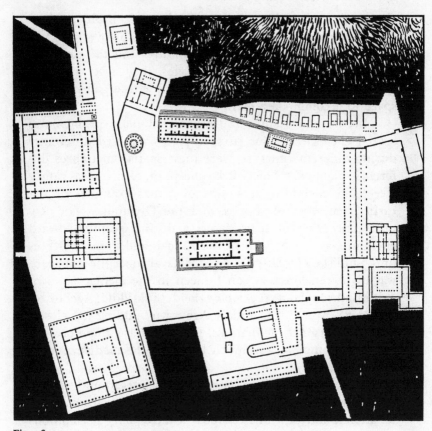

Fig. 26.
Plan of Olympus, Greece.

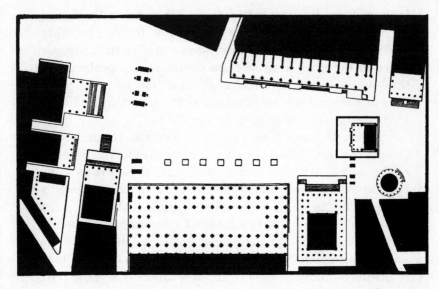

Fig. 27.
Plan of The Roman Forum.

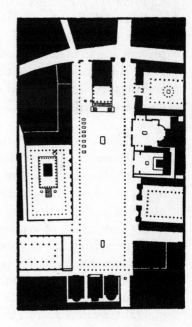

Fig. 28.
Plan of The Pompeian Forum.

form and rhythm to contemporary demands, and not as a preconceived idea in mediaevally narrow terms. In other words, **Sitte's primary endeavor was to further such organic order in the town as grew from contemporary problems of life**—which would have included, no doubt, even the problems of the automobile, provided Sitte had anticipated such a state of things, which he of course did not.

Sitte's philosophy in the above point is fundamental. In spite of this, just this point has been regarded by many critics as his Achilles' heel. Obviously, these critics have been unable to discriminate between fundamental thoughts and physical facts. If these critics instead had taken pains to delve deeper into Sitte's mode of thinking, undoubtedly they could have found the proper answer to this controversial space problem in accordance with the fundamental laws of all town-building; that is, in accordance with those laws that Sitte championed. They could have done this, notwithstanding the augmented spatial demand caused by the automobile. **With good will this could have been accomplished just as well as one is able to design buildings to satisfy the present augmented demands for air, light, and space, and yet to do it in accordance with those same fundamental laws of architecture which guided even the mediaeval builder in his narrow space.**

The foregoing pages may serve as a short explanation of Sitte's town-building philosophy along its three main directions of thought: the "informal moment," the "correlative moment," and the "spatial moment." It must, however, be observed that the division into these three moments is not Sitte's own mode of reasoning: it is our mode of approaching Sitte's direction of thought. We have done so in order to explain his experiences in town-building studies in an extracted form. The same applies to Sitte's understanding of fundamental laws, for Sitte did not formulate these fundamental laws in a distinct manner: he merely told his story in a direct way and with the support of much explanatory picture material so as to offer the reader the opportunity to exercise his own thinking, and through this to formulate his own understanding of these fundamental laws.

Were we now to formulate our own conception of these fundamental laws as they can be found through Sitte's mode of reasoning, we would on the whole arrive at the same conclusions as we did when studying manifestations in nature.

First, concerning the informal moment, it is a fact that every building of Sitte's town material, whether from classical or mediaeval days, was a genuine creation and, therefore, expressive of its time and people. In other words, every building was conceived through the principle of "expression," which called for freedom in creation, and could not, as said, be chained by doctrines demanding sterile formality.

Second, concerning the correlative moment, in all his published material Sitte stressed the good correlation of forms in such a strong manner, that there was left no doubt in the reader's mind that this correlation was imperative by command of fundamental principles; that is, the fundamental principle of "correlation."

Third, concerning the spatial moment, Sitte's emphasis that the plaza of the town must be conceived in the same organic manner as the room of the building, makes it clear that town-building is an architectural problem and must be conceived through the true principle of architecture; that is, through the fundamental principle of "organic order."

In these principles lies the quintessence of Sitte's town-building philosophy, just as we found that the quintessence of nature's construction lies in the same principles.

Sitte's influence in the Germanic countries and in Northern Europe has been remarkable. In 1902 the first edition of his book was published in the French language under the title: "L'Art de Bâtir des Villes," but it has had little direct effect in a soil where the formal school of "Urbanism" was predominant; yet its indirect effect can be easily traced. It is unfortunate that Sitte's book has never been translated into the English language, for it would have been of considerable value to the English urban development. In spite of this, the English soil was fertilized by Sitte's ideas, and England did not delay joining in the new movement, for as early as 1898 Ebenezer Howard published his book, "Garden Cities of Tomorrow," and with practical work began to actualize his thoughts. A more extensive influence was exerted throughout England by the remarkable writings and work of Sir Raymond Unwin.

It would have been of great value for civic art in the United States, if Sitte's town-building principles had been digested. These principles would have served as a healthy balance against that pseudoclassical influence of Haussmann. Sitte's ideas could have been as easily adjusted to American conditions as they were adjusted to English conditions by Sir Raymond.

C. HAUSSMANN VERSUS SITTE

The civic rehabilitation efforts, as we have seen, followed mainly two distinctly different lines, the formal and the informal; that is, the "stylistic" and the "organic." The formal was classical both in spirit and form. The informal was, if we may say so, mediaeval in origin: in the beginning, it was mediaeval even in spirit and to some extent in form; its principles, however, were beyond the times.

The former movement developed to a considerable degree through the realization of an actual problem and because of historical circumstances it became more or less personified in Baron Haussmann. The informal movement was based on esthetic considerations; it was a fight for forgotten principles, most effectively promoted by Camillo Sitte.

Since each of them—Haussmann and Sitte—was a leading protagonist in his respective direction of urban development, it might be of value to contrast these two personalities.

Haussmann was primarily an organizer and executor, and because of these qualifications he was appointed to direct the improvements of Paris. During this work he became a qualified town-builder in those particular fields that he had to deal with. How large a personal contribution he made to the architectural aspect of Paris, and how large a portion of this work was executed by his fellow-workers, is hard to determine. But there is no doubt that Haussmann's influence was most decisive in many respects. Obviously, he had a good understanding of rhythm, unity, and form balance in the city's organic construction.

Besides all of this, Haussmann, as said, was confronted with a definite problem to solve. Because many of the monumental plazas and lay-outs of Paris had been built before his time, it was Haussmann's task to continue these projects and to unite them by an elaborate network of boulevards. The greatness of his achievement lies in the fact that he undertook the development of his plan in a natural way—one thoroughly in accord wih the spirit of Paris—and did not attempt to force a strange, theoretical, and preconceived lay-out on the city. Perhaps it was in his favor that he was not a scholar of architectural orders, but a clearly thinking realist.

Being a realist, Haussmann based his work strictly on existing conditions without any clear vision of future requirements. Accordingly, his Paris scheme developed from contemporary conditions in a manner that was too rigid to allow enough of adjustments to satisfy new and vital demands of the future. Consequently, Haussmann's achievement was not of such a nature as should have inspired a certain school in the building of cities—which it surprisingly has done.

From a modern point of view, Haussmann was not a town-builder in the right sense of the word, for he improved only certain conditions for certain limited purposes; that is, he considered—or rather was forced to consider—only a few of the problems in the entire field of civic problems. The exterior aspect of the city was of greater importance to him than were the vital needs of the population. To be just, however, large scale sanitary problems were executed, and large sums of money were spent for such improvements. But the problems of light, air, and openness—which are today of primary importance—were to a great extent neglected. True enough, these needs were not in the foreground at that time, but a town-builder of those days, when an extreme congestion was no longer compulsory, already should have visualized the necessity of more light, air and openness, and should have provided at least possibilities of future adjustments along such directions of thought. With respect to this, it is significant to note that Paris in the year 1800 had about 1000 acres of park land within its outer boulevards, whereas in the year 1900 it had only about 300 on the same area. Certainly, this was not an improvement.

Haussmann became a town-builder because of outer circumstances. Sitte, on the other hand, had a natural inclination to this profession, and although his creative genius as an active town-builder was not outstanding, so much the sharper was his analyzing eye. Studying his art-form by traveling in various countries, he learned to understand the language of architecture in a comprehensive sense. Through this he was able to visualize the art of building in a broader sense than did his contemporaries in general. According to Sitte's conception, architecture meant more than a mere building, for it included the entire field of forms that had to deal with man's accommodation; where the building was a part of a street, the street a part of the street-pattern, and the street-pattern a part of the whole town. Understanding of architecture in such a broad sense, guided Sitte. Through the strength of his personality he translated this understanding into written form. And so he became the renovator of town-building.

By the actual execution of a certain problem, Haussmann

constituted an example in town-building. Here the physical result was apparent for anyone to adopt, whereas the principles remained obscure—provided Haussmann, after all, considered principles. Sitte, on the other hand, re-established fundamental but forgotten principles. These principles could not be copied, but through them the creative art of town-building could be revived. For this reason, his work was of constructive influence in the progress of town-building.

Sitte was an admirer of classical and mediaeval towns. From these he gathered his study material, and through this material he brought the forgotten principles into light. Because of these historical sources, many have been and still are suspicious of the real value of Sitte's contribution, denying that his ideas can be adapted to modern conditions. It has been frequently stated that the bent street lines and the picturesque plaza formations, so typical of the mediaeval era, do not fit the modern community.

It is true enough that Sitte did have a personal leaning toward mediaeval form-conception, and it is just as true that many of those activities in town-building which were influenced by his ideas and executed by his followers were not adequately significant from a contemporary point of view. Even his staunch admirers have been guilty of misconception in this respect. It must be borne in mind that Sitte lived in a time when copying in architecture was accepted rather unscrupulously, and when, because of this, admiration of one's work often resulted in the imitation of that work. Sitte's case was no exception from the general course. In fact, many followed too strictly the picture material that was published in Sitte's book, not always understanding the basic principles which he aimed to emphasize through the published picture material. Sitte cannot be blamed for this.

Sitte used examples from the past as his material of study. This was a sensible thing to do, for it was the only available material that could give him guidance. He could not have considered contemporary examples for such a purpose, for it was just against these that he directed his attacks. Of course, Sitte could have just as easily discovered the fundamentals of design in nature, and, if such had been the case, his fundamentals would not have become involved in that confusing labyrinth of preconceived styles, but would have been accepted as fundamentals in any circumstance. And there would have been no misconception of stylistic deviations, whether mediaeval or otherwise.

Be it as it may, Sitte deserves full credit for his contribution; and we must consider this contribution of basic value even to the modern town-builder, provided that he intelligently goes down to the roots of Sitte's thoughts. By doing so, he can transpose these thoughts according to his own personal leanings, and can interpret them to fit even the most modern demands. Everyone concerned with modern civic problems, whether he admits it or not, has been influenced by Sitte, directly or indirectly, willingly or unwillingly. Even those who disregard his ideas and see in them only old-fashioned romance, are considerably indebted to him for much of what they are able to accomplish themselves, no matter how extreme their viewpoints.

Sitte's challenge considered principles which are from time immemorial, not time and taste which are subject to change. This certainly was Sitte's point of view, for he remarks himself, that, "it is not a preconceived idea of this research to recommend so called picturesque beauty of old towns for modern purposes." In other words, he pointed out rather clearly that it was not his aim to utilize mediaeval examples to illustrate how towns of his time should have been built, but to explain those principles which in earlier times consciously or subconsciously influenced civic efforts toward organic coherence. In all creative eras this has been obtained through honest expression of contemporary life. In accordance with this timeless principle, even the towns of today must be an expression of present contemporary conditions, and of no other conditions.

This was the fundamental thought of Sitte's challenge. It was neither an old nor a modern idea. It was more; for **it was—and is—one with a universal all-time significance.**

D. FORMAL VERSUS INFORMAL

Both the Formal Continuance and the Informal Revival have produced good results, and both have led to deplorable mis takes. This has been more a matter of individual accomplishment, than of which system was used. In the field of design, as in any field, a strong creative personality is beyond systems; whereas the weak mind is apt to bring into disrepute whatever he undertakes. The virtues or vices of the two movements in question, therefore, cannot be based on individual achievement: they must be based on the solid foundation of fundamental laws. Let us then investigate these two movements of town-building from this angle of fundamental laws, in order to form an idea of their respective possibilities as bases on which civic problems of today and of tomorrow could be founded.

The Formal Continuance was dressed, for the most part at least, in some classical style which more or less had its origin from ancient Greece. Because of this, one might dwell in the misconception that the Greek lay-out was formal in the same sense as was the stylistic form of the Formal Continuance. Such was not the case, however, as we already have learned. The Greek lay-out was well-balanced, but not symmetrical, for the creative strength of the Greeks lay in their sure sense for proportions and in the grouping of masses into a harmonious ensemble where symmetry had no place. In studying the various lay-outs of the Greek era, we will learn that this sense seems to have been, without exception, the decisive guide. Earlier, we mentioned that eminent example of the Acropolis plateau where all the main features were built within the same short period of time, and yet informally

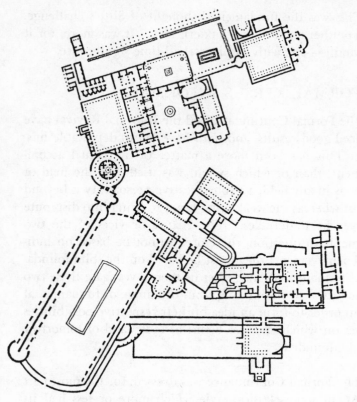

Fig. 29.

Emperor Hadrian's villa,
near Tivoli. A vivid grouping
of buildings, masterfully fitted
into the Roman landscape.

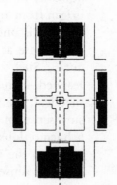

Fig. 30.

Diagram of a sterile axis system
of planning: the thoroughly unimaginative "Civic Center" type.

related one to another and to the whole. It is true, of course, that the Greek temple—like the Parthenon of the Acropolis plateau—had a distinct middle-axis, but this middle-axis was of no significance in the planning of the lay-out at large. Only a slight glance at the Greek lay-out—at any Greek lay-out—makes it evident that the freedom of living balance of forms and masses was more important, to the Greek mind, than a sterile symmetry. In other words, the Greeks did not plan according to a fixed axis, but according to a highly developed space-conception and a careful consideration of surrounding landscape characteristics. A theoretically established formality could not have inspired such a sensitiveness, but instinct had all the freedom to decide. Because of this freedom of instinct, even the most official plan-developments were made individually informal. It was this quality of informal freedom that made the Greek building ensembles spiritually vital and architecturally strong.

So was the case even with the Romans, as we have already seen in the Roman and Pompeian Forums—and as can be seen, perhaps more distinctly, in Emperor Hadrian's Villa, near Tivoli.

Notwithstanding the borrowed style, the general conception of the Formal Continuance was quite unlike that of the Greeks. Because of doctrinal understanding of architecture, the lay-outs were developed in a spirit of strict regularity. A sensitiveness such as guided the Greeks, existed only in a weak form and exerted little influence on the planning work. The mathematical spirit of the divider was brought to the fore, and the stylistic lay-outs breathed the dry atmosphere of the divider's commanding insensibility in terms of stern symmetrical strictness. This symmetrical strictness had nothing in common with the Greek instinctive drift toward organic order. It was a mere theoretical leaning toward stiff military regularity.

In this manner, the Formal Continuance accelerated in its development far away from existing conditions toward a

stylistic autocracy that had little in common with these conditions. Any further development of this movement would naturally continue in this same spirit of stylistic autocracy, and would offer dangerous prejudices to an age where the truth that "form follows function" has been widely accepted. The Formal Continuance, therefore, belongs to neither the present nor the future. **It belongs to history**—let us hope— **and as a historical manifestation we have presented it here.**

The Informal Revival, on the other hand, notwithstanding its first appearance in mediaeval attires, was much closer to the Greek understanding of town-development than was the Formal Continuance. The latter borrowed the outer forms of the Classical era, whereas the former accepted its principles. The Informal Revival was, for this reason, as free as was the Greek development. Just as the latter expressed freely the Greek life in all its various aspects, so could the Informal Revival express freely the contemporary life in all its variations. Because of the modesty of its means of expression, the Informal Revival could bring order even to the humblest corner of the town. And because of the flexibility of its means of expression, it was able, occasionally and when appropriate, to mould itself even into strict formality. With all these vital qualifications, it seems to us, the Informal Revival is fit to serve as a good guide for all present and future town-building.

However, the Informal Revival had to face a hard handicap. It must be observed that the movement was born in a time when the imitative form had its highest tide. Therefore, although the Informal Revival as to spirit and conception was nurtured in the creative auras of the Classical time and the Middle Ages, its application to contemporary life had none of these creative advantages. The creative instinct of the time was low, and could not be vitalized through artificial means. This was not only a hard handicap to the Informal Revival, but it even brought the movement into disrepute, at least in certain circles. The movement is not to be blamed for this. On the contrary, the Informal Revival deserves much credit for having dared a venture of creative nature in a time so saturated with imitation. Or perhaps the movement already had the vision of a new and creative era to come?

Behold then this:

Curiously enough, **in just those places and countries where the Informal Revival was born and accepted, the first attempts toward a new creative form took place.** Now, whether this was purely coincidental or a logical trend does not matter; but **the fact remains that these attempts have since then gained in strength and spread themselves, and, as things stand now, the new form already exists.**

Vitalized by this new form, the Informal Revival must be so much the more considered the best adviser in all future town-building.

We have investigated the underlying forces of the two cardinal movements in town-building during the latter part of the nineteenth century and the opening decades of our century, in order that it may be easier to approach actual problems of today. For, when we come to speculate hereafter in terms of today and tomorrow, it is important to have examined those foundations which previous eras have essayed to build. This does not, however, suggest an adoption of old methods for modern purposes, for the demands and technics of today are very different from those of the past. Therefore, as we are about to step from the past to the present and to open the doors for future town development in a constructive spirit, it is of vital importance to bear two facts in mind. First, we must bear in mind that the mode of town-building always has sprung and always must spring from existing conditions of life; and as our conditions of life and those hereafter are bound to be revolutionarily different from those of the past, we must open-mindedly keep ourselves free from such traditional ideas as could obstruct an unbiased development of our cities. And second, we must bear in mind that those principles that are from time immemorial and inherent in the nature of things, must guide town-building matters even today, and hereafter.

In this latter respect we have found in the foregoing:

in the Introduction: that the universal principle of architectural order must be accepted as the leading star in all town-building;

in Chapter One: that this star of archiectural order was the leader during the Middle Ages, and for this reason their art of town-building stood on a high level;

in Chapter Two: that when this star of architectural order ceased to be the leader in town-development, decay was inevitable;

in Chapter Three: that only when this star of architectural order was reinstated into leadership, constructive results took place.

And so, even now and hereafter, this same star of architectural order must direct our efforts in a successful building of towns and cities.

Consequently, during the whole course of the following Part Two—where we are going to discuss contemporary and future town problems only—no matter which of these problems there will be discussed, **they all will be consistently discussed with the presupposition that the physical solution of these problems must be based on the principle of architectural order.**

PART TWO:

TOWARD THE FUTURE

4. PROBLEMS OF TODAY

MUCH of the planning work of today must deal with the correction of earlier mistakes, which—let's put it frankly—are the result of a serious neglect of one of the nation's most vital problems. In quite many instances, these past mistakes are virtually impossible to correct, and most likely they will remain in the urban organism as hindering inconveniences for times to come. These inconveniences constitute a clear warning. We cannot, therefore, too severely criticize those of yesterday for their failure to prevent these mistakes. And we must be equally prompt in criticizing ourselves for any like omission.

While still involved in the jumble of these reflected difficulties, we are at the same time finding ourselves entirely in a changed era. Old dogmas no longer hold good; new methods are not as yet backed by experience; and we are forced to grope obscurely in order to find the road forward.

Present day civic development is indeed revolutionary, and in all probability will continue so for a considerable time to come. For these reasons the future is bound to be uncertain. We may know what is taking place today, but just how this will reflect upon the conditions of tomorrow cannot be clearly predicted. This makes the planning work largely of instinctive speculation.

From the midst of this spectacular turmoil of changing conditions, it has been difficult to realize how rapidly many towns have mushroomed into extensive cities. Most of this development belongs to a period covering only a few decades, during which time we must mark: the general rush to the cities due to various causes; growing congestion which has been still more aggravated because of the erection of tall buildings; the extension of the cities' boundaries out into the surrounding country; the founding of satellite communities about the mother cities; and above all, the rapid increase in quantity and variety of traffic means. Considering the possibility that these happenings may indicate only the beginning of a continuous development toward a future which we are able to sense only vaguely, we are facing a great problem with many implications.

Growth has been so rapid, in many cases, that there has been little opportunity for a thorough study of the situation. Tragically, not even the necessity of such a study has been understood, with the result that many large cities are now in a perplexed state of bewilderment. To be sure, conditions have grown, not only beyond man's control, but even beyond his conception. With this in mind, and with the realization that matters hereafter must be more thoroughly studied and handled, we have reason to ask: will the rush to the cities continue as heretofore, complicating the situation all the more; are we heading toward a continuous or temporary stagnation in urban development; or, is a dissolution of the city to be expected, and if so, in what manner?

It is impossible to answer these questions exactly. The problems must, therefore, be solved independently of the answer. In fact, prophetic powers are not necessary, but instead it is so much the more necessary to be prepared for the right solution, no matter what the conditions and demands in the future may be.

A. URBAN DISEASE AND ITS CURE

The field of action in urban development is broader now than it has been ever before, for the number and size of urban concentrations has greatly increased. Villages have become towns; towns have become large cities; and in countless cases neighboring townships have been swallowed by the expanding force of the nucleus city, in which process these expanded areas have become a solidly packed heterogeneous mass. Because this packing has taken place with a lack of adequate leadership, it is clear that many different functions have been indiscriminately jumbled together, blocking and disrupting one another and the city as a whole. The inevitable result of this has been: disorganized congestion, decline, dilapidation, blighted areas, and then, slums. Alas, not infrequently, large areas in the heart of the city have become the centers of a contagious disease which threatens the whole organism. In many cases the overgrown city is like the flat lichen on the Northern cliff, where expansion outward causes the withering of the center.

As the situation is, there is urgent need for proper counsel. As for this proper counsel, however, one must bear in mind that the rapidly growing big city is a rather novel thing. Not so far in the past, the big cities could be counted on the ten fingers of one's hands; but since the rapid growth of cities finally has begun as to number and size, it is this very age of ours that now has to deal with the dire consequences of this growth. Therefore, when we speak about urgent need for proper counsel, this cannot be had through earlier experiences and by using past methods of town-building. Such an approach would constitute a grave error. Indeed, **it is most important to understand more than has been so far understood, that past methods of town-building are not valid anymore, and that present and future methods must be based on entirely new premises. And these new premises can and must be found only in and through the existing difficulties.**

Meanwhile, to alleviate the difficulties, the "practical" planner takes the shortest cut. When traffic becomes unbearably heavy, he widens the street, and still more traffic pours in. When concentration intensifies and land values increase, he zones tall structures in order to maintain land values, and bad conditions become worse ones. The slums he clears by piecemeal mending, and the old infects the new in short order. **Urban conditions cannot be cured in this superficial manner.** Deeper must the planner delve into his problems in order to discover the real cause of the difficulties, and then from these discoveries work out the proper methods of cure. The planner must know, as well as the doctor, that when the head aches the stomach might be out of order. The planner must know, as well as the doctor, that when the stomach is out of order the cause may well be found elsewhere. And the planner must be aware of the fact as well as the doctor, that vitality cannot be transfused into a dead organ. The dead organ must be removed, and the transfusion effected in a healthy part of the body. The planner must know all this, for, in much the same manner as the doctor acts, must even the planner act upon the withering body of the overgrown city. **He must unearth the roots of the evil. He must amputate slums by a decisive surgery. And he must transfuse vitality only into those areas that are protected against contagion.**

Obviously, one of the main causes of urban decline can be found in the growing disorderly compactness, for this brings into the city the disturbing interferences of manifold and different activities which have nothing to do with each other. In such circumstances, it is impossible for the city to function normally, and to prevent decay. If the inner organs of the human body were mingled in as chaotic a manner as is the organism of the overgrown city, the result undoubtedly would be sickness and death. In any organism in nature, such a lack of order would ultimately result in disintegration. Nature is aware of such dangers, and therefore she has instituted basic laws to prevent this.

These laws of nature are well worth careful investigation, particularly since we find ourselves now in much the same situation as we were in the introduction, when organic life was the object of our study. Again we must examine happenings at the source of things.

Let us therefore see what nature can teach us.

Any growing organism in nature is a body containing a countless number of cells, each of them located in its proper relative position. By constant cellular multiplication, the organism grows, each new cell expanding into that adjacent space which is provided for growth. This provided space brings flexibility into the growth, and at the same time it protects the organism from internal frictions such as would hinder healthy growth. A tree grows and assumes final shape in much the same way. Its boughs instinctively spring from its trunk in such a manner as to allow ample space about them for the subsequent growth of smaller branches and twigs; and these in turn instinctively space their growth to provide room for leaves and smallest shoots. In this manner is flexibility introduced into the growth of the tree; and in this manner each growing part of the tree is protected from adjacent growth. Here we discern, also, that flexibility of growth prevents disturbing compactness and that sufficiency of space protects the details as well as the whole during the growth. In those cases where flexibility and protection are not provided, decay is the result. Such is the case, for example, when in the tight growth of the deep forest, those branches, stems, and trees which are smothered by lack of space are doomed to wither. Such is the case in any cramped circumstance, whether this happens in cellular life or in the life of peoples and nations. For, in order to be able to live, one must have space in which to live. So must be the case, **for "flexibility" in growth, and "protection" of growth, are fundamental issues in any manifestation that lives and grows.**

When fundamental principles were studied in the introduction of this analysis, there was no particular mention of flexibility and protection, because of the fact that they are innate in the mother principle of organic order, yet latent while the organism is relatively static. Such was the situation in the mediaeval town, for example. As soon as the organism begins to grow, these said principles enter into action. This is the case in the dynamic city of today, **and for this reason the fundamental significance of flexibility and protection must be emphasized when the problems of today are considered.**

Generally speaking, the guidance of the principles of flexibility and protection, as applied to civic problems, means first, **to plan any section of the city so as to make the city's normal growth possible without disturbing other sections;** and second, **to undertake such measures as could guarantee the protection of established values.** In other words, this means: to safeguard continuous healthy growth through "flexible" planning; and to stabilize values by taking "protective" measures.

The above holds good in new civic developments. In those cities which are already overgrown, however, flexibility and protection must be instrumental in so organizing conditions that any development toward the future must happen in accordance with the demands of these said principles. To obtain this presupposes a well-studied, comprehensive and gradual surgery according to a pre-established scheme. The objectives of this surgery must be three-fold: first, **to transfer activities from decayed areas to such locations as are functionally suitable for these activities, and in accord with the pre-established scheme;** second, **to rehabilitate those areas by the foregoing action vacated for such purposes as are best suited here, and in accord with the pre-established scheme;** and third, **to protect all values, old and new.**

The process of applying flexibility and protection to urban developments must mean a physical, economic, and spiritual reconditioning of the urban territory at large, and a stabilization of those results gained. This must be the primary aim of the process. The actual result of the process, however, is that the unprotected compactness of the urban body evolves toward an open system of several protected community units. In other words, the actual result is: **"decentralization."**

B. TOWARD DECENTRALIZATION

The above reasoning makes it clear that decentralization is a logical derivative from and through the principles of flexibility and protection, if the aim is to free the city from the contagious danger of slums. Now, slums are cancer in the urban body, and it is a well-known fact how cancer must be cured. If the cause of this blight is not removed in time, the disease will inevitably spread itself, for palliative remedies are no good in the long run. And because the practical planner has been slow in using decisive methods in removing this urban cancer, it is now mandatory that the town designer thoroughly examine the situation and act accordingly. He must shun half-measures, and use surgery when necessary. If this surgery is used logically and methodically, with a long-time process of civic improvement in mind, it will, as said, be the best instrument in the furthering of decentralization.

Also, when the principles of flexibility and protection have had the chance and time to influence the city's reorganization and growth, the city ceases to be that compactly concentrated body, so characteristic of the cities of yesterday. It evolves toward a new type to come: the "decentralized city of tomorrow."

Although the general need of urban liberation from the existing deteriorating compactness must be considered the fundamental reason for decentralization, many other factors contribute to this tendency. One, for example, is the increasing demand for freer and airier living conditions. There are several underlying grounds for this demand.

Advance in the field of medical and social sciences has brought recognition that the health problems of the town community are problems of basic importance to the welfare of the population. Because of this, the population has become health conscious. Having been so far forced to live in dark rooms, the town-dweller longs now for more light and sunshine. Having been cramped in narrow quarters, he now desires fresh air, more space, and more opportunity for outdoor exercise. And having been accustomed to exist midst a stony desert of building masses, he now prefers to be surrounded by gardens and the freshness of nature. Moreover, scientific advances in the understanding of the great spaces has made man space conscious. Psychologically speaking, this has led man into an entirely new environment where his mind, instinct, and intellect are constantly nourished in an atmosphere of openness and encouraged toward a growing desire for this openness.

So is the situation on the psychological side. On the physical side there is a reflected situation. New modes of living cause changes in the modes of planning. The previous crowding of building masses for the sake of concentration, calls now for a change to more openness and more free space for gardens and recreation fields. The introduction of reinforced concrete, steel, and glass into building construction encourages an open mode of building design. Meanwhile, technical progress introduces an ever-growing number of new conveniences which make conditions develop toward better standards of living. Even this, on its part, is a spur in the general tendency toward airier conditions about one's living place. The more this tendency grows, the more it forces the city's boundaries to expand themselves toward the surrounding lands.

In the progress of industry, the development of modern traffic means is without doubt the most manifest achievement. These modern traffic means, if they do anything, herald an era of intense decentralization, for they make an extensive metropolitan area readily accessible.

Since the discovery of the earliest "horseless carriage," motor vehicles of all kinds have been constantly improved. The transportation facilities, therefore, are already now fully adequate in the service of decentralization. But, because of the lack of proper planning, people are not able, as yet, to make full use of these facilities. It is obvious that the street pattern from olden days cannot safely or efficiently satisfy modern traffic. Streets are crowded with moving or stagnating vehicles; traffic officers and ambulances are on constant guard in keeping things in order and in saving lives; sidewalks are lined with unending rows of parked cars; and the air is noisy, filled with gas and odor. Indeed, we have the best traffic means at hand, yet we have assuredly the worst traffic conditions.

Any real traffic solution in the modern city requires entirely new principles of traffic organization, and thoroughly new methods of road planning. Because the street scheme of olden times is no longer adequate, a new one must be born where broadminded and unbiased understanding must take the lead. The city-planner must realize that an inadequate street circulation affects the urban body as unfortunately as poor blood circulation affects the human body. For this reason it is important that he find the right remedies. And in this respect the planner must first of all open adequate arteries so that both the city and the population can spread themselves toward the country—toward air, light, and nature.

Another significant factor augmenting the pressure toward decentralization is the steadily increasing population. A few statistical facts in this respect might be illuminating.

In the dawning years of the nineteenth century, there were in Europe 22 towns with a population of 100,000 or more, whereas there were none in the Western Hemisphere. Only London and Paris were large, the former consisting of approximately a million inhabitants, the latter of but half of that number. Considering Europe at large, only 1.6 per cent

149

of the total population inhabited the towns. The opening year of the twentieth century unrolled quite another situation, for the number of towns with 100,000 or more population had increased to 160, of which a great number were large cities. The urban population constituted 40 per cent of the total, notwithstanding the fact that the total European population was now much more numerous than it was a hundred years previously.

The United States exhibits a like situation of urban growth, yet with a faster tempo and with a greater number of large cities. Of the total 14 million population increase between the years 1910 and 1920, only a million and a half found their way into rural districts, whereas the rest was added to the urban population. Today the population of our cities constitutes almost 60 per cent of the total. In view of the fact that this flow to the cities is of a relatively recent date and probably—in spite of occasional stagnations—will continue to exist for a long period to come, our time must be prepared to meet the situation.

However, the centripetal wave from the country toward the city has caused a centrifugal wave from the city toward suburbs, satellite towns, and neighbor communities. This latter wave is a logical decentralization process which takes place particularly in the overgrown cities. As a natural manifestation this decentralization process goes on without the efforts of the planner.

Considering the mentioned centrifugal wave in the light of the present increase of civic decay, it is apparent that if things are not conducted in such a manner as will lead to proper decentralization, the future surely will bring sad consequences. The disorderly spread of the city of yesterday and today has already occasioned so much decay that any further such spread would plunge urban conditions into an irreparable state of confusion. Unless the surgery of decentralization is undertaken **in time** and is conducted in **organic sense,** coming generations will witness constantly growing slum areas. In **"organic sense,"** must be the key-word. Therefore, **when we now and hereafter speak about decentralization as a rehabilitation process in the overgrown cities, we mean this in the sense of "organic decentralization."**

Notwithstanding the logic of decentralization, it seems to meet with opposition from some quarters. We are not considering now such opposition as derives from conservatism for the mere sake of conservatism, nor do we mean opposition caused by egotistic speculative motives. We are considering opposition on the part of those persons whose sincere and honest interests in the city's welfare are beyond doubt and whose concern springs from worth-while points of view. As for this opposition, many believe that increased density increases efficiency in business activities, whereas decentralization, particularly when carried too far, might bring about difficulties in this respect. "In modern business life, the easy contacting of people is an essential thing," the advocates of this opposition maintain.

For our part we are fully in agreement with such a direction of thought, for without doubt, logical efficiency in business is essential, and for this reason we are going to discuss this matter rather thoroughly, later on. In order to avoid misunderstanding, however, we will at this moment explain the basic idea of business efficiency as we see it applied to organic decentralization.

Decentralization should not aim at an utmost dispersion of people and their activities. It must aim at a dispersion of the present compactness into concentrated units, such as centers, suburbs, satellite townships, and like community units; and furthermore it must aim at the organization of these units into **"functional concentrations of related activities."** Because of the fact that, from these "functional concentrations," unrelated and otherwise disturbing activities are to be eliminated, it then seems obvious that necessary contacts could be established so much the more directly and efficiently and easily.

This must be the basic idea according to which any decentralization scheme must be carried out, in order to be "organic." In fact, the prime origin of the decentralization idea is to be found just in this kind of development, that is, **the development from disturbing confusion to functional efficiency.** Such must be the logical procedure in any walk of life, for any business enterprise consisting of a number of various branches cannot have all these jumbled into a disorderly mess: the various branches must be organized so as to concentrate related activities into a unified system, and by this to achieve necessary efficiency. It is just this kind of logical business organization that we are endeavoring to bring into the decentralized community. This is an important objective, we think, for it does help, not only the city's functioning as such, but even the functioning of every business organization within that city. And once things have been brought into such an order, then, we are sure, even the busiest business man will prefer decentralization, for he will clearly see its advantages.

C. HOUSING MAN AND HIS WORK

The problems of functional efficiency bring us directly to the problems of housing. For, certainly, in any striving toward functional concentration of related activities, "related activities" must mean to a considerable degree a satisfactory interrelation between man's living place and his daily working place. A satisfactory interrelation in this respect makes life both more efficient and more livable. It eliminates much of that daily traveling to and from work, which contributes so strongly to the abnormally nervous restlessness of the present day city.

It is a well-known fact that in the gradual growth of the small town into a large city, the formerly adequate relationship between living and working has been ignored. The larger this growth has been, the more time must one spend in the daily commuting between one's places of living and working. And as a large percentage of the population is compelled to take part in this daily commuting, naturally then the earlier state of quiet order in the city has become severely affected. The mission of decentralization is to correct this situation.

It is not necessary in this introductory study to go deep into the details of housing—now considering particularly housing of man. There is, however, one point concerning this problem which is essential when looking from the angle of decentralization. **It is the selection of a proper site for the housing development so as to make the development an integral part of the decentralization scheme as a whole.** That is, a housing site must not be decided until the relationship between the housing development in question and the city-wide decentralization scheme has been settled. For a housing development should not be an irrelative action: it must be a correlative step in the decentralization process at large. Otherwise such a development would be an irrelevant achievement of temporary nature only, and because of its very nature of being irrelevant, it is the best instrument in the furthering of that disorder we are so eagerly and diligently endeavoring to cure.

Unfortunately, a large proportion of contemporary housing is not organic, but haphazardly located. All too often the site is selected merely from the point of view of easy land acquisition at the moment. Large sums of money are spent, more as a matter of emergency than as a thoughtful movement toward organic planning. This is a high price to pay for potential slums to come, for that's what most of this kind of housing amounts to. **Such is the inevitable fact, as fundamental laws cannot be ignored.**

The first concern in any housing development, as we see, is to know **"where"** it must be located in the general lay-out. The second concern must be **"how"** it should be developed.

As to this latter question, it must be remembered that according to the spirit of the art of town-building—as was set forth in our introduction—housing must presuppose homes and healthy environments, and not just walls and roofs for physical protection. Such must be the commanding maxim which everyone dealing with housing problems must follow.

This is as self-explanatory as is the construction of the bee-hive to fit the characteristics of the bee-society. It then would seem unnecessary to dwell further upon this matter. Yet, because this much revered machine age of ours is apt often to reverse even the most natural things, a few words must be spent.

In some quarters the citizens are regarded as some sort of "homo units," of which each one is to be provided with certain accommodations worked out in advance according to generally systematized standards, and mechanically perfect. These systematized standards are imposed upon each unit regardless of disposition, and each gets a "cell" in which to live. Such an approach to housing is unsound, not because of the perfect mechanical equipment that the system is apt to offer, but because people have always been and always will be individuals and not mere units. To linger in "cells" by the hundreds and thousands, everyone in his own, would constitute a perfect filing system, provided people were or could be made alike. But inasmuch as a man is not and never can be made a standardized creature, such a housing idea would sooner or later create dissatisfaction, unhealthy deviations from normal social order and, ultimately, social unrest.

Mechanization is not in itself faulty, but it renders its most positive service when it does not occupy an illogical position of complete dominance. **The human side of the problem must not be so subordinated that man becomes merely a number filed into a certain numbered unit.**

Turning now our attention from housing of man to that of man's work, we meet even here a situation similar in the mode of approach to the one we met in the case of man's housing. For, even in housing of work, functional distribution and grouping needs to be considered as an organic part of the whole organism. Even here the problem, "where," must be first solved.

Housing of work is of course a many-sided problem, for there are all kinds of work to be executed in the city. Thus we can note homework, crafts, shop work, professional and educational work, public utility work, transportation and harbor service, miscellaneous activities in the official and business districts, and finally, light industry and heavy industry. In many of these cases, it is rather obvious to hit upon a logical solution on the basis of adequate correlation between living and working. In other cases again, a lasting habit of inadequacy has bred contentment with inadequate conditions. Much of the effort of decentralization, therefore, must be directed against those content-ideas, and this must happen through the enlightening of people toward better demands by means of proper planning. This is the case particularly concerning industry, both light and heavy.

Speaking particularly about heavy industry, there is reason for asking whether or not it should be located in the heart of the large cities, as it often is. The answer must be most decidedly in the negative. Previously, we have examined the circumstances under which heavy industry began to move into the towns. Looking with the eyes of today, one might stamp that action as short-sightedness or, one might accept it as a logical step to have been taken in those years. However this might be, the said step has constituted a hampering prejudice, for even today this attitude of yesterday is accepted, despite changed conditions. The result of this is that industry, even if originally located outside or in the outskirts of the town, is fast becoming an ever increasing obstruction within the city. It should be obvious what this means to the three factors involved: city, industry, and workmen. Every gardener—who in constantly dealing with growing plants, bushes, and trees has been made aware of natural tendencies—could have told the logical consequences of this sort of a growth. He could tell even now that trimming and replanting is a good thing to bear in mind. We, on our part, could tell many things of this trimming and replanting insofar as industry is concerned. We could mention cases where industry must be relocated, the sooner the better; where actual relocation has been carried out, yet not far enough to prevent new disturbances; and where good conditions have been accomplished by open-minded planning. But all this is unnecessary, for things surely speak for themselves. They seem to speak a clear language, for the fact is there; that an industrial decentralization tendency already exists, and that this tendency seems to be growing stronger with time. Civic organization must take corresponding steps, and must consider decentralization of industry—in organic manner of course—one of the essential civic problems of today.

There is small need of pointing out what a helpful forward step this industrial relocation would constitute. Large industrial territories, often located in the best sections of the urban area, would be released for other much-needed purposes. Industry on its part no longer tightly crowded, could function more efficiently in more flexible quarters and with improved transportation facilities. This relocation of industry would mean a corresponding relocation of workers to better environments and to more livable homes. Those areas thus vacated—perhaps already blighted or slums—would offer an excellent opportunity for rehabilitation.

D. ECONOMIC AND LEGISLATIVE

Organic decentralization is only an empty gesture, unless it is founded on sane principles of economy and supported by adequate legislative enabling measures. These two points of view—the economic and the legislative—constitute the practical corner-stones of the decentralization development. Yet, in these two points of view, many seem to discern insuperable barriers in the realization of the decentralization ideals. As a matter of fact, though, it is just this kind of a skeptical attitude of mind which is the very barrier itself. If all instead were animated by a reverse attitude of receptive open-mindedness, for sure, the economic and legislative impossibilities would soon be completely metamorphosed into encouraging possibilities.

We do not consider ourselves experts enough in these fields to be able to offer any exact device, generally or specifically. Notwithstanding our limitations, we are going to venture a suggestive program, according to which the gradual process of decentralization should evolve to make it economically possible. And, in addition to this, we are going to venture a recommendation of a few points in which the present legislation must be changed in order to facilitate the decentralization movement. But, inasmuch as these considerations will be discussed later on, we will at the moment confine ourselves to a few basic remarks only.

Considering first the economic questions of the decentralization process, it must be remembered that the prime objective of the process is the physical, economic, and spiritual conditioning of the city. Three major points must be observed in this respect: first, **the creation of new urban values on the broadened area of decentralization**—which implies that every step of the process is an economically positive action; second, **the rehabilitation of decayed areas for new uses** —which likewise means a multitude of actions of which each is economically constructive; and third, **the protection of all values, old and new**—which is equivalent to the stabilization of economic values. Also, every move of the decentralization process, when organic, is a distinct and methodical pursuit of sane and stable economy. And inasmuch as the duration of any such process would cover at least several decades, the exact times for the various actions could be selected so as to make them fit with the economic program of the process.

The above shows that decentralization is a comprehensive system of economically sound actions extending over a long period of time. It then would seem obvious that the movement constitutes a saner approach to civic problems than that lack-of-system of today which, generally speaking, over a period of years has destroyed a large part of those values that it has tried to establish. It would be enlightening to make a survey of all that has been built in the disorderly grown cities during a few decades—say, during thirty or forty years—and then to investigate how large a part of this building work has been depreciated into slums during the same period of years. Yet a survey is unnecessary, for even a passing glance at the situation gives a convincing answer. And that answer is most discouraging.

Considering such a waste of values on the disorderly side, it would seem a matter of common sense that organic decentralization should be encouraged by those having the city's economic success at heart. It is precisely they who should, therefore, be eager to assist the planners by bringing the economic problems of decentralization into a workable system. Just they should work out unified economic systems of such important issues as, for example, planning, construction, taxation, et cetera. These all belong to the province of economic experts, for surely, we can be of no more service in this matter than to emphasize the obvious fact that, **unless the economic problems of the city are solved in accordance with that "methodical pursuit of sane and stable economy" such as decentralization can offer, the growing cities are doomed to follow the old road of disorder**—which is not economically sane.

The prevailing civic legislation has evolved from the static conditions of the past where the legislative measures have been crystallized to protect concentration against any new changes in the generally accepted manner of building towns. Consequently, these measures of the past do not fit the present era which demands radical changes in the civic organism. New legislative measures must therefore be undertaken to enable civic organization to develop logically according to the tendencies of the time. Exactly what these measures should be, must naturally be conceived in connection with the planning work itself.

No doubt, a fight is to be anticipated between the new tendency to decentralization and the old legislative restrictions. In this fight the champions of decentralization are on the right side, for the purpose of true legislation must be to support sound evolution rather than to obstruct it. Outworn stipulations of old conservatism, therefore, must give way to the superior forces of the new. The forces of old conservatism, we suspect, will be characterized by indifference to vital civic improvements, lack of vision, mental stagnation, and speculative selfishness. Progressive planning, on the other hand, will rely on an open-minded attitude toward the vital demands of life, and on a strong common spirit. Which side will eventually win the battle depends much on which one can marshal the stronger forces.

The above summary may serve as a short introduction to the economic and legislative discussions to take place later on. There is no point in delving deeper into these matters, until the field has been prepared from which they must spring. Once this has been done and the nature of organic decentralization has been fully explained first, then the economic and legislative questions and answers will be shaped more clearly. At that time more exact statements can be made.

E.   TOWARD A NEW FORM ORDER

It is easy to convince people that the city's physical development must be based on sane principles of economy. But it

seems not to be as easy to convince people that this development must be based also on the fundamental principles of
architecture. Such is the fact, however, and in the introduction this fact was made clear by stating that, "just as any living
organism can be healthy only when that organism is a product
of nature's art in accordance with the basic principles of nature's architecture, exactly for the same reason town or city
can be healthy—physically, spiritually and culturally—only
when it is developed to a product of man's art in accordance
with the basic principles of man's architecture." In this introduction it was furthermore stated, that "any investigation
of town-building matters must be essentially an investigation
of architectural standards." These principles, self-evidently,
must be applied even to our present investigations of the decentralization movement. This means, firstly, **that any building designed into the city must be expressive of the time of its
construction, and of no other time.** And secondly, it means
**that all the buildings in the decentralized community must
be shaped so as to achieve a good correlation of building units**
—in a contemporary sense of course, that is, in a "decentralized sense of openness." The significance of these two demands we must examine in the following.

When we say that any building designed into the city
must be expressive of the time of its construction, it naturally
presupposes that the present time must have an expressive
form of its own.

But, does it really have one?

Previously, when we discussed the Informal Revival, it
was maintained that the movement was born in a time when
the imitative form had its highest tide, and that this fact was
a hard handicap. On the other hand—as was furthermore
maintained—there appeared, later on, many attempts to proceed along a new and creative course in the search for an expressive form of the time—and when time passed, this new
form gained strength and was widely spread. As things stand

now—it was finally stated—the new form already exists.

Now, one might accept this statement at its full value. Or one might regard it as a mere emotional overstatement of little consequence. But whether one accepts or hesitates to accept, one thing is certain: no matter what the status of the present form-development may be, **this problem of form must be subject to a careful consideration so as to be able to sift the chaff from the grain in the search for an honest form of our own. For, honest our form "must" be.**

Looking with the eyes of today there is enough of time perspective to understand that, after the general downfall of form and taste during the nineteenth century, a new orientation was most urgent. In fact, the opening years of the twentieth century witnessed much pioneering in the search for a new form-expression of the contemporary life.

To be sure, this pioneering was not an easy matter because, after the long-lasted ornamental sweet-dreams and decorative nightmares, the road onward seemed pretty hazy. The writer of this knows these difficulties ever so well, for he was midst this pioneering from the very start. It was a well-known fact in those days that this pioneering had to be a clear-headed steering between the Scyllas of that over-used old, and the Charybdises of those all-too-often-random forms of sparkling novelty. It was a well-known fact that there were many exaggerations, many mistakes, many compromises, and many fallings back on the old. It was likewise a well-known fact that, whenever a constructive thought was brought forth, that old man "style" was always present, haunting and harassing things. So for example, when it was said that "form must express material and construction"—which is perfectly correct and fundamental—there was readily produced a style-form to represent this maxim, no matter whether the object of design was a concrete bridge or a silver necklace. Again, when it was said that "form must follow function"—which also is perfectly correct and fundamental—then "functionalistic" style forms were readily used, no matter whether the function was there or not. So things have been carried out all along the long road of progress. Thus, even today when speed has become an important issue of design, everything is "streamlined," no matter whether the object of design is a racing car or a lamp-post. For sure, architectural problems have been handled much in the same spirit as if the question had been about ladies spring hats or fur coat trimming.

Style in architecture must not be understood as a fashion of the day, but as an expression of the age. Even if many style-varieties might appear, mirroring the shiftings of life, nevertheless these varieties must be based on such fundamental form-characteristics as are ultimately going to shape the coming style of that respective culture in the making.

On the long orbit of the Western cultural progress, beginning from the earliest childhood of its history, we discern three milestones of genuine style, rising high above the others. They are the Egyptian, the Greek, and the Gothic formorders. There was a long period of time between the culminations of the Egyptian and Greek forms. Likewise the interval between the Greek and the Gothic was broad. It was bound to be so; for a new style—by virtue of being style in the right sense of the word—could take roots only when conditions of life during the progress of a long period of time had developed into a new cultural order. Then this new cultural order became expressed in a corresponding style-order. Again, when this cultural order had run its course, its styleorder also had run its course. It ceased to be creative style; it became a historical style, which never **should** have been applied by posterity—but which, alas, **has** been applied.

The Gothic order was the last genuine style in the Western world. Much time has passed since it weakened into flamboyant inconsistencies and finally ceased to exist as a living style. The Gothic was followed by the Renaissance high-tide of a great and distinctive style formation. This

Renaissance style-formation, however, was not a genuine one, but a reflection of the Greek form-conception—and later-on so much of a reflection as to make it imitative. Its ramifications, the Baroque and the Rococo, developed subsequently into respective styles of their own, although more or less in a sculpturally decorative sense. After their times—as we know—there was a long time of style digestion and assimilation, of style "revivals" and "rebirths," and of all that fumbling hither and thither, till there was nothing more left over than a dry and empty eggshell—the chicken gone, grown and eaten, long, long ago.

Yet behold, what has happened during this long period of fumbling with that dry and empty eggshell. Indeed, just this very period was in many respects significant as a great revelation to mankind. To begin with, it must be borne in mind that man's knowledge of the construction of the universe, both macrocosmic and microcosmic, has been considerably broadened so as to offer entirely another conception of space and of its organization than was man's conception heretofore. Moreover, it must be borne in mind that intercommunication between peoples and thoughts has passed through revolutionary changes. This has been true particularly during the most recent years, when all kinds of communicative means have appeared, both for fast traveling and still faster interchange of thoughts and ideas. One needs only consider the fact that in our days any thought and idea can be flashed in less than a second's time to any corner of this globe, no matter how remote—and one realizes how completely conditions have changed. Naturally, all this has been and is apt to affect man's attitude toward the problems of life, spiritual as well as material. A multitude of new conditions have arisen and still more are bound to arise; many new problems must find their solutions, and a new form-development will be much in demand.

In fact, in comparison with previous times, the domain of form has been multiplied as life has become more complex, more diversified, and more craving for comfort, mechanical and otherwise. This domain of form has been still more multiplied because of the fact that science and industry have brought about a great number of new materials and construction methods. All this offers the best opportunity for a new form-conception, entirely along new lines, such as earlier times scarcely could have imagined. Besides, all this is apt to stir up the dormant creative imagination—one would think.

The prime supposition for a new style, as said, is a change of condition of life toward a new order—for a new form-world needs a freshly new soil from which to grow. Insofar as the soil is concerned, the conditions of present day life are new and original beyond all past experience. The suppositions for a new form-world, therefore, are excellent. As a matter of fact, we are already far advanced along the new road. Nay —to repeat—the new form already exists.

It must be observed, however, that when we speak about a new form of our time, we do not speak about a new "style-form" of our time. On the contrary, the more the matter of style is postponed, the clearer one is able to develop a direct and expressive form. For, beyond doubt, **a sincere search for form by ignoring an intentional search for style, is the safest way—toward style.**

Yet, just this much-mentioned matter of style seems to be continuously the chief stumbling-block in the progress of form. Because publicity is an important issue in present conditions, unfortunately style novelties are often given much more prominent places in form-development than is given form-development itself. Such undertakings as World's Fairs, Local Fairs, and like spectacular things hinge much on their publicity values to be gained by means of strikingly novel forms. Accordingly, a great number of such exhibition buildings are designed into showy features—often too showy, we should say. Whether this is good or bad, we refrain from stating—for it depends on the aims of these affairs, whether they mean commercial success or cultural progress. But from the point of view of sound form-development, such a procedure is dangerous, for it gives the great masses of people the impression that these showy things represent "modern style."

There are hundreds of motion picture theaters and similar show and shopping places, with their bold and blatant signs and glamorous light effects, where the designers obviously were unable to bridle their Pegasuses. Whether or not this kind of design is good for business, we do not know and do not care to know. Our only concern is the spirit of vulgarity which through this has been brought closer to everyday life. There are many places, such as exhibitions, shops and show-windows, where the new design has been and is displayed. With satisfaction it can be stated that in these respects, generally speaking, a constant improvement has taken place, much to the good of normal form-development. Particularly the growing generation of architects is gradually becoming imbued with a sane conception of the demands of the time—and, **particularly in those cases where enough of stamina has overcome the temptation to tricky jazziness** there seems to be much enthusiasm and capability among the young. This, indeed, is a hopeful sign. Nevertheless, as things still are, one often gets the impression that modern architecture and bar-room decoration are much the same thing. Thus it happens, not so seldom, that hotels and homes establish their bar-rooms in "modern style," while the rest parades in that old outworn stuff.

The difficulties in form-development arise from the fact that the design profession is to a large degree insincere. Many are eager to follow modern thought, but do not care to delve deeper into the matter in order to learn what modern thought really means and what the underlying principles are. Often one sees architects dealing with "modern" forms—yes "modern" to the limit—although they still yesterday were inveterate stylists in Greek and Gothic terms. Often one sees architects being "experts" of town-design—yes "experts" to the utmost—although they still yesterday created discord by erecting ill-fitting structures without any thought of town-design and its most primary requirements whatsoever. **How could one trust the sincerity of a philosopher, if he overnight turns his direction of thought to the opposite, for the mere sake of being up-to-date!**

The deepest thoughts are not born in noisy streets and market places; they are born in silent solitude. Analogically, the sincere form does not emerge from ambitious adorning of World's Fairs and such spectacular affairs; it originates from the modest work for silent home atmosphere. Really, if we were to undertake a survey of the best and most direct form-development that modern thought has produced, we would not be surprised to find this in the kitchens, pantries, and bathrooms of the homes. Here, form has escaped styles and other side-influences; it has been conceived clearly and simply to serve its purpose, and it has been moulded gracefully with good taste. Here, we can learn a lesson of how form-problems must be solved, for here they have been honestly solved.

From these kitchens, pantries, and bathrooms of the home, this learned lesson could help us to solve the problems of the rest of the home in a like manner of honest approach. From these homes we must proceed further to solve the problems of streets and plazas in a like manner of honest approach. From these streets and plazas we must proceed further to solve the problems of towns and cities in a like manner of honest approach. Once we and all the other designers alike have done this, we have solved all the architectural problems of towns and cities in a direct and functional manner. And, provided this has been done with good sense for proportion, rhythm, and fundamentals—for sure, **"our form" has been all the time with us.**

But what about our "style"?

Well, the future art-historian may deal with those things, if so is his pleasure.

So far, the aforesaid concerns the first-mentioned phase of the new form-order; that is, form-shaping of individual buildings so as to make these buildings expressive of the time of their construction. Still the other mentioned phase must be discussed; namely, the one concerning a proper correlation of these individual buildings—and, as for this, it was already said that such a correlation must hereafter be conceived in a "decentralized sense of openness." So it must be, because of the fact that all town-development of today must satisfy the increasing demand for air, light, and space.

Now, when we speak about the demands for air, light, and space, we do not mean that this demand is entirely a recent trend. Certainly, those palatial developments, described in our analysis of the formal moment in town-building, were at least airy and spacious with their plazas, gardens, and extensive parks. But that was the case only with these palatial developments themselves, whereas the rest of the town remained cramped, dark, and gloomy. Therefore, when we now speak about the demand for air, light, and space in a contemporary sense, we mean a "general demand."

On the whole, this general demand for air, light, and space had its origin from those days when the time became conscious of town-design in the terms of the Informal Revival. But as this Informal Revival at the beginning sought its examples mainly from the narrow conditions of the Middle Ages, the demand for air, light, and space was not always satisfied; and it took therefore a considerable time before the consequences of the new era became evident. However, the groundwork was laid for organic thinking in town-design, and matters were bound to proceed progressively along this line. And, as the gradual development of mechanical means of communication accelerated the possibilities of an open mode of planning, the new conception of architectural town-formation in terms of openness developed accordingly.

As for this new conception of architectural town-formation, we have even here—as was the case with architectural design in general—enough of time-perspective to study the matter in the light of a logical evolution. In this evolution we can easily discern several distinctly different inclinations, of which we will mention some as illuminating examples.

First, we will mention that attempt to continue with the mediaeval mode of informal planning—particularly of smaller towns, suburbs, and satellite communities—yet to adapt it to contemporary conditions with increased openness and with smoothly-running curves so as to ease the growing traffic flow. This mode of informal planning became particularly the prevailing trend in those countries where Sitte's challenge was accepted and his advice followed, and it resulted in a great many fine community developments of that intimate "home town" type.

Second, we will mention those attempts to form individual town-communities of the so called "Garden City" character, where the demands for spaciousness have been adequately provided for. Such was the trend particularly in England; and in this respect the activities of Ebenezer Howard and Sir Raymond Unwin have been mentioned in another connection. Already the name, "Garden City," assures that this kind of town-development was based on building types in a human scale and, therefore, that it was apt to bring humanly livable conditions into the town.

Third, we will mention such planning-type where the correlation of large scale buildings has become expressive of the big city of our time, yet where the best principles of building correlation of both the Classical and Mediaeval eras have been kept in honor, notwithstanding the augmented openness of planning. This kind of a planning-type constitutes perhaps the bulk of such contemporary town-development as has followed the ideas of the Informal Revival.

Fourth, we will mention the development of such planning where the leading thought is to bring a maximum of sunlight into the interiors of the buildings by means of a proper orientation of these buildings. Basically, this thought of orientation is a logical one, provided of course that it is logically balanced with other and perhaps more essential demands. Things have not been always conducted so, however, for in great many cases the thought of orientation has been illogically over-emphasized to such a degree that a satisfactory correlation of building masses has been neglected and a monotonous repetition of these masses has been the result. Surely, this kind of unbalanced planning is the fruit of too much theoretical reasoning, where form-sensitiveness is given but a slight chance to direct.

Fifth, we will mention the tendency to an open mode of planning by the erection of tall structures, with much space between these structures. And by tall structures we mean now particularly skyscrapers—individually planned, or groups of them. On the whole, this mode of planning, so far, is still much in the making, inasmuch as it consists for the most part of frequent and bold picture material for professional books and magazines. There is, however, something refreshing about these ambitious schemes, for, although they often-times spring from a super-glorification of our machine age rather than from a sincere aspiration for better homes, they no doubt are necessary actions in the course of things: they fertilize the soil for ever new ideas, and through this they breed progress and positive harvest. Let's be amiable and put it so.

We could mention many other examples of town-formation in the signs of open mode of planning, but we deem it unnecessary for our purpose. These already-mentioned examples mark the most conspicuous inclinations in the progress of contemporary town-building.

All these catalogued different inclinations of open town-formation mirror, on one side, the gradual technical development of those means which can make this openness possible; and on the other side they mirror all the leanings between the intimate development of the small community and the ambitious craving for effectiveness by means of architectural mass-formation. In all probability, it is in the broad field between these two extreme leanings that the future development of architectural town-formation is going to have its course. No doubt, during this course, a multitude of new ideas will be born to fit the changing demands of life. And as any time must have the freedom to solve its problems according to its own conception, there is nothing more now to be added, except that two fundamental points must be observed. First, it must be observed that **any architectural town-formation must happen in accordance with the best understanding of organic order so as to achieve a favorable architectural atmosphere.** And second, it must be observed that, **particularly in the residential sections, the paramount problem must be to achieve such design-character as can bring home atmosphere into these sections.** For in all instances the oft-repeated thought must be borne in mind, that **the more there is infused home-atmosphere into the urban communities, the deeper the roots of healthy social order will grow.**

F. NECESSARY CLEANINGS

While we are in the mood for bringing order into towns and cities, there is still another point concerning order—or why not say "decency"—which should be corrected before much else can be accomplished in the way of town-improvement. We refer now to that dirt and disorder which frequently is spread all around; and we mean, furthermore, all those signs, bill-boards, and like things, such as are displayed along streets and plazas and which, for the most part, are of such a quality as is apt to foster poor taste and cultural degeneration. Surely, these things are of no credit either to city governments or to the town people themselves.

The entrance to the mediaeval town led through an imposing gateway with towers, symbolic emblems, and heavy fortification walls. Outside this gateway, the open country-side spread itself; inside it, was the picturesque town. So to speak, this entrance-gateway was a milestone between art of nature and art of man. In a great many instances this entrance-gateway expressed, in architectural terms, the best of the town's aims, to impress friendly visitors favorably.

The entrance-gateway of a modern city is vastly different. It has been said that the railroad station is the entrance-gateway of the city of today, and that its architectural forms serve the same purpose in the present-day city as was served by those of the entrance gateway in that olden town—the purpose of favorable impression. This is true when one enters the place by train and one's first impressions are derived from the said depot and its perhaps orderly surroundings. But how often does this happen. Impressions are received rather from the wide outskirts, passed mile-by-mile before the station is reached—and what kind of outskirts, alas; notice them with a keen and critical eye. Littered factory grounds and dirty back-yard clutter, old junk, half-rotten fences, sheds leaning precariously, and shattered windows—these are the things displayed for one's enjoyment; and in these beauteous places one can see the unfortunate, dirty, and perhaps diseased slum-dweller. One wonders why it is necessary to advertise one's home-town by such means. Undoubtedly, such conditions are the result of shocking negligence, for at least a semblance of order is not costly. A dirty face is not a matter of money; it is lack of decency.

A single ordinance by the authorities could alter the situation; a minimum of planting could change the picture in reforming the said gateway to bring honor to the population. But so accustomed are people to such conditions, in any city they enter, that they seem immune from its ugliness.

But the pompous depot with its dirty back-yard approach is only one of the many entrance-gateways to the city. There are also the main highway arteries. In the case of these, the problem is not one of cluttered factory-areas and slum-districts, but of the fronts of profitably situated buildings.

As one approaches the city, bill-boards of all sizes, design, and color border the highways—obscuring and uglifying the landscape. Gasoline stations, loud and blatant in form and tint, dot the roadside. As the city is neared, these gasoline stations grow in number and color; and as the country highway changes to the city street, huge commercial advertisement scaffolds compete with bill-boards, lamp-posts, telephone poles, and all that trivial rubbish so dear to the suburban builder. In the night, when only the effects of the glimmering lights can be seen, the scenery might be picturesque and sparkling. But in the daytime it is a nightmare. Please, look at that "famous Broadway"!

Methods of advertisement can bring delight to business districts and make street pictures vivid and colorful, if handled with good taste. Why, then, select the worst kind of means and thus make streets unattractive and vulgar? Street-adornment is not the concern of the individual alone who advertises his merchandise and strives to attract public attention for mere private profit. It is a matter of public concern, and must be under official control. When a radio crooner hums his honey-sweet songs, anyone can act according to his inclinations by either listening or turning the "music" off. But when buildings, streets, public squares and parks are plastered with ugliness, nobody can escape it. Surely, no one has the right to infect both ground and air with discarded garbage. Why, then, has anyone an unbridled right to scatter his **mental** garbage around the town?

Is all this blatant street advertisement really necessary to encourage the buying of all those varied articles displayed in shops and show-windows? Likely not. Everyone knows where to buy a pair of shoes, even the stranger can read it just by a glance at the window, for here the merchandise and the character of the shops are clearly exhibited. Here, perhaps, sensible lettering and enlightening trade-marks could give additional guidance, and thus could be the practical, economical, and esthetic solution of this problem of advertisement. But when all the sellers are in a constant competition, using most forceful methods of attracting universal attention, matters progress in ceaseless crescendo for the worse. What if all the merchants along the street screamed at the top of their lungs to attract attention: would it help?

The destructive influence of uncontrolled advertisement must be taken into consideration, and measures enacted accordingly. This must be done before other improvements can be effective. **And because this kind of exaggerated advertisement is a disease of the present era, its cure must be considered one of the problems of today.**

G. COMPREHENSIVE PLANNING

We have endeavored to present as many-sided a program of civic problems of today as we deem necessary in this introduction. There are, however, still a few words to be said about the mode of approach to these problems, and about the manner in which this approach must be organized.

No civic problem can be solved independently without considering other integrally interrelated problems. Failure to approach the solution of civic problems from a comprehensive understanding has been the basic fallacy of planning in general, and particularly in the planning of fast-growing cities. Even today, planning-eyes are not open to discern the broad scope and integral nature of civic problems.

Earlier, when civic embellishment was the fashion of the day and the "civic center" was regarded as the supreme issue, such efforts had little or nothing in common with the solution of vital planning problems at large. Such decorative scheming was much a matter of civic pride, and only rarely concerned itself with improvements of fundamental planning character where the welfare of the people was the governing thought. Later on, when the imperative need for improvements in the growing traffic-confusion necessitated a great number of street-regulations, those regulations did not consider the various traffic problems in an organic integrity, nor were they studied in correlation with other problems involved. Such, unfortunately, continues to be the course even today for, indeed, traffic solutions are still for the most part local concerns and piecemeal studies. Again, when the housing of people becomes, as it does at present, increasingly urgent, the air is filled with housing and more housing, and everyone is eager to solve his problems without knowing "where" they should be solved. Well, how could the tailor fit the buttons on the coat before he has cut the coat and knows where the button-holes should be? Similarly, how could the planner know where his local problems should be solved, unless he has examined the situation at large? For the local problems constitute only a few "buttons" on the plan, and these must be correlated to the "holes," and to the whole. Failure by the planner to consider the entire range of problems will occasion new and worse confusions.

To prevent such confusions, there is one and only one procedure; and that is to undertake a thorough study of the whole situation. This means **comprehensive planning.** A master-scheme must be worked out, covering those areas and problems in question—a plan both flexible and dynamic so as to prevent obsolescence; and a competent and permanent planning institution must be entrusted with its development. This planning institution must be free from politics and intrigues; it must have the faculty to study and re-study, and the power of planning and replanning so that, however conditions may develop, flexible changes can be made to meet new demands. In this work, any interfering influences by speculators, politicians, or any underground workers whatsoever, must be consistently and insistently prevented.

The first step in any planning must be to set up such a competent, permanent, and authorized planning institution.

5. CONCENTRATION

THE foregoing study of the problems of today has made it obvious that organic decentralization must be regarded as the leading theme in contemporary town-building. Consequently, all planning efforts must be focused particularly on this movement and on its various phases, and not on the existing concentration. On the other hand, it is necessary to have a clear picture of the concentrated status in the cities before the full implication of decentralization tendencies can be understood. It must, namely, be borne in mind that those reasons that made concentration necessary in the past, have in the course of time been gradually changed to those reasons that now make decentralization urgent. The causes of this change we must learn to know.

The prime reason for concentration is the fact that man by nature is a sociable creature. Man's normal tendency is to live in groups, and his actions are largely governed by herd-instinct. In man's struggle for existence, his position is both inwardly and outwardly strengthened when he acts collectively. Inwardly, collective action offers protection, courage, initiative, joy, and inspiration. Outwardly, it impresses respect and fear. Because of herd-instinct, men are inclined to feel and think in groups. So religions were born. So'society came into being. And because of this same inclination, the community sprang into existence: men gathered together, they lived in close contact, they formed camps, hamlets, and villages; and when greater numbers gathered, villages expanded into towns, towns into cities, and cities into those extremely concentrated great metropolises of the present era.

Because men lived in concentrated circumstances, they became bold and pugnacious. This caused fear in opposite quarters; protective walls were built, and defensive concentration was so increased as to make conditions extremely congested. In such a manner the congested town was born because of fight-and-fear. But, as this congestion was bound to last for a long period of time, it became regarded as a predestinated characteristic of every town. Therefore, when this congestion later on, because of changed conditions, began to follow an opposite course, it was stupefying. Men's minds were so settled in the old concentrated mode of thinking that they were unable to grasp and assimilate the new. The long-lasted congestion had moulded a definite type of homo: the **town-dweller.**

The spirit of the former town-dweller still exists, for even the modern **city-dweller** is stung by an insect. It is not, however, the same bug of fight-and-fear that produced the town-dweller of olden times: it is the fly of diversion.

The modern city-dweller—to draw a typical picture of average inclination—is incapable of self-entertainment, and is therefore dependent on the diverting entertainment of others. Because he has been nurtured in noise, he feels the pulsing of life through the city's noise, and is distracted by an enigmatic fear when alone in silence. The city's whirring and rattling are a constant nervous strain and stimulus; and when this abnormal incitement ceases to act as an agitating spur, that silence which follows is strange and uncomfortable to him. In such a silence, the city-dweller subconsciously feels an echo of that hollowness which is caused by the city's din, but which he does not feel in the city itself, just because of this very din.

When visiting silent country lands, the city-dweller takes others with him in order that the party's chatter may distract him during those hours when he is away from that captivating restlessness of the city. In direct contrast with this, the country-dweller once in a while leaves his rural solitude to spend a few hours of excitement in the city; but he soon tires and gladly returns to his quiet rural tasks.

Thus it is: **the country-dweller prefers concentration of mind in his decentralized life in the country, whereas the city-dweller is apt to decentralize his mind in the concentrated life of the city.**

These facts should not be overlooked when psychological questions are considered in connection with the change from concentration into decentralization. In this respect, it is important to bear in mind that there is a distinct relationship between man and his work; which, in the city's case, means that man makes the city and the city makes man. In other words, man creates the crowded concentration, and this concentration in turn produces the typical city-dweller.

In the case of decentralization, the same reciprocity holds true. For when the decentralization movement takes root and grows, it will tend to free man's mind from restraining congestion—and this free mind, in its turn, will speed the decentralization movement. Thus, man's attitude of mind, and the planning of cities, will develop together and reciprocally toward increased decentralization. During this gradual and reciprocal progress, a new type of man will be born: **man who has become influenced by the positive qualities of both town and country.**

A. COMPULSORY CONCENTRATION

Indeed, that concentration caused by fight-and-fear was compulsory, if anything. So was the situation in those mediaeval days when human life did not count so much, and when almost every place to dwell had to be a fortified stronghold. Fear for the enemy and the resultant necessity of protection caused concentration around castles and convents. These were solidly built and were provided with complete means of defense. As the people from the surrounding country-side gathered about these castles and convents for protection, towns were born, and an enlargement of existing fortifications was needed. Accordingly, the mediaeval town became surrounded with heavily-built walls, crenelated towers, and watery moats. Because of the frequent fighting in the Middle Ages, and because of the fact that the means of warfare made concentrated defense necessary, extreme concentration was an inevitable result. And, as said, this congested town character gave rise to the subsequent psychological attitude that the town, merely because it was a town, should of necessity be extremely compact—much in the same sense as there seems to be a prejudice, still today, that a few square feet of urban land constitute a fortune.

When conditions changed and the necessity for local protection lessened, the gates of the town were opened and the crowded population was permitted the freedom of expansion. This freedom was not much used, however, and consequently the spread of the town was slow. Centuries of tight living had so accustomed people to narrow quarters that their mentalities were moulded accordingly.

So was the situation in the European countries where the mediaeval congestion established traditional concentration. Much of this tradition was, in one form or another, brought to the new lands in the Western Hemisphere. In spite of this, town-development in the United States was very different. The necessity of defense existed, of course, but it was entirely of another nature since a few fortresses here and there were sufficient. The towns were free to expand as they liked, the streets were relatively broad, the gardens were spacious, and the country-side lay open and sunny, inviting the community's spread. No such extreme concentration, as we see, was imposed upon the American towns as was inflicted on the European ones.

Notwithstanding this, even the towns of the United States were in those days forced to concentration. This was caused by another reason. It was of a technical nature: it was the lack of adequate means of communication.

The earlier lack of adequate means of communication and the subsequent development of these means, constitute the most fascinating study when concentration is contrasted with the gradually evolving decentralization. This study will reveal the nature of concentration in its true light, and will even so render evident the logic of the decentralization movement.

In early days, walking was the sole means of communication. Horses were for warriors and knights only, and, although carts and carriages were used, they were too few in number to be regarded as a means of traffic in the town. Accordingly, any planning of towns in those days had to be based on the presupposition that everyone had to get along with his own two legs. Such conditions continued to exist for thousands of years all over the civilized world, and it seemed as if man in his problems of traffic was forever confined to human legs, horses and carts, although he was able in other fields of life to exhibit progressive changes. A few random examples from various times might best illustrate this situation.

It has been said that Paris in the middle of the sixteenth century had only two horse carriages for hire. Although this statement may not be an exact one, in any case it presents an illuminating view of contemporary conditions. As Paris at that time had a population of 250,000, and was the most important city, it is easy to imagine how conditions were in general, even if there had been a few more carriages in Paris than those mentioned two. However, as time passed, there could be noted a distinct growth in the number of carriages. This growth was slow, that is true, for matters in earlier times did not proceed in the same tempo as they do today. So, for example, almost one hundred years had passed, from that above mentioned Paris case, before London had a sufficient number of carriages to be considered a means of traffic—yet for the patrician class only. Even this limited convenience did not last long, for in the year 1635 a royal proclamation put an end to it. This proclamation declared that horse carriages had become a nuisance in the city, for not only were His Majesty and his much beloved Queen perturbed by the traffic, but the princes and noblemen as well. Besides —as the proclamation continued—such traffic demolishes the pavement. Consequently, the good Londoners were forced to stick to their own two legs.

Such prohibitive measures could not continue effective for long. Of course not, for a century later, London with its population of 700,000 had two thousand private carriages and one thousand public ones for hire. This meant an average of one public carriage per seven hundred persons. Such an average was not very large, to be sure, but it was a considerable advance in comparison with earlier days, and in contrast with many other places it was an excellent progress. By comparison, Berlin half a century later, in 1815, had only thirty carriages for the use of its population of approximately 200,000, which meant an average of one carriage per six thousand.

But things accelerated. Berlin had, in the middle of the past century—also not even a full century ago—one thousand carriages for its population of 500,000; whereas Paris, with its population of 1,500,000, was provided with sixteen hundred carriages. This meant an average of one carriage per five hundred persons in Berlin, and in Paris about one carriage per thousand. Also, there were still many pedestrians in the streets.

So much for examples.

Meanwhile, traffic facilities of various kinds were under development, foreboding a new era. The railroad was gradually becoming a useful means of intercommunication between the city, its suburbs, and neighbor townships. An outgrowth of this railroad was the urban street car. This latter, however, was rather ineffective in its earlier days because horses were used as the driving power, thus making traffic comparatively slow. When electricity first supplanted horse use—which, observe, happened only a few decades ago—speed was increased and the chains of compulsory concentration were considerably loosened. Yet the revolutionizing era of gasoline motors, pneumatic rubber tires, and automobiles, was not there as yet.

Viewing now the matter of concentration in the light of the aforesaid, one realizes how things during the past centuries have gradually but steadily brought new impulses into town-planning. During this progress, the necessity of concentration has gradually shifted toward the possibility of decentralization and, ultimately, to an urgent demand for it. The most surprising discovery, however, is the recentness of the use of mechanical means in urban intercommunication. Considering, moreover, the fact that the most rapid development of mechanical traffic means and the intense use of these means in urban service has happened just during two or three of the latest decades, we have reason for wondering what the conditions in this respect are going to be, say, three, four, or five decades hence. **We have much reason for wondering, for, in fact, our present mode of planning must to a great extent satisfy the requirements of those future conditions.**

B. SPECULATIVE CONCENTRATION

Speculation, in itself, is not necessarily of negative value. As an encouraging vitalizer of the city's multifarious undertakings, it often is instrumental in keeping things going. Without this kind of stimulus, the city would soon become numb, indifferent, and sleepy.

Unfortunately, however, speculation is not always of such a positive value, for human nature often violates that common spirit so essential to the welfare of the city. This common spirit must not be violated, for it is the uniting and reconciling faculty which fuses the population together in the striving for common good. This was already indicated in the characteristics of herd-instinct where the underlying idea must be mutual protection, help, and inspiration, and not selfish interests to benefit a few, and to harm others.

Speculation in the city is concerned particularly in land-values. During the city's growth this land-value speculation is a by-product, often a deplorable one, where speculators of one kind or another become involved in the manipulation of building-grounds in trying to get their share of the possible profit. In the residential and suburban sections of the city, this kind of speculation usually operates normally, for sufficient land is available so that land-values regulate themselves within reasonable limits. The situation is different in the congested regions of the city proper, for here speculation frequently becomes unreasonable, causing a prejudicial divergence of interests by thus upsetting the economic balance of the city.

These divergences were seemingly latent as long as a natural concentration was imposed upon the city, and no change of conditions was generally regarded as possible. In such circumstances, everyone was compelled to accept prices and costs whatever they may have been. But when changing conditions began to forecast the community's expansion, this attitude of resignation shifted to one of irritation, where speculation was ready to influence the situation and divergence of interests became active. Speculative concentration was contrasted with speculative decentralization; the former trying to maintain its position, the latter discovering and championing new opportunities.

As matters are today, long-lasting concentration has established the standards of land-value on a rising scale. The present tendency toward decentralization, on the other hand, is apt to make these standards uncertain. In this value change, rise of land-value is profitable to the landowner; the remainder of the population—which directly or indirectly contributes to the landowner's profit—is affected to the contrary. For this reason the landowners, generally speaking, favor concentration; whereas the rest of the population is perhaps inclined to prefer decentralization. But inasmuch as the landowners of the congested centers are relatively few in number as compared with the entire population, rise in land-value is disadvantageous to the vast majority. Also, we have this situation: minority and personal interests versus majority and common interests. And because the balance in this manner tips in favor of the minority, there is reason for questioning: "Who should have the right to control planning of cities so as to decide land-use—from which land-values derive?"

A constructive answer to this question is important, particularly because of the fact that it is not a rare thing that high speculation throttles the city by controlling, and to a large degree paralyzing, the efforts to organize a natural process of expansion. It is equally important that this answer be found on the basis of such principles as are valid no matter what the situation may be. And it is furthermore important that this same answer could be discriminative as between one kind of speculation and another.

Now, looking upon the controversy between the exaggerated tendency to speculation and the city's freedom of natural expansion, the right answer to the above question on the basis of principles is easily to be found. To start with, this we have established as an unquestionable maxim: "the primary purpose of the city is to provide adequate living and working accommodations for its population." Every kind of speculation which supports, promotes, and encourages urban development in the spirit of this maxim, not only has the right to exist, but is highly desirable. Conversely, such speculation as tends in effect in the opposite direction, must be regarded as noxious and must be carefully restricted.

Speculation, as we see, is a two-edged sword with two-fold effects, depending on its ethical nature. It can therefore be divided into two main classes:

The first is that type of speculation which, thanks to far-sightedness, is able to forecast the city's natural and potential development, and by means of speculation advances that development. This is a good co-operation with the city, and it is therefore fair-and-square that such far-sightedness be recompensed. And that answers our question insofar as this type of speculation is concerned.

The second is that type of speculation which, thanks to its authority—actual or by obscure means obtained—restrains the city's development, with resultant harm to the community and with good profit for the speculator himself. This type of speculation constitutes a destructive element in the community and, therefore, it should be allowed no power of influence. In reality, however, it is just this restraining type of speculation which most frequently keeps unnatural concentration alive, directly or indirectly.

Going deeper into things, it is obvious that this restraining type of speculation has its historical background. Much of the landowner-speculator's power of influence in civic affairs is an inheritance from those olden conditions where the landowners exercised their influence in the running of the town, but where speculation was entirely out of question because the town was at standstill, land-values stable, and future potentialities still an unknown quantity. This kind of urban status established the traditional attitude that those possessing land in the town should have the power to determine the general land-use in that town. As long as compulsory concentration prevailed, this practice constituted a harmless mode, a dead clause. There was no other alternative, for land was used as it was, and nothing else could enter into the situation. But with the gradual change from compulsory concentration into vital decentralization, the individual landowner's traditional rights to control land-use has opened great opportunities for that kind of speculation which is apt to hamper decentralization in its desired course. In other words, that tradition of the olden times, so natural and workable in concentrated circumstances, has now become an unfitting and obstructing tradition in decentralized circumstances. This is plain and clear, for inasmuch as the former standstill of concentration is as different from the present trend to decentralization as night is from day, it is quite natural that a mode of procedure which was suitable for the former cannot satisfactorily serve the latter.

Consequently, a new mode of procedure such as is suitable for decentralization must be constituted in the regulation of land-use control. And however this new mode of procedure is constituted, it is of prime importance that the planning authorities be given enough of power to counteract all obstructing efforts of speculation. For, surely, decentralization must not be directed so as to encourage obstruction to the good of the speculator. It must be directed and controlled by an impartial authority to the good of the community itself. This, let us hope, will give the death blow to the restraining speculative concentration.

C. VERTICAL CONCENTRATION

The erection of tall structures tightens concentration in a vertical direction. This is the case particularly in the congested sections of the big cities of today. And because the skyscraper is the epitome of this upward trend, it must be made the object of our examination.

Despite that admiration and pride which the skyscraper seems to inspire, it has in many respects become an obstructing element in those cities where unlimited skyscraper growth has taken place. The consequences of such growth were not foreseen in due time, and no revisions in the street-system were made to provide for the newcomer. As matters stand now, the skyscraper is the big, self-conscious, and egocentric member of the building family in the city. Figuratively, he noises himself abroad, pushes others aside, and begins to dominate the situation in a boasting manner—till others become disturbed and wonder what to do with that fellow.

Really, due to its very character, the skyscraper has brought many new problems into the city. The skyscraper is tall, and because of its height the neighborhood is affected by the shadow. The skyscraper is voluminous, and because of its volume land-values are unbalanced. The skyscraper is massive, and because of its mass the quiet scale of the surroundings is overpowered and the city's form-coherence deranged. Despite these issues **of primary importance,** the skyscraper is regarded as the outstanding product of contemporary architecture, "the taller the better," and has been allowed to grow with almost no limitation—till one begins to wonder . . . ?

There is considerable reason for wondering whether or not the skyscraper may prove an obstacle to the decentralization movement, for, with respect to many of the objectives of this movement, a great number of tall buildings would act in opposition to these objectives. So, for instance, while decentralization endeavors to bestow upon the city adequate amounts of air, light, and openness, and to restore normal land values and sane economic conditions, the skyscraper is causing shadowy depths, abnormal land values, and considerable economic disturbances. And while the art of town-building strives to establish favorable form-unity in the city, the skyscraper counteracts all such laudable endeavors.

As a free unit and separately fitted into an appropriate lay-out, the skyscraper is surrounded by air, light, and openness, of course. But in any mass construction of skyscrapers, much of these worth-while qualities are lost. This is the situation particularly when skyscrapers have been imposed upon the cities as a generalized erection along narrow streets.

In such circumstances, these skyscrapers have caused such deep and shadowy canyons in the street labyrinth of many of the large cities, as to make these streets mediaevally dim. Isn't this contradictory? For, while the skyscrapers pretend to be the last word in the building enterprises of the present mechanized era, their effects, insofar as air, light, and openness are concerned, have in fact led to much the same result as were the effects of building activities during the Dark Ages; that is, during that period so much criticized by the mechanized minds themselves.

The answer to this always is that with modern advances in ventilation, air-conditioning, electricity, and such like, much can be accomplished by a substitution for natural conditions. This is true enough. But that is beside our point. For, irrespective of practical problems, the mass erection of tall and bulky structures close one to another does not satisfy one's desire for fresh air, sunshine, and space—which is a normal psychological demand, so characteristic of our age and so fundamentally sane. Therefore, in order to fulfil its claim as a genuine product of modern times, the skyscraper must adjust itself to meet the genuine physical and psychological demands of modern times. And if the skyscraper, after all, is to be accepted in the future city of organic decentralization, it must be accepted on such conditions only.

Once the skyscraper was introduced in the city, landowners began to make use of their self-obtained air-rights by erecting tall colossi of maximum bulk. Extreme density was the ultimate effect. Now, thousands upon thousands crowd narrow streets originally planned for limited traffic only. And when a single structure houses many thousands, who several times during the day pour in and out, it can be imagined what a whole street bordered with these giants has to stand. Those who have experienced this kind of phenomenon—and have thought about it at any length—must realize that matters are not as they should be. It is true, of course, that many inveterate congestion enthusiasts, having been accustomed for years to such conditions, might not see our point. They might not see it just as, for example, those who are constantly used to noisy and superficial dinner-music-entertainment often have become deaf to the fine qualities of symphonic music. In spite of this disagreement, however, we insist that the causing of constant over-crowded conditions is far from intelligent scheming. The crowding of large masses of people might happen occasionally for exceptional reasons and, for sure, such casual crowding can be exciting and stimulating. But when an over-crowded traffic has been superimposed upon the city as a permanent state of things, it is almost absurd to call it "traffic."

It might be true that many a big city, even of the old type, has its congestions. The skyscraper, therefore, should not carry all the blame. But even in such cases the conditions should be improved rather than made still worse by careless air-right allowances.

Careless air-right allowances for erecting skyscrapers cause not only the said congestion, but even an extreme concentration of business activities. Because of this extreme concentration, land-values have been raised to an abnormal level, often creating an unsound playground for big speculation. As the aim of such speculation is to maintain, or rather to increase, concentration, the economic equilibrium of the city is endangered.

Generally speaking, however, the abnormal land-values are too theoretical to be actual, and too exaggerated to be stable. Sometimes these values might work in accordance with one's expectations, particularly when the general conditions in business are lively, or tending upward. But fluctuations in business effect fluctuations in land-values, and for this reason the value of land must not be fixed according to exaggerated expectations, but according to normal conditions. Normal conditions, again—as both economic principles and common sense indicate—can be maintained only when a workable balance exists between production and demand. Here, and just here, we discover the skyscraper's weak point as an economical feature in the city, for, due to its colossal volume, the skyscraper easily creates overproduction of space for rent. Thus, when the air-rights of several enormous structures have been fully utilized and the demand for space has been satisfied, the adjacent lots must take the consequences. All too often, perfectly good properties in the immediate neighborhood can serve as parking lots only.

The manner in which such unfair competition influences land-values is neither novel nor surprising. A great deal of experience testifies to the fact that the unrestricted skyscraper can be economically dangerous. As the unrestricted erection of skyscrapers is an outgrowth of sanguine prosperity, and as cities unfortunately experience depressions as well as times of prosperity—and particularly deep depressions after high tides of prosperity—the whole procedure, then, is built on such presuppositions as almost deliberately invite catastrophic effects, sooner or later, and often.

The foregoing makes it evident that there are many objections to the mass erection of skyscrapers, and that these objections arrive from practical and economic considerations. There is, however, one more consideration, one of esthetic nature. In the foregoing it was said that the skyscraper is massive, and because of its mass the quiet scale of the neighborhood is overpowered and the city's form-coherence deranged. The more the skyscraper has been given freedom to grow, the greater this danger has become. And the more speculation takes the lead in this process, the worse can be the architectural aspect. Surely, the city's form-coherence must not be left at the mercy of commercial speculation.

When the skyscraper was first introduced in the city, no measures were taken toward a reorganization of the existing street lay-out to meet the demands of this new civic member.

The old city-plan, having been designed for very different conditions, continued to guide urban growth, notwithstanding the fact that the skyscraper in itself demanded a radical change in the plan pattern of streets. Unquestionably this was a grave mistake on the part of those officials responsible for the town's physical order. They should have realized the obvious fact that there must be a workable relationship between the mode of disposing building masses and the lay-out of streets and building lots; and that the existing narrow streets and limited building lots were not suited for such big structures as the skyscrapers had the inclination to develop to. One cannot squeeze extraordinarily big feet in normal shoes; one must trim the shoes according to the size and form of the feet. The town-planners of those days should have realized in time the meaning of this analogy.

Now let us ask: has there, on the whole, existed a practical need for skyscrapers? Or have they been erected merely to exhibit man's technical skill, and to satisfy vanity?

The skyscraper has become a frequent feature of the skyline in the larger cities of the United States. This is most plausible, for the skyscraper is a natural product of American psychology, engineering, and architecture. It is surprising, however, to observe that Europe has been slow to consider the skyscraper and that so far its execution has scarcely begun there. Modern inventions, provided they satisfy a real need, are usually spread in short order throughout the civilized world; yet the skyscraper, even if a modern achievement of consequence, has been localized almost to a single country. The reason for this cannot be found in the quick growth of the American population with such an intensity of land-use throughout the country as might make urban concentration compulsory. Such reasoning would have no backbone, and conditions overseas would contradict this. Besides, that great development of individual and collective transportation means in the United States—largely exceeding the corresponding development overseas—should, so one would think, further decentralization toward the open country rather than toward vertical urban concentration by means of tall buildings. Nay, the reasons for the skyscraper's appearance must be found elsewhere.

The first structure of the skyscraper type was erected in Chicago. Because this city at that time was growing most rapidly, one might get the impression that through a vertical concentration a favorable solution of the immense growth was imperative. Only a short glance at the map of Chicago, however, shows clearly that any growth could have taken place in a horizontal direction, for ample land was available for the most intense expansion. Consequently, the skyscraper idea in Chicago obviously did not spring from practical necessity.

Yet that idea, once born, could have proven the ideal solution in those circumstances where, because of limited areas for expansion, a necessity for vertical concentration really existed. Manhattan, that narrow stretch of land surrounded by water and with great anticipations of its growth, is the most conspicuous example in this respect. But even here, only a small percentage of the island is, so far, covered with buildings beyond normal height. Besides, why should the heart of New York be necessarily over-concentrated on that narrow land, when the broad areas of Brooklyn and Long Island were at hand? The East River is no unsurmountable obstacle, for many great cities are divided by bodies of water as broad as that river. Therefore, the narrowness of Manhattan, often presented as a reason for the skyscraper's necessity, is not a valid argument.

Concentration of a large population does not of necessity create a need for vertical growth. London—to take the most enlightening example insofar as size is concerned—was larger than was New York when the latter began its mass erection of tall buildings. Yet, while the ambitious New

Yorkers believed it imperative to expand high into the air, the well-balanced Londoners were satisfied with their horizontal stress. The Britishers, of course, had ample technical opportunity to go into the air, but such was not their inclination. Obviously, the necessity of skyscrapers was not convincing to them.

Nor are we convinced on our part.

In those instances, however, where the skyscraper was wanted for ambitious reasons, its necessity was easy to explain.

Skyscrapers were first erected in the large cities of the United States, but soon the habit spread as a favored vogue to cities of less importance. Even many a small town has now its skyscraper, as a matter of civic pride.

Manhattan is the great leader, of course.

Whole-heartedly I admit that my first impression of Lower Manhattan was impressive. It seemed as if the lofty skyscraper masses rose directly from that vast Atlantic, colorful and airy in the light of the descending wintry sun. Indeed, it was a picture never to be forgotten.

As I progressed up the Hudson River, constantly changing views emerged, each one conveying a strong impression of the pulsing life within the city—that working ground of millions of human beings rushing in the perpetual restlessness of the ever growing competition for daily livelihood. High above this nervous rush, the steel and stone forest of skyscrapers rose toward the sky; the mighty work of human hand in superhuman dimensions; man but a tiny ant in the midst of his ambitious work.

The picture of New York is colorful when the sun is low and spreads its warmth over building masses. The skyline forms a silhouette of glowing light against that deep background of indigo.

The picture is airy, when fog softens the atmosphere and the skyscrapers cut their silvery outlines on the silver sky.

The picture is majestic, when myriads of lights dot the

black curtain of night and the stars of man blend into the sparks of heaven.

The picture is ever new; when looking from skyscraper pinnacles at the plastic panorama fading toward that distant blue, when surrounded in Central Park by that colorful silhouette of lofty forms, when in Lower Manhattan's narrow streets with sunlight cutting its golden streams through those deep shadows.

The picture is ever new, ever fascinating.

Indeed, Manhattan has its charm. It has this, however, much thanks to the atmospheric play of light and color on the towering masses. But when the metallic sky lies gray and gloomy over the city and the dull atmosphere lounges over land and water, the skyscraper forest springs starkly from the ground like chimneys after a fire. The buildings show their masses in dry nakedness, and the pleasing play has gone.

Manhattan has color and atmosphere. But it is lacking in coherent form.

Yet both are necessary.

A military march has both color and form; there the vibrations of brass give color and cadence gives form. If the brasses are silenced and the drums continue to beat cadence, the rhythm of form is still present. There still is life. There still is inspiration.

The landscape, the grove, the tree, all have their rhythmic charm of form even after the color of the foliage and the effects of light have gone.

But Manhattan is lacking in form in this sense.

Form in this sense, however, might not be considered an essential matter, for the magnitude of Manhattan is perhaps its supreme virtue, it seems: the larger, the more imposing.

In fact, the dreams of Manhattan's growth to a super-skyscraper metropolis seem ambitious. It is the Babylon of the future; the symbol of the great country of the Western

Hemisphere; the focus of the life of the country; the mirror of the aims of the nation. Increased population is to mean increased importance; greater congestion is to mean more vitality; growing traffic is to mean augmented activity; and loftier growth toward the sky is to mean amplified expressiveness of form. The theme of Manhattan is one of constant crescendo, a growing fortissimo of action and form. Man is but a worn cog in an enormous machine—ceaseless—restless —ruthless.

At least, so Manhattan impresses sound common sense.

The art of town-building—as we understand it—must not be satisfied with such ambitions as Manhattan seems to have. Its aims must not point toward magnitude. Its aims must be modest. Yet, in its modesty the art of town-building must be ambitious, for it must deal with the best of man. Its fundamental objective must be to provide a healthy environment for man so that the best within him can grow in strength. In concert with this objective the art of town-building must strive to build its manifold problems into a workable organism. According to this workable organism the cities can grow, no matter how great the growth ultimately may be; and even if the city were to become the greatest of all the metropolises, its magnificence must not be measured by the quantity of its masses and the intensity of its traffic, but by the quality of its physical and spiritual order.

The art of town-building must be loyal to its principles even with regard to the skyscraper. It must be willing to accept the skyscraper, provided the city-plan is prepared accordingly and the building is fitted properly there. This means that the skyscraper must be a natural product of the plan, it must be a healthy organ in a healthy organism, and it must function in accordance with other functions, practical and esthetic alike.

Yet, having considered all the pros and cons as to whether or not skyscrapers after all should be built in cities, the art of town-building concludes that **the only function left over to skyscrapers is their contribution as architectural features in the city.** Once this point of view is accepted, it is for the civic organization to determine where and how skyscrapers should be allowed to grow.

Prior to the skyscraper-era the town conformed to the topography of the land. From this low-lying silhouette rose varied building masses, towers, and the manifold gables, turrets, and pinnacles of the various buildings. These gave a lively variety to the town's skyline, and expressed through their respective formations the character of the buildings themselves and of the city at large as well. Accordingly, the skyline was formed into a true reflection of the town's purposes, functions, and aims—both physical and spiritual. Differences in size, in scale, in mass, and in the architectural treatment of detail, formed a significant correlation between the public and private buildings. Because logical planning resulted in a good distribution and grouping of the various official and cultural activities, rhythmic effects were automatically infused into the formation of the skyline with appropriate intervals and accents. Intellectual and public activities were strongly expressed in the general picture. Cathedrals and church towers rose high. Municipal buildings formed marked groups expressing official authority. And cultural and educational institutions occupied prominent locations, contrasting with the commercial and private sections of the town.

In this manner, the skyline of the town was built into rhythmic balance of accents and modulations. It was a skyline fully expressive. **It stressed the pre-eminence of spiritual purposes and aspirations.**

With the appearance of the skyscraper, however, the significant balance between the spiritual and the material was disturbed. The first tall steel-skeleton building sounded the trumpet call and challenged the logical formation of urban rhythm based on spiritual pre-eminence. This was an inevitable result, for as a rule the skyscraper is concerned primarily with commercial and business activities. Consequently, the material side of the city's functions are over-accentuated in the skyscraper city, whereas the spiritual moment is given only an inferior place in the shadows of the tall skyscrapers. Thus churches, libraries, and museums lie buried in deep canyons, walled by gigantic masses. And one wonders how the Cathedrals of Cologne and Amiens would feel if treated in the same cruel manner.

However, the materialistic side of life cannot be neglected, for it is an important factor in all conditions and particularly in the present era of widespread national and international trade relations, and as such it must come into expression in the city's architectural formation. On the other hand, because of the fact that this materialistic emphasis tends too much to dominate the city's formation, it is so much the more important that spiritual values be embodied in the city by infusing into the materialistic building masses true architecture and good form-coherence. **For, after all, true architecture and good form-coherence are the cultural and spiritual essence of both the art of building and the art of town-building. Therefore, if these art-forms are to live up to their aims and principles, here then is an important case to consider.**

Viewing the skyscraper problem in the light of the above, it is evident that the construction of uncontrolled and self-sufficient skyscrapers should be prohibited. For it is precisely thanks to the blunder through which such buildings have been allowed to grow, that has risen much of the practical, economic, and esthetic difficulties in the city. Controlled and coherently fitted skyscrapers, on the other hand, should be encouraged insofar as they serve the city functionally, and are of esthetic value in the city's formation and skyline.

With this in mind, **and only with this,** we greet the dawning of the individual skyscraper—and a favorable grouping of them—for only in this way can the skyscraper be of positive value in the city. It can be of positive value particularly in the decentralized city. Really, in the functional concentrations of the decentralized city, the skyscraper constitutes the climax of concentration.

D. CULTURAL CONCENTRATION

The bee, when flying from flower to flower gathering material for honey, forwards propagative processes in nature. Herd-instinct functions in a similar twofold manner, for while it offers physical protection by bringing people together, this action tends to encourage initiative and inspiration. And when initiative and inspiration are praised for fostering positive cultural values, herd-instinct must really have the credit.

This bringing of people together is important from the point of view of culture, inasmuch as cultures are not the achievement of isolated individuals, but the result of collective and concentrated endeavors of nations and eras. Surely, cultures could not be born without fertilizing concentration. Hence the urban community is a cultural necessity. It only remains to know how to organize this urban community so as to achieve the best cultural result, and for this reason we must ask: "Should the urban community be concentrated, or should it be decentralized?"

The basic reason for cultural concentration in the city is to offer everyone the opportunity to make contact with cultural achievements, strifes, and intellectual activities of one kind or another. Mere contact, however, does not raise the mental level of the individual: this takes place only when one's mind has had time to digest those sentiments, thoughts, and ideas which the said contact has stirred up. Two distinct steps are therefore necessary in cultural progress: first, to receive cultural impressions, and then, to digest these impressions.

To receive cultural impressions is a matter of short time, relatively speaking, and can be accomplished in concentrated circumstances. To digest these impressions, on the other hand, is a slow process requiring both time and solitude. When this latter becomes too intense so that it does not allow sufficient time and solitude for absorption, the result can easily be the opposite to that intended. Spiritual food affects the mind in much the same way as material food affects the body; that is, high-pressure learning, like excessive eating, dulls the mind and thwarts the taste. Instead of inner cultural growth, it produces shallow civilization, inducing the mind to seek easily digestible nourishment, commonplace and vulgar divertisement.

There is much of this kind of divertisement to be found in the concentrated city. It must be observed that cultural concentration in the city brings even anti-cultural concentration there: opposite poles strive to balance one another. To which side the balance will incline in this competition, depends on manifold reasons, but undoubtedly the extremely congested city is apt to occasion an unfortunate balance. It produces spiritual slums.

Returning now to our question, whether the urban community should be concentrated or decentralized in order to bring the best cultural result, the answer can be read from the above, and it reads as follows:

It makes little difference whether the opportunity of having cultural contacts takes place within the concentration of the extremely congested city or in the functional concentrations of the decentralized urban community. But to absorb constructive cultural thought and to have it live, necessitates a healthy and quiet atmosphere in which to contemplate. As the congested city, generally speaking, cannot offer this opportunity, and as organic decentralization at least **offers** possibilities of such an opportunity, there can be but the one answer to our question; namely, that the decentralized urban community is to be preferred to the concentrated one, insofar as culture is concerned.

In the above we have investigated the matter of concentration from various angles and in each case we have arrived at the conclusion that all future town-building must happen in the spirit of decentralization. Now our investigation of concentration from the point of view of culture, gives that same answer. **This is the final and decisive answer, inasmuch as man's cultural problems must be considered the paramount problems of all humanity.**

6. ORGANIC DECENTRALIZATION

NOTWITHSTANDING the fact that decentralization is an unmistakable trend of modern times, civic authorities have surprisingly often been cautiously conservative and scarcely aware of the utterly new problems they face. They may have partially comprehended current happenings and may have taken positive measures of improvement, but frequently they have failed to reason as to what the future consequences of these measures might be. When the road of progress has been built in this stey-by-step manner of not knowing where it was going to lead, it has been paved with blunders. It seems that man sees clearly only after he has tried a mistaken direction and found it to be wrong. For this reason it is not surprising that, even after conditions of life and technical progress had made decentralization possible, there was much confusion as to the right course. The movement was strange, and its consequences concealed.

In most cases there was little thought of comprehensive investigation before the city had already begun to spread itself into adjacent lands. Existing suburbs were enlarged, new suburbs were founded, and satellite towns sprang into being in haphazard manner. Regional land-owners sought to attract with their property advantages; real estate agencies founded their business on enticing promises; and suburban planners produced their spiritless lay-outs, scattering them at random with no control. For sure, decentralization was left freely to spread itself, creating difficult dilemmas for years to come.

In such manner did urban growth usually take place, especially when that growth was rapid and when phlegmatic officials left the city's fate in the hands of the incompetent, of the indifferent, or of those interested in speculation. In many communities however, to render justice, decentralization was satisfactorily managed, to the great advantage of subsequent growth. But even in these cases it was impossible to have a thorough understanding of all the chances and dangers of decentralization, and to escape all blunders of judgment and execution. With but slight risk of error, it can be stated that scarcely a single city of consequence was fully prepared to meet its problems. This lesson of past experience should constitute a healthy propaganda for the necessity of organic decentralization.

Decentralization of any city is a problem in itself. No generalized rules therefore can be applied, unless especially adapted to meet local requirements. Our investigation of the matter, consequently, is going to deal primarily with essentials.

The reasons for decentralization already have been investigated, and through this it was made evident that the movement is logical and sound. One point in particular stood out in this analysis as an imperative step to take; namely, the physical and spiritual rehabilitation of the urban areas at large. With regard to this, it was found that such aims can be obtained only by making the decentralization process "organic." Moreover, it was found that only through organic decentralization can lastingly healthy results be achieved.

In this spirit of "lastingly healthy results" will the arising and increasing problems of organic decentralization be investigated in the following.

An eminent example of
randomly "scattered" de-
centralization.

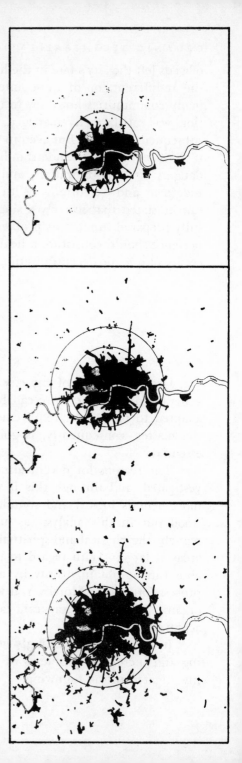

Fig. 31.
London: Area built over 1840.

Fig. 32.
London: Area built over 1860.

Fig. 33.
London: Area built over 1880.

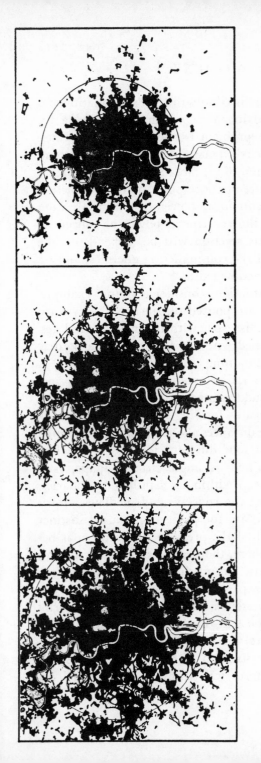

Fig. 34.
London: Area built over 1900.

Fig. 35.
London: Area built over 1914.

Fig. 36.
London: Area built over 1929.

A. THE PHYSICAL MOMENT

Organic decentralization distributes the city's population and land-use into those outlying areas which are available for growth. In a sense the problem is one of physics, because certain energies in the city's dynamic changes cause a trend toward expansion. In view of the fact that concentration and decentralization constitute opposite poles, a certain reaction must arise when the centrifugal power of decentralization becomes stronger than the centripetal power of concentration. How effective this reaction will be, depends on the difference of strength of the counteracting energies, and on how much freedom of action exists.

To illustrate the situation, consider a simple example. If a few drops of water are poured on the table, they form by cohesion into a roundish spot with distinct border lines. If the water spot is pressed with the finger tip, the borders tend outward, yet maintaining their original shape. A stronger pressure creates radial extensions of a star formation, more or less. A sudden pressure, however, causes the liquid to splash centrifugally, forming small groups of different sized spots at varying distances about the original globule.

The water assumed four different forms. In the first instance, the water retained its single circular shape, as if cautiously anxious to keep within its capillary boundaries. Its form was like that of the concentrated mediaeval town where the cohesive necessity for protection caused distinct fortification lines. With slight pressure the water spot became denser at its periphery, though not sufficiently so as to break its cohesive borders. In much the same way, the congested town tended to expand when the necessity for concentrated defense was lessened, but was still compulsorily centralized because of the lack of means of communication. With yet greater pressure, the boundaries of the water spot were broken due to the strength of the outwardly pushing force, and, where that force was strongest, there radial extensions were formed. In urban terms, this is comparable to a city where railroads and street car lines had partially freed the internal congestion along these lines. In the last instance, however, where a sudden and strong pressure was applied, the centrifugal force was sufficiently strong to occasion an entirely new configuration, and the water was scattered about the table surface; forming itself, because of cohesion, into individual units of various sizes at varying distances from the center of the applied pressure. This action symbolizes the decentralized city of the future.

This last instance, in which the water was distributed into individual spots, is of particular importance in our case of organic decentralization. First of all, it is a good illustration of those physical forces that are behind the decentralization trend. And although this distribution of water into individual spots happened in a random manner, we might as well assume that this "random manner" was only seemingly so. For, if all the innumerable and diminutive forces that were produced in the short second of the finger pressure could have been exactly measured and organized, the seemingly accidental configuration of water would have resolved itself into an intentionally organized process of energy reactions. Looking at the water distribution from this angle, the process, metaphorically speaking, was a miniature picture of organic decentralization.

The process of the city's decentralization is much larger in scale. It is more comprehensive in its causes. And, fortunately, the time of action is long enough to allow an all-sided study of the situation.

B. THE CHEMICAL MOMENT

The preliminary conception of organic decentralization— comparable to our experiment with the water spot—means the dispersion of the city into surrounding lands. So far,

however, this is only a general idea concerning those areas
available for growth, and not an investigation of the adaptability of these areas for the various functional purposes of
the city. Real organic decentralization begins with the distribution and interrelation of the city's manifold activities.
In a sense, this is comparable to chemical processes, for the
progress of organic decentralization acts and reacts like a
slowly and constantly working chemical process where a
gradual change from disorder into a workable order is manifest. So to speak, chemical laws direct the conversion during
which the various urban functions, formerly haphazardly
distributed in the city's confusion, become now adequately
interrelated so as to assume functional groupings. These
groupings, as the conversion proceeds, begin to form themselves in certain suitable locations on the broadened urban
area, and with workable interrelations with other groupings.

It is important to understand organic decentralization
in the light of a logical sequence of "chemical" processes—
figuratively speaking. It shows that the movement springs
from the city's inner potentialities in an indigenous and rule-
bound manner.

Continuing now our discussion in "chemical" terms,
the functions of the individual member of the community
may be regarded as the molecule of the functional substance
of the city. This means that the various activities of the
individual inhabitant constitute that unit which, when re-
peated and combined into innumerable groupings, forms the
totality of the city's activities.

These individual activities can be divided into two main
groups: "everyday activities," and "casual contacts." Those
activities of the first group, to be satisfactorily arranged, must
be concentrated; whereas those of the second group, taking
place less frequently, are more independent of location and
could therefore be decentralized.

Also, already in the "molecular" functioning of the city,

we are faced with the two basic tendencies of organic decentralization—concentration of the individual's living and working conditions, and decentralization of the city's various activity groups.

The individual's everyday life includes such activities as home life, work inside or outside of the home, procurement of necessary supplies, child and adult education, and physical and mental development. In the case of such indispensable everyday activities of one's existence and livelihood, it is a sensible thing that they be concentrated as much as possible within a certain area so as to eliminate the compulsory use of mechanical means of communication. Such an arrangement is logical; it is practical; it is time saving; and, above all, it is human.

Such an arrangement, though, is nothing new.

The farmer, in his daily life, spends the day about his farm buildings, plough-lands, and meadows. He does not rush from place to place to get his work done, but quietly organizes his usual day within the comparatively limited area of his farm. Consider also the natural relationship between living and working in the hamlet, village, and small town. In this quiet and livable atmosphere, much can be found which the large cities would do well to emulate. **Because this relationship between living and working is based on natural selection, and because it contributes so greatly to fuller and happier living, it must be accepted as the primary premise in the creating of functional order in urban life, no matter whether the community be small or large.**

As long as a community is small and has grown naturally with a purpose of its own, its problem of functional concentration is automatically solved. This is usually the case with an integrated and independent town. Because such a town is more or less static in both size and population, it is to a considerable degree independent of that nervous life in large centers. And as long as conditions remain at this "primeval" state, the town can get along without the planner's immediate concern—although even here proper planning is essential.

The planner's immediate concern must be rather with those complex community units that are not independent. Here conditions are different, for as soon as such community units are parts of large cities, exterior influences come into play. Preventive measures then are urgent, and can be achieved only by restricting these units to a maximum size so as to leave protective free land between them, respectively. In this manner, harmful interaction is eliminated.

A direct derivative of adequate interrelation between living and working is the functional community. This functional community is that earlier mentioned manifestation of "functional concentration of related activities"; that is, a community unit where the bulk of the population can exist without being compelled every day to rush back and forth into the congested heart of the city or elsewhere in order to make a living.

In the functional community, walking must be considered the basic system of individual transportation. It is that means which was almost entirely employed in olden times; therefore, many might be prone to regard it as primitive and antiquated. Particularly those enchanted by present-day excellent mechanized means of transportation might consider such traffic ideas—that is, the elimination of modern facilities—rather futile in solving contemporary problems.

We are not suggesting the elimination of modern traffic facilities. Modern traffic facilities must be utilized to their fullest when this utilization is practical and appropriate, but no planning must have as one of its aims **the compulsory use** of these facilities **for everyone in everyday work.** It is not those modern traffic facilities which cause the urban paralysis of today. It is the poor organization within the city which makes the use of these facilities compulsory and, consequently, makes conditions restless and unhuman.

In days gone by, living and working were for the most part closely interrelated. This was not because our forebears reasoned more clearly than we do today, but because there were not adequate means of communication to establish matters otherwise. But when easy and rapid communication was made possible, towns were free to expand, and living and working were separated. Such a separation is generally believed to have been a necessary consequence of urban growth. This belief, however, is not exact. The separation of living and working did not take place merely because there was expansion, but rather because the cities were not prepared to meet the new situation intelligently and because the planners did not realize the far-reaching consequences of such a separation. Therefore, as the urban growth continued, this separation was accepted as a necessity, and was even regarded in some circles as a symbol of an advanced mode of planning. Today, daily travel to and from work has become a habit, streets are crowded, and traffic has become a nuisance, in spite of the excellent modern mechanical means of transportation.

But little calculation is necessary to discover how impractical this system really is. It is not unusual for a person to spend some two hours of every day merely traveling to and from work. This means that **two months of the year's twelve months of daytime** are spent in crowded and restless traveling. To make matters still worse, this journey happens day in and day out over exactly the same route: dulling process indeed! In actual distance this commuting frequently amounts to from ten to fifteen thousands of miles per year. Just think how much of the wide world one could see to the everlasting benefit of mind and soul, if the same time and mileage were used for a real tour! It is true that many enjoy the daily traveling to and fro, believing that it is part of their daily work, or feeling it an exciting and integral part of their business. Others again prefer to dwell as far away as possible from their place of work, regarding living and working as two different phases of their daily activity. Those who pre-

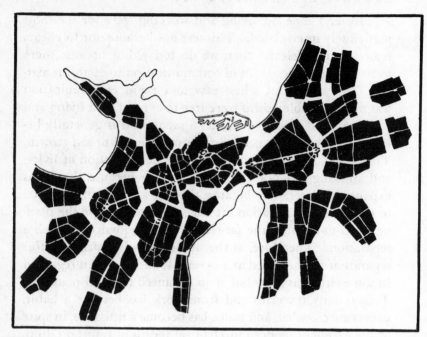

Fig. 37.
Decentralization pattern of
Greater Tallin (Reval), Estonia.
Eliel Saarinen, 1913

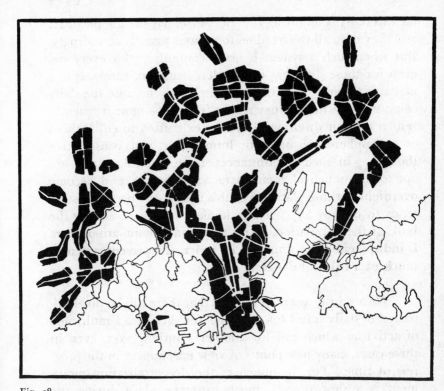

Fig. 38.

Decentralization pattern of
Greater Helsinki, Finland.
Eliel Saarinen, 1918.

fer this daily commuting can, of course, pay for the pleasure, and they have all the freedom to arrange matters accordingly. But when such a system is made compulsory for everyone, even for those disliking this restless situation, surely, it is a negative system. It is negative, especially because the daily commuters—whether they realize it or not—most frequently return to their dwelling places too exhausted to enjoy them as atmospheres of intimate human life and constructive thought. In such circumstances, these dwelling places are apt to lose much of their character of homes, and become overnight parking places. For this reason, the present system tends to destroy any friendly home atmosphere among the bulk of the population. **And as friendly home atmosphere is indispensable for sound social order, the present system is much of a cultural danger.**

We are fully aware of the fact that there can be no elimination of daily travel for everyone, for there are a multitude of activities which call for another solution. Yet, even in these cases, many new points of view may appear in the progress of time. For, inasmuch as the decentralization movement is a slow process, much can take place during the change of conditions of which the urban dweller of today has no conception, as yet.

Much can take place already now, for in many respects we have a clear conception of how to arrange matters. It has been said that there is little reason why heavy industry, for example, should be located in the heart of the city. The logical step then must be to correct past mistakes of this nature. When this heavy industry will gradually be moved to new manufacturing suburbs, it will relocate other functions such as housing of workmen, and technical and administrative staffs. Light industry will decentralize in much the same manner, for it will spread itself into the various units of the decentralization areas where better living and working conditions can be had. Considerable amounts of business, particularly such as is concerned with the supplying of daily needs, will automatically follow the centrifugal trend. Many other members of the multifarious urban household will find suitable and improved conditions in the new communities which, step by step, will be built in accordance with modern needs and methods. All these already constitute a considerable part of civic functions, and their removal will lessen the present density.

It is generally conceded important that the various branches of business and the civic administration as well, must be located in the heart of the city. In these cases it would seem difficult to arrange the cities' centers so as to bring them into accord with the idea of proper interrelation between living and working. On the other hand, when large areas of the present centers have become vacated, these might prove to be suitable residential districts for those having their work in the cities' hearts. In this manner almost everyone might ultimately have the opportunity to enjoy adequate home conditions near his daily occupation. Were this so, indeed, the cities would be far more pleasant places in which to live and work.

When discussing the chemical moment of decentralization, it was said that, as the conversion proceeds, the functional communities begin to form themselves in certain suitable locations within the broadened urban area and to assume workable relations one to another. This action takes place because discriminative selection brings functional order to the city by dividing its activities into those mentioned two basic groupings—"everyday activities," and "casual contacts."

Inasmuch as the casual contacts of a decentralized city necessitate intercommunication between the various activity centers, this naturally presupposes much longer routes of travel than is the case with concentrated everyday activities. On the other hand, by locating everyday activities within the individual community borders, the need of mechanical means

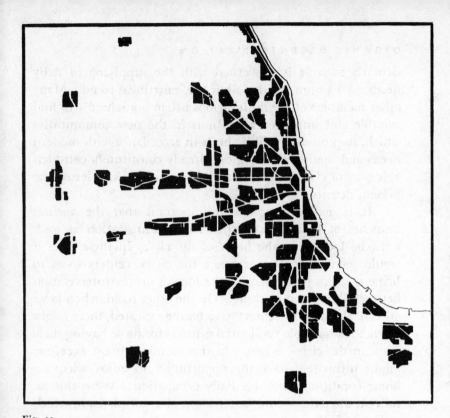

Fig. 39.

Decentralization pattern of Greater Chicago.
Cranbrook Academy of Art, 1935-1936.
Student: George A. Hutchinson, Jr.
Instructor: Eliel Saarinen.

Fig. 40.

Decentralization pattern of Greater Detroit. Cranbrook Academy of Art, 1933-1934. Student: Walter P. Hickey. Instructor: Eliel Saarinen.

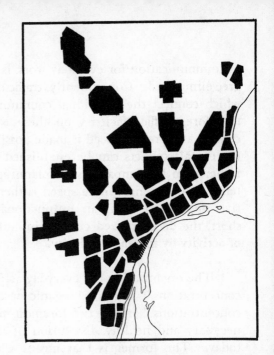

Fig. 41.

Decentralization pattern of Greater Hartford, Conn. Cranbrook Academy of Art, 1933. Student: Bradford Tilney. Instructor: Eliel Saarinen.

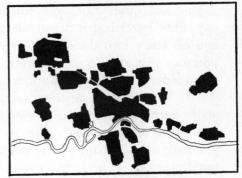

Fig. 42.

Decentralization pattern of Athens and Piraeus, Greece. Cranbrook Academy of Art, 1940. Student: Christopher Chemales. Instructor: Eliel Saarinen.

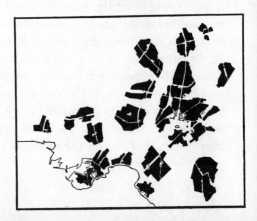

215

of communication for everyday work is to a considerable degree eliminated. Consequently, traffic on those main arteries which connect the individual communities is lessened and, therefore, traffic efficiency on these is correspondingly increased and greater speed is made possible. In this manner, the casual contacts can be established by velocity of travel rather than by compactness of planning. A good traffic system permitting maximum speed is therefore of greater relative importance than an unfunctional concentration. In short, **the decentralized city retains sufficient concentration of activity by increased velocity.**

The organization of "everyday activities into functional concentrations," and the "organic decentralization of these concentrations," are the two foremost means of achieving the necessary and healthy dissolution of the compact cities of today. The former is that means which brings humanly livable and quiet conditions into the various units of the city. The latter is that means which brings functional order and efficiency into the city at large. It is therefore of importance that any decentralization movement be conducted in accordance with these two means.

In this manner, as decentralization proceeds along the above outlined dual thought—and in accordance with a pre-established master scheme—the city's transformation assumes gradually such a shape as was described in connection with our "physical" experiment with water; where "the liquid splashes centrifugally, forming small groups of different sized spots at varying distances about the original globule. Moreover, this transformation moves simultaneously toward such an organization as was described in connection with our "chemical" experiment, where "chemical laws direct the conversion, during which the various urban functions, formerly haphazardly distributed in the city's confusion, become now adequately interrelated so as to assume functional groupings." In other words, **the ultimate result of this transforma-**

tion is that there has been gradually formed, around the nucleus of the original compactness, an organic grouping of new or reformed communities of adequate functional order according to the best principles of forward town-building.

The ultimate result is: ORGANIC DECENTRALIZATION.

C. ILLUMINATING EXAMPLE: NEW YORK

Organic decentralization is a logical process, based on practically sound and humanly positive considerations, and allowing a slow and gradual solution. It is not a working program of immediate execution. With regard to this, it must be borne in mind that precisely in the large overgrown cities the greatest need of organic decentralization exists; and yet, within these cities, the compact conditions have become so thoroughly ingrained that any rational reorganization along a decentralization scheme seems scarcely possible. During a continuous process of concentration, the overgrown cities have become petrified into stony deserts of tightly packed structural masses. Simultaneously, they have developed into an elaborate accumulation of land and building values, and of assets and liabilities. Civic legislation, having emerged from and in the spirit of concentration, has become the paramount instrument in maintaining these values, assets and liabilities. Obviously then, concentration has a strong foothold in the overgrown cities, whereas decentralization seems to have but a slight chance to bring relief to the situation.

"Existing values" and "existing legislation," as we see, are the two main difficulties to be surmounted in order to make decentralization work. But inasmuch as they will later on be scrutinized separately and thoroughly, let's disregard them for the moment—or mention them only in passing as our scrutiny proceeds—and outline a theoretical procedure, indicating how decentralization in other respects is possible

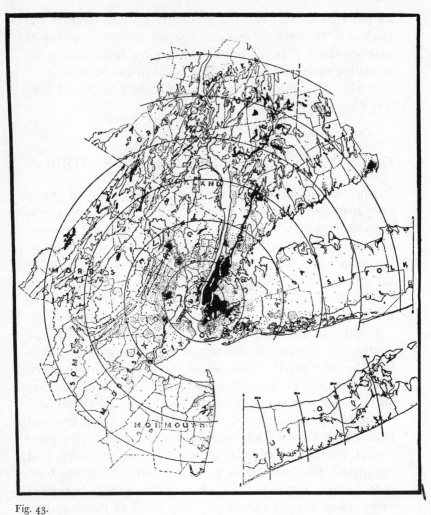

Fig. 43.

New York and Environs showing estimated distribution of population according to
U. S. census of 1920.

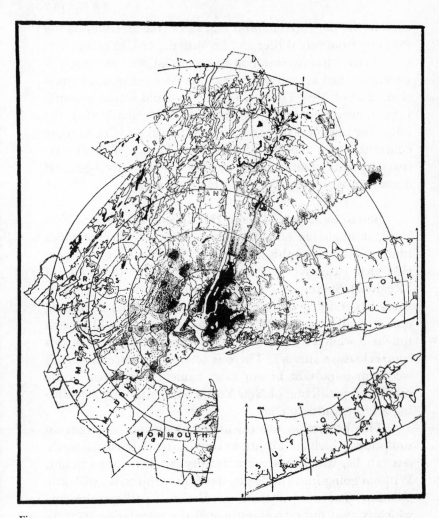

Fig. 44.
New York and Environs showing estimated distribution of population for a total of
21,000,000, estimated for 1965.

even in the largest communities. Let's take an illuminating example from actual life; and because the task in every overgrown circumstance is not an easy one—at least seemingly—we might then as well select perhaps the most difficult situation: that of New York. In order to avoid misunderstandings, however, we will begin with the remark that the following outline will not constitute positive advice to those concerned with the planning of New York. **With due respect for this planning, our outline will be only a general discussion with New York as a mere example.**

Before we set out to tackle this difficult situation of New York, it might be enlightening to mention some previous undertakings along this same line. First of all, we will mention that extensive study which goes under the name of "Regional Survey of New York and its Environs." This study has resulted in a great number of volumes of printed matter, maps, charts, and illustrations; and it would take us too far if we were to try even a superficial description of this comprehensive survey. There is one point, however, which we deem important in our case; namely, that scientifically calculated prediction of New York's population increase during a few decades to come.

This prediction was calculated along four different assumptions which are all just as convincing as scientific methods can be, when future uncertainty is taken into account. Without going into all the details of this subject, we will only mention that one of these predictions—perhaps the one which is most indicative—estimated the population increase of Greater New York to twenty-one millions in the year 1965. How exact this estimate will prove to be, cannot be said and does not matter, for what difference does it make whether the population has increased to that enormous number within the said time period or within so or so many decades more? The general trend in this increase is the significant point.

But the thing that interests us in particular about this

predicted population increase, is the illuminating map that shows the approximate distribution of these twenty-one millions of people on the land areas of Greater New York. And the most surprising point in this respect is that the increased population is distributed almost exactly along the same land areas and in the same ratio as is the case in the Greater New York of today. This means that the density of New York population after a few decades will be more than doubled; that the intensity of activities will be more than tripled; and that the load to be carried on the traffic arteries of those days to come, will have proportionately a still higher increase—if nothing is done about it. It is true that this same Regional Survey states that "a proper distribution of industrial, business, and residential areas is necessary," but, on the other hand, no positive suggestions have been made as to how to direct this said decentralization along organic channels. On the contrary, the published map of circumferential highway routes indicates that the core of the present compactness— Manhattan Island—will for years to come remain the sole, supreme, and constantly growing concentration of the whole metropolitan development. Moreover, the published map of radial routes does not show the sort of planning which could inspire the founding of new centers elsewhere. And finally, the new Riverside Drives—both the Eastern and the Western—are most apt to facilitate still more concentrated activities on Manhattan proper.

Considering the already crowded situation along all the traffic channels, particularly along those leading to and from Manhattan, one can easily imagine what this situation is doomed to be when the population increase has reached that predicted number of twenty-one millions—and what it is doomed to be still more, when the increase passes the fantastic thirty million mark a few decades later, as the same calculation continues to predict. Already now there are all kinds of underground traffic channels, such as tunnels for trains and individual vehicles, subways, sub-subways and

Fig. 45. New York and Environs. Progress
on Circumferential Routes, 1928-1932.

Fig. 46. New York and Environs. Progress
on Radial Routes, 1928-1932.

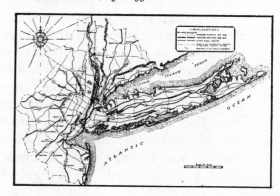

sub-sub-subways. Already now there are all kinds of elevated, super-elevated and super-super-elevated roads and railroads which all must carry their respective loads to full capacity. Surely, in the future days there must be many times more of these traffic channels, both underground and overground. The ground must be perforated by an ever increasing number of tunnels and tubes to make it look like a worm-eaten trunk. The octopus of overground lines will stretch its arms over town and water, hither and thither, so that ever more land areas must be yielded for that ceaseless moving around—and one wonders whether that old man and master-schemer, King Solomon, had a hint of this situation when he issued his remarkable proverb, "Where there is no vision, the people perish."

It is not our intention by the foregoing to stress the desirability of decentralization in the case of Greater New York. Those many volumes of the Regional Survey breathe this desirability themselves, at least to a certain degree. So, for example, we read there as follows: "considering all the trends that are occurring in the population distribution, it seems apparent that the policy of the city should be directed toward encouraging more open development." In other words, this unofficial survey of New York and its Environs recommends, to the official authorities of New York and its Environs, that decentralization should be applied to the case of Greater New York. In which manner and to what an extent this decentralization should be carried out, has evidently been left to the authorities themselves to determine. But undoubtedly, those behind the Regional Survey have anticipated, in the inner chambers of their respective egos, that someday something drastic must be undertaken to protect the city from that disastrous fate it is heading toward because of its continuous growth. On the other hand, one must not overlook the fact that this survey has been worked out in that electric atmosphere of present day New York with its overwhelmingly great economic values at stake, and that this fact has perhaps made the surveying minds conscious of the realities of today rather than of the possibilities of tomorrow. Hence, we suspect, the cautious mode of presentation. So much for the Regional Survey of Greater New York.

Turning our attention now to another phase of this New York situation, there exists published material—of rather recent date *—about a proposed Master Plan of the City of New York, prepared by the duly authorized City Planning Commission of that city. It might be enlightening to examine this proposed plan by comparing it with the above discussed Regional Survey. It is true that a clear comparison cannot be had, for whereas the Regional Survey takes into consideration all the broad areas within a radius of about fifty miles, with Lower Manhattan as the focal point, this new proposed Master Plan deals only with those areas which are under the jurisdiction of the City of New York itself; namely, the areas of Manhattan, Brooklyn, Queens, Bronx, and Richmond. Because of this difference in scope, the respective conceptions of population-increase go widely apart— at least seemingly. For, while the Regional Survey is sanguine about its tens of millions of population-increase, the proposed Master Plan has the following temperate prediction to make: "It is recognized that New York's population, like that of other large cities, is approaching stability. The 1940 census has done much to confirm this conclusion, indicating an increase of but 6½% during the past decade, compared to the 23% growth in the decade 1920-1930."

This surely sounds differently than what we were told a moment ago. In actual fact, however, the difference is not as essential as it might seem at first. For, besides that mentioned difference in scope insofar as land areas are concerned, it must be borne in mind that in the growing cities there takes place an accelerating centrifugal movement of popula-

---

* November 20, 1940. City Planning Commission of the City of New York: Proposed First and Second Stages of the Master Plan of Land Use.

tion from the central parts of the urban complex toward the encircling regional areas. This movement, naturally, causes a considerable decrease in the growth of the residential population in the central parts of the city—as the above quoted statement of the proposed Master Plan indicates. As for the whole metropolitan area, on the other hand, this centrifugal movement from the center, plus that constant centripetal movement from the country at large, bring an ever-increasing number of people to the whole urban complex—as the calculations of the Regional Survey predict. The consequence of this is that there is on one side a logical decrease, and on the other side a dynamic increase. Also, on the whole there are no essential contradictions between the sanguine predictions of the Regional Survey and the temperate statements of the Master Plan, as far as concerns population increase.

However, the temperate statements of the Master Plan are misleading even in another point, unless one particular fact is borne in mind. It must namely be remembered that migration from the center to the outskirts does not mean that the traffic load on the streets and arteries to and from the center is correspondingly lessened. Indeed, it is far from so. **Because of the fact that the bulk of those having migrated to the outskirts still retain their business activities in the center, the augmented daily commuting causes just that kind of traffic disturbance which is so detrimental in the growing cities of today. To disregard this hard fact is to disregard one of the most essential causes of the serious traffic problems of our time.** For, after all, it is not the number of people and their living places which cause the difficulties; it is the amount of traffic on streets and arteries.

There is still one more point to be made clear.

When the statement of the Master Plan indicates "an increase of but 6½% during the past decade, compared to the 23% growth in the decade 1920-1930," it confronts the "boom decade" of 1920-1930 with the "depression decade" of 1930-1940, and it almost seems as if the conclusion had been drawn with the assumption that all future urban growth is going to happen in terms of depression. To champion such an idea, we are sure, was not the intention of the Planning Commission. But as, in spite of this, there seems to linger a widespread opinion to a similar effect, we must mention something about it in passing.

It may be true that during times of depression there is less inclination for people to move into town communities—for even in urban matters, as in other phases of life, there are downward periods just as there are upward ones—but, indeed, those reasons which have caused and still cause urban growth remain active and evidently will continue to be so in future. It is therefore dangerous to believe that a temporary stagnation in the growth of the urban population were a sign of a gradual complete stagnation. Such a belief is only apt to foster unpreparedness and inaction in civic matters.

However, all these calculations of population increase—whether those of the Regional Survey or of the proposed Master Plan—are not of deciding consequence insofar as organic decentralization is concerned. In fact, the population of the New York areas is already now too large and too compactly accommodated to make decentralization an easy matter. The chief problem, therefore, is not to count the number of individuals, present or future, but to arrange livable conditions for these individuals, no matter how large the number. In order to be able to accomplish this, the population increase must be so disposed that over-saturated circumstances in all parts of the urban territory can be prevented. So must be the endeavor, and the goal. And if we after all have discussed the matter of population increase, it has been done in order to get a clear picture of the situation, before we set out to tackle the difficult problems of New York ourselves. Besides this consideration for our own purpose, we have discussed the matter of population increase in order to animate caution. For, **on our part we still harbor the cautious opinion that the population of Greater New**

York will continuously grow and bring new and augmented difficulties—if nothing is done about it.

Returning once more to this proposed Master Plan of the City of New York, we are familiar with the fact that it has been met in many circles with much opposition. This opposition—we trust—is based on sincere intentions. Nevertheless, we dare to maintain—equally sincerely—that this same Master Plan is a document of great significance. True enough, it does not consider organic decentralization in a broader sense: of course, it could not have done so because of its limitations of jurisdiction, but its originators—we believe—have been imbued with the spirit and understanding of the right decentralization principles. At least so is our impression, and to explain the reasons for this impression, we might do it best by citing a few extracts from the published report of this proposed Master Plan.

First, there is expressed the necessity of far-sighted planning, thus: "New York of today would have been a more convenient, a more efficient and a better and happier place, if its amazing growth could have proceeded in accordance with some form of far-sighted direction, but it is never too late to plan."

Second, there is expressed the necessity of flexible planning toward the future, thus: "The plan itself has purposely been kept general instead of precise and detailed. It can readily be amended if judgment changes as to conditions and objectives. It is a plan of the future, not a map of the present."

Third, there is expressed the necessity of protection by means of green-belt developments, thus: "In order to secure the amenities and advantages of more open space, and at the same time separate these large communities one from another, the Commission suggests the principle of gradually developing park-belts and reservations of open space, public and private, to serve these communities and neighborhoods."

Fourth, there is expressed the necessity of developing functional concentrations of related activities, thus: "In order to reduce the amount of time that the average New Yorker must spend to and fro, the Commission anticipates that both business and industry will be further decentralized within the limits of the greater city. This involves increasing the space for existing principal business centers outside of Manhattan, and providing for the growth of new secondary business and industrial districts."

Here we have four statements, each one of **basic consequence.** The first statement stresses the importance of far-sighted civic organization so as to achieve more convenient, efficient, and livable conditions. In other words, the statement means that all planning, to be successful, must be based on "organic order." The second and the third statements recommend, respectively, the principles of "flexibility" and "protection" in all planning work. The fourth statement suggests the organization of functional concentrations on the urban territory. As we see, these four points are familiar from our previous discussions of organic decentralization.

Besides these four points, there are furthermore two points in this published report which we deem important to mention in this connection. These consider respectively the "scope" and "character" of the gradual rebuilding of the disorderly city into an orderly one. So we continue to cite.

First, pertaining to the "scope" of the rebuilding program, we read as follows:

"It seems reasonable to expect that most of the existing substandard areas, with their old law tenements, will be eliminated within not much more than one generation." *
And furthermore we read:

"At some time in the future, nearly all the buildings that stand today will have been replaced. Monumental structures such as great museums, libraries, churches, and important public edifices, may last for centuries. Most of the other

---

* "One generation," naturally, must not be too literally understood.

structures—apartment houses, tenements, dwellings, offices, factories, and lofts—will earlier have passed their day of usefulness. It will not be a question of forcing their replacement. They will no longer be suitable for their purposes, and will have been voluntarily demolished to make way for buildings which will better serve new needs. Many structures will be replaced within the brief span of one generation; more will assuredly yield in the next succeeding generation. It is the inevitable process, not the time element, that is important. For this reason the Commission has not attempted to set up a time schedule for realization of the suggested Master Plan of Land Use."

Second, pertaining to the "character" of the rebuilding program, we read as follows:

"Recent trends in building-design and site-planning indicate that obsolescence of existing structures may proceed faster than has been the case to date, as people are rapidly becoming accustomed to thinking in terms of good large-scale developments. The process of rebuilding is therefore expected to take place not lot by lot as in the past, but whole blocks and groups of blocks at a time. A better opportunity will thus be given to achieve well-knit residential communities complete with the small parks and playgrounds, public and semi-public buildings, and local shopping centers requisite to a satisfactory neighborhood environment. As all this can happen in areas that are already close to places of employment, it may be termed a 'recentralization' of the residential pattern which in recent years has shown a tendency toward excessive dispersion."

Surely, this rebuilding program is clearly conceived and entirely in harmony with the present trend in town-building where that maxim of valiant progressiveness must be accepted, that **"yesterday is sheer history, and that the spirit of tomorrow is in the making already today."**

We house only one hesitation. This hesitation, however, is not caused by lack of confidence in the Planning Commission, but originates from the fact that the Commission has not had the authority to study the problems of New York as a comprehensive and unified organism of the whole metropolitan area. If the commission had been duly authorized in this respect—well, in such a case our problem now would be only to applaud the Commission's Master Plan of Greater New York, and accept it—at least in its main points —as a good example of how decentralization problems must be carried out. But as the Commission has **not** been duly authorized in the above respect, we then—as faithful champions of comprehensive organic decentralization—must from now on go our own way in order to find out what the said Commission would undoubtedly have done, provided it had been sufficiently authorized.

Now that we are going to tackle the problems of New York, we must first of all repeat an earlier remark; namely, that the following outline will not constitute positive advice to those concerned with the planning of New York. **It will be only a general discussion with New York as a mere example.** May we add to this remark still another; namely, that the following outline is not going to penetrate deep into the matter. It is going to skim, so to speak, a few of the many essentials only.

Furthermore:

By no means do we intend with the following to convince the genuine New York dweller that his home city must be altered in order to make life more livable there. He probably would not get our point, for we and he speak two different languages in town-building: we are concerned with town-building from an organic point of view in general, whereas he is concerned with his home city from the New Yorker's point of view in particular. He has grown up with New York, and New York has grown up with him. It is therefore a likely thought that a mutual agreement exists between the genuine New Yorker and his home city.

Speaking about the problems of New York, the first thought, naturally, must concern that over-crowded Manhattan. Already, when studying the proposed Master Plan, we observed—quietly—that Manhattan Island is rigidly and compactly planned. And when the protective green-belts were mentioned in the Commission's report, it was stated rather definitely that "the opportunities in Brooklyn and Manhattan are not so good." From all this we gathered that matters on Manhattan are pretty tightly settled, and that there is nothing to do about it.

Perhaps this is true?

We doubt, however, the validity of such an opinion, for, incidentally, we have a printed report about "Slums and Housing"—of the year 1936 *—where we find it clearly shown that about forty percent of the occupied area of Manhattan calls for rehabilitation "as bearing strong slum characteristics." Moreover, according to this same report it is amazing to observe that these decayed areas are just so distributed as to form the non-decayed areas into three distinct town communities, provided the rehabilitation of the decayed areas would take place outside of the land areas of Manhattan—as it should, to a large degree at least. Following through this fortunate disposition in the formation of the said three communities, there could be developed a "Downtown concentration," a "Middletown concentration," and an "Uptown concentration." It seems almost paradoxical that the process of disintegration, despite its downward course, has reached a point where the disposition of the blighted conditions is conducive to an organic rebuilding. It seems as if nature, during the period of man's urban folly, had utilized her wise sense of selection to help man in the necessary rebuilding. Now is the time for man to take advantage of the fortunate disposition of these disintegrated areas.

Following, furthermore, the information supplied by the above mentioned slum clearance study, one can find almost

* James Ford: "Slums and Housing," Vol. 1, Fig. 83.

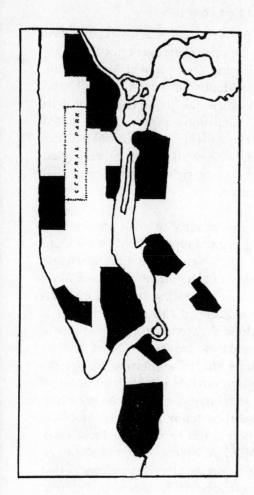

Fig. 47.

Slum study areas on Manhattan.

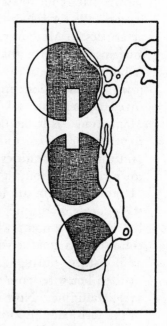

Fig. 48.

Three logical concentrations on Manhattan.

the same situation even on the areas of Brooklyn. Most likely the same is true even on other territories. The whole sphere of New York's influence, therefore, should become subject to a comprehensive blight-investigation, so as to open people's eyes to see the decayed situation in an "organic sense"—if we may say so. By "organic sense" we mean disposition of decay in a manner from which an organic rehabilitation could be directly derived; that is, in such a manner as on Manhattan, where decay has so spread itself as to make possible the formation of three town concentrations as logical derivatives of logical rehabilitation.

Now, supposing such a comprehensive blight-investigation really had been accomplished, we then would find ourselves at the cross-road of two possible directions along which further to proceed—one leading toward increased compactness, the other toward decentralization. Which one of these two directions should be selected is by no means an arbitrary matter. On the contrary, it is important indeed to select the right direction, for **in this very selection there lie hidden momentous consequences for all future development of the city of New York.**

To select the first-mentioned direction, toward increased compactness, means that the rehabilitation of the decayed areas is going to happen on these very areas themselves, with the obvious result that the present compact status will be pinned down for generations and, furthermore, with the ultimate result of an inescapable disintegration of the rehabilitated areas into new slums to come—which is nothing surprisingly new, for we have learned how compactness evolves. And these new slums to come will cover much broader areas than do those of the present time. This is perfectly plain, for one must bear in mind that the mentioned prediction of New York's population increase—calculated by the "Regional Survey of New York and its Environs"—even if partly true, is enough of testimony of what the future is bound to experience in terms of compactness, if nothing is done about it in time. And "in time" in the case at hand must mean "today." It must mean so, **for the slum situation, "just of today," offers the most opportune moment to direct New York's development toward far-sighted openness.** On the other hand, if this most opportune moment in New York's development is slighted in an Old School routine manner, the future millions and still more millions of New York's population, then, will be doomed to suffer from the consequences of the present Old School routine manner.

Considering such a serious prospect, it is of utmost urgency that a keen sense of responsibility must guide present actions; and this means that even the other mentioned direction—that toward decentralization—must be examined. For, **how could responsible leadership in planning matters abandon such a logical course of development as the present decentralization trend really is, before the potentialities of this trend are examined first?**

Well, to examine the decentralization potentialities of New York, naturally, means an examination of that oft-mentioned blight situation so as to enable one to map out the coming rehabilitation—in "organic sense." This must be the first step in the pioneering toward a far-reaching planning pattern for the future Greater New York. An essential point in this respect is that there must be achieved a mutual agreement of co-operation—at least in principle—between those many authorities having to deal with the vast and various land-areas now in question. This is essential from the point of view of a unified system of action. Moreover, it is essential that the planning work must proceed in a spirit of research, where an unbiased open-mindedness prevails and where "impossibilities" and "shrugs of shoulders" have no place. This must be particularly true insofar as economic and legislative hesitations are concerned.

As for these economic and legislative hesitations, we started our New York investigations with the remark, that "inasmuch as they"—namely, the economic and legislative problems—"will be later on scrutinized separately and thoroughly, let's disregard them for the moment, or mention them only in passing as our analysis proceeds." Accordingly, we will mention now—"in passing"—that insofar as particularly economic hesitations are concerned, we will in due time arrive at the conclusion that there can be found a logical solution of those economic problems caused by decentralization, provided these problems are met boldly.

For example, there is the problem of "land-value."

Yet, what does "land-value" mean? Surely, land in itself constitutes no particular value, it is the **use** into which land has been put and **the location of that land** in the plan pattern which constitutes land-value. Therefore, when this "use" of land is transferred to another site, equally advantageously located in the new decentralized plan pattern, even its economic quality—"value"—is automatically transferred to that new site. By transferring property rights in this manner from one site to another, the problem of land-use shiftings, consequently, is a simple matter of trading and bookkeeping.

In concentrated circumstances there was but little reason for land-use shiftings. Hence the value of land, generally speaking, was permanently tied to its site; and accordingly the psychological tradition was constituted that site and value are inseparably one and the same thing. In decentralized circumstances, however, this tradition becomes a harmfully restricting thought which must be readjusted to fit these new circumstances. And as decentralization is not merely the trend of the time, but even the **only** means in the fight against decay in the overgrown and overgrowing cities of today, it is vital that one's mind be receptive in this readjustment.

Please, bear in mind that we are not advocating the abolition of existing values. Rather, we are advocating the security of these values by their logical relocation—of course, on condition that these values are normal and not speculative. For, as long as there is "use" of land, there is a corresponding "value" of land, and this holds true no matter where the land is used or where its use may be transferred, provided the new location is appropriate for its use in the general configuration of the community.

Applying now—with good will and sincere desire—the above prospects of economic decentralization to the present blight conditions in New York, one will find that it is worth one's while to undertake, **at least a survey** of the situation, in order to learn whether or not the decentralization opportunities in this particular case are insurmountable. **And through this survey one soon will discover that they are not.**

Of course, cautious conservatism—and lack of good will, perhaps—may still breed insurmountabilities. There are such things as assessed values, for example. In this respect the value estimates are almost always too high to represent actual values less their yearly depreciation—and these assessed values, therefore, must be readjusted. This must hold true in any circumstance, regardless of whether the property values are retained on the old locations, or transferred somewhere else. As for a transference of these assessed values—and of property values in general for that matter—it must be understood that even the taxation of these values is subject to a corresponding transference: for the unification of a taxation system, embracing the whole enlarged metropolitan area, is a logical consequence of organic decentralization. Also, even in this respect, good will can find an acceptable solution on the basis of sound economy. As we see, then, even the assessed values and their taxation do not raise insurmountabilities—no matter how eagerly a lack of good will desires to see it happen.

Besides these assessed values and their taxation, there might be found even other economic hesitations, if the aim is necessarily to make organic decentralization seem economically insurmountable. We, too, could find many stumbling blocks in this respect—and very easily—were we not so keenly sure of the importance of organic decentralization.

So much about the economic point of view.

Again, as for the legislative point of view, we will even in this respect mention—"in passing"—that in due time, when the legal issues are going to be scrutinized in this analysis, we will arrive at the conclusion that, in order to make organic decentralization possible, the existing civic legislation needs to be changed in six major points only; and that each one of these changes is in perfect accord with the generally accepted conception of ethics, rights, sanctity of ownership, and with all the other phases that constitute the foundation of our social and spiritual understanding of life. Consequently—and our further investigation confirms this opinion—insofar as civic legislation is concerned, there are no obstacles to a logical development of organic decentralization, other than the slowness of human beings to understand the meaning of contemporary events and to adjust their actions accordingly.

The afore-discussed pioneering toward a far-reaching plan-pattern of the future Greater New York—on the basis of the present blight situation—is comparable to the "physical moment" of organic decentralization. So far it is only "a general idea concerning those areas available for growth, and not an investigation of the adaptability of these areas for the various functional purposes of the city," as was previously stated. "Real organic decentralization," it was furthermore stated, "begins with the distribution and interrelation of the city's manifold activities." In a sense this is comparable to "chemical" processes, for "the progress of organic decentralization acts and reacts like a slowly and constantly working chemical process where a gradual change from disorder into a workable order is manifest. So to speak, chemical laws direct the conversion during which the various urban functions, formerly haphazardly distributed in the city's confusion, become now adequately interrelated so as to assume functional groupings." This we have already established.

Let us now study the planning problems of Greater New York in the light of this "chemical moment."

Let us, therefore, undertake a theoretical experiment with the whole metropolitan area of New York, including large districts even beyond the present metropolitan territories. Let us put all the many problems of these areas under our "chemical" process. This process, acting slowly and during a long period of time, would break up the present inorganic miscellany of functions. It would group these functions into organic functional units. It would move these thus-formed functional units into new locations more suitable for the various activities than are the existing locations, and into a workable relation with the city's organization at large. All this would happen in accordance with our conception of organic decentralization.

According to far-sighted planning, a large part of those docks which at present encircle Manhattan could someday be moved to more adequate locations. Such an action would free the waterfront for other important uses which would be more suitably located here. Through these shiftings, integral shipping-communities could be created, each embracing those functions related to it.

It is not difficult to discern how it came to pass that the shores of both the Hudson and Eastern Rivers have become lined with docks, warehouses, and industry. When New York was a small town on Lower Manhattan, it was fully logical that all the shipments should take place along its shore lines. But when the town began to grow beyond all expectations, far-sighted planning should have had an inkling of the consequences and should have limited this unwise encirclement by providing areas for new docks elsewhere. But as the day of unrestrained and unstudied growth was at hand, almost every available inch was used. Today, the shores are crowded with ships and the narrow land packed with docks, warehouses, and merchandise for and from the four corners of the globe. The streets are so crammed with heavily-loaded trucks as to make them seem themselves slowly moving warehouses. Indeed, the situation is much like super-confusion of hyper-congestion; and this is piled on a land area which is only two miles in width and which has many other vital functions to fulfil.

All this has happened during the past century, until today the limit has been reached. It is now high time that far-sighted planning reverse the process, and that the development of a hundred years to come take place in a direction opposite to that of the past hundred years; that is, toward decentralization instead of concentration. As the present docks become too old and outmoded, they should be rebuilt step by step in other locations. As the warehouses dilapidate, they should be reconstructed step by step in other places. As many other things become overcrowded, they should be removed step by step elsewhere. Thus the shores and adjacent lands could be gradually freed from the present uses. They could be replanned—and to a large extent planted.

The industrial situation should be considered from the same angle, not only on Manhattan proper, but on the entire territory in question. It is far from practical that industry remain within the most congested areas in the city, although for reasons already discussed it has become embodied there. The city should be freed from the disadvantages that beset it through having industry crowdedly located, and new industrial centers should be founded in those locations where adequate transportation facilities can be easily had. Undoubtedly, such an action would enable industry to function better; it would greatly improve the living and working condition of the workmen; and it would contribute greatly to the health and efficiency of the city as a whole. These points have already been stressed again and again; yet they are worth stressing again and again as far as Manhattan is concerned, for it is increasingly evident that Manhattan should not be jammed with all types of sundry manufacturing and, therefore, there should be no hesitation in taking decisive steps.

Furthermore, far-sighted planning should relocate many other types of urban activity that have become disadvantageously distributed in regard to their respective uses. So varied in character and suitability are the land areas about New York, that satisfactory locations for any functions can be found there. Many of those activities of purely business nature could be assorted, regrouped, and favorably relocated on the broad area of the territories of decentralization. In this manner, decentralization of New York would become an insistent and continuous process of readjustments. These readjustments on their part would cause other readjustments of a corresponding nature. Much of residential Manhattan would be liable to become open land areas, as former working sites and their corresponding areas of living were relocated somewhere else. Instead, new residential areas of varied character could be planned here to serve those work centers still retained on the Island.

Ultimately, when the greater part of this rehabilitation process had taken place, we would find our good New Yorker —or rather someone of his offspring—living in an open and sunny residential neighborhood of comparatively low density and working in an adjacent well-planned business district. We would find him living and working in such conditions, no matter whether we consider downtown or uptown Manhattan, or any other area of the decentralized Greater New York. Green lands and play-grounds would now replace many of those areas where slums once spread themselves, and the former inefficient congestion of haphazard growth would have been reformed into orderly functioning of forward planning. The varied means of transportation could at last assume their maximum efficiency. Yet, considering the spirits and bodily well-being of the town people, organic planning would have offered them even the possibility of walking comfortably from home to work.

Years, and years hence.

D. VISION

Of course, these ideas of New York's decentralization must run the risk of being branded as sheer dreams. It is so, not because the task were impossible to be carried out in the long run—both practically and economically—but because most minds have been adjusted to consider such planning a mere impossibility. In this respect man is a peculiar creature: he sees that a thing which was regarded yesterday as an impossibility has become a commonplace possibility today; yet rarely is he able to realize that the impossible of today may well turn into the usual of tomorrow. Accordingly, any profound consideration of the future is beyond most men, because their training has not been conducive to a serious viewing of the world of tomorrow. To them, those who consider such questions as are related to the future, belong to that rather bizarre world of "dreamers."

Certainly, all this kind of planning which has now been discussed, is dreaming. **Dreaming it "must" be. Planning a priori is dreaming, for it is that indispensable scheming toward the future which is innate already in the child as he keeps his budding imagination hopefully alert; and which scheming has, during past times, infused vitality into individuals, families, communities, nations, and into humanity at large; and without which scheming man were but a prosaic matter-of-fact-specimen of daily matters-of-fact.** The first imaginative steps in any progressive movement have always been taken by those all-too-rare individuals who happen to be imbued with vision. In fact, on these men, so frequently and disdainfully classified as "dreamers," hinges man's continuous effort to improve his future.

But planning is more than dreaming. **Planning is that conceiving faculty which must recommend ways and means of transmuting the possibilities or impossibilities of today into the realities of tomorrow.** It must be concerned with the welfare of future generations, and it must find the solutions to satisfy this concern. In this spirit must planning be understood. Lack of this spirit shuts the doors for a satisfactory development toward better conditions for man.

All large cities of rapid growth and intense concentration have their problems of decentralization. All these cities must look ahead. All these cities must "dream."

When things are so, may we then ask, "Why is such a dreaming so infrequent in the planning of cities." The answer is that far-sighted planning is so seldom accomplished mainly because the average mind overestimates existing "impossibilities," and refuses to believe that an orderly rehabilitation of the disorderly city over a period of years is feasible. He considers only the existing land-values, and fails to realize that land-values were established by man under certain circumstances, and that they are neither inviolate nor unchangeable. He regards existing civic legislation as necessarily permanent, and tries only half-heartedly to create new legislative stipulations in accord with changed conditions.

When planning is too greatly concerned with existing conditions, evolution is sterilized, the city is prevented from moving forward, and the possibilities of solving future problems are restrained through present inaction. **How could progress be achieved when the primary presuppositions for progress are obstructed?** Unintelligent would it be to attempt to pour wine from a bottle while pushing the cork more tightly into the neck of the bottle. Yet planning, in refusing to withdraw the corks of existing land-values and legislative stipulations, is following an equally unintelligent course. Surely, such planning cannot be far-sighted.

Far-sighted planning is free from these difficulties. Far-sighted planning is well aware of the fact that organic decentralization cannot be successfully carried out when controlled by antiquated rules of concentration. To attempt to do so would be as senseless as to keep consistently cutting the boy's coat according to old measurements, although the boy grows bigger year by year. No! Land-values and civic legislation of yesterday and today are not those of tomorrow where the new values and new legislation must evolve from the planning work toward tomorrow itself. Therefore, "revaluation" and "relegislation" must be the directives of any planning that can satisfy future demands—just as much as constant "re-measuring" must be the key-word that can produce fitting coats during the boy's growth. "Revaluation" and "relegislation" will produce new physical realities, which in their turn will occasion new values to be balanced against the old, during the planning work. This planning work must happen in the spirit of tentative research, which must grow in freedom independently of present conditions—because of which freedom this tentative research is able to discover and ascertain possibilities of the best solutions of future problems.

Despite the logic of this kind of planning, the skeptic is prompt to criticize. "It is a dream," says he. "Future conditions are unknown; why, then, bother oneself with matters which may develop in a totally unexpected manner?"

The planner must be the first to recognize the indisputable fact that the future is unknown. For this reason he must be eager to encourage flexibility of planning. He must constantly try to prepare for future possibilities by freeing the city from restrictions which are no longer valid, yet which hamper any appropriate development toward the future. As coming events cast their shadow before them, it must be the planner's task to analyze that shadow and to prepare—logically, scientifically, and with vision—for that which he believes **will** and **should** develop. All stubborn conservatism, tending to close all possibilities by obsolete stipulations, prevents any adequate answer to the unknown but foreshadowed demands of the future. **Only through progressive striving for openness can future problems be adequately solved. Only because the bud opens itself into flower, can the fruit be developed to form new seed for new plants to come.**

The planner must search for the logical, the practical, the economical, and the human. He must be certain that these qualities will always be kept in esteem, whether the city increases or decreases in size, regardless of how the habits of life change, and irrespective of whether the present mechanical trend continues or not. He must be certain that orderly conditions will always be preferred to disorderly ones.

The planner must know that every New Yorker, if given his choice, would prefer an organic planning of Manhattan with ample open areas of green, provided of course that the practical problems had been at the same time satisfactorily solved. The planner must know that the orderly regulation of the shores of the Danube in Budapest will always continue to be enthusiastically appreciated. He must know that the environments of the Seine in Paris will always be enjoyed and will greatly contribute to the charm of that city. He must know that the magnificent harbor development of Rio de Janeiro will always be considered an achievement where nature's beauty has been fully respected. He must know that Chicago's Lake-front will continue to be considered of a great value to that city. And he must know that any civic achievement where nature's art and man's art are brought together into a sublime solution will always be met with unanimous contentment.

Indeed, the planner must know that all these are viewpoints which will not change. **There must be no wavering, therefore, in directing urban development toward a goal which the future will accept with profound gratitude.**

"It is just a dream," the criticism goes on. "Does not all this mean that much of the existing city is doomed to vanish in order to provide for the new? Might not one as well advocate the building of an entirely new city? How can any such program be economically feasible?"

If, one hundred years ago, the New Yorker had been told that his home town might grow to its present size, he probably would have shouted emphatically: "What! How could such a tremendous growth be economically possible! No! It is just a dream!" He would not have realized that when growth takes place, year after year—gradually, slowly, continuously, and consistently—monetary questions are subordinate to this growth and to the increased demands of newer ways of living. If the early New Yorker had but partially visualized the possibility of such a tremendous subsequent growth—and but in part foreseen its consequences—surely, he would have begun to ponder, to plan, and to organize. He, and his descendants alike, had then endeavored to direct their home town toward a saner growth by prudent scheming, year after year, decade after decade. Had such been the case, the present generation would have much to be grateful for. And the attitude of today would be one of open-mindedness and vision rather than of conservative inertia because of those tough "impossibilities"—and of that stupid "dreaming." Unfortunately, however, the early New Yorker was neither open-minded concerning the physical problems of his city, nor did he reveal any particular vision with respect to its future. Present difficulties are the results of these failures. It is only to be hoped that these difficulties, **from now on,** will encourage a planning vision which will escape further troubles for years to come—while new demands arise.

As time passes, new demands arise in every large city. Because these new demands are liable to bring about new difficulties and inescapable increasing disorder, it is time that planning questions be considered in a forward-thinking manner. One must realize how short-sighted it is to interpret urban growth in terms of a few years, believing that the money necessarily must be immediately at hand. It requires but little of imagination, it would seem, to understand urban problems in a broader scope; for there are decades, centuries and ages ahead, during which the city will continue to pass through fluctuations of growth, standstill, decrease, and of growth again. During these fluctuations, new demands arise and new problems must be solved. And the city must be prepared to meet these demands dynamically, year after year, decade after decade.

It is true enough that most of the improved results can be achieved only in a more or less distant future. In spite of this it is vitally important that the start be made today. **This start must be made on paper—which is relatively cheap. It must be made by means of human thinking—which oftentimes seems still cheaper. Why, then, raise the question of large sums of money, before matters are studied without the using of these sums of money?** For, so far, the question is only of design research, and not of physical execution.

This procedure in question is just the same as in many and different walks of life. So for instance, any far-sighted institution—scientific, technical, industrial, or educational—must foresee and prepare for future problems through constant research; looking beyond the seemingly impossible, and thereby paving the way for actual realization of that seemingly impossible. Without this constant research work, these institutions would soon sink into sterile repetition, and would gradually become useless institutions.

Similarly alert must the procedure be in the planning research for the city's future.

But when the actual execution of these research results begins, it takes place—as can be remembered—first, by "creating new values on the enlarged areas of decentralization"; second, by "rehabilitating values on the present blighted areas"; and third, by "protecting all values, old and new." It must be a well-organized and economically constructive evolution which happens gradually, constantly, and consistently. During this process, money is needed, of course. Money is always needed when cities are developed, whether the development proceed in one direction or another, disorderly or orderly. If the direction is toward increasing disorder, money is used to create values which to a great extent do not last, as experience has shown. If the direction is toward organic order, the money is used to create stabilized values, as experience has shown. **This latter direction, however, is the fruit of that dreaded "dreaming."**

"It is but a dream," it is still maintained. "How could building-grounds be wiped off the map without introducing ruinous economic conditions?"

Which one introduces ruinous economic conditions: order or disorder? Is it economical planning when large areas of building-grounds decay in an amazingly short time into slums, spreading the disease even to those sections which so far have been orderly and healthy? Surely not! And when order endeavors to stop this disease by creating protected values and stable conditions, why then call such an action ruinous? When short-sighted and antiquated ordinances allow almost unlimited air-rights that raise land-values into excess and because of this raise neighbor land-values are destroyed, perhaps for ever—for sure, this is not a dream—nay, it is a night-mare. When disorder goes on in this manner like the Angel of Death, ruining ever more values, it is tolerated, and civic legislation does not have the courage to look things straight in the eye. But when logical order is recommended, to rehabilitate and preserve the general status of land-values in the city, it then is feared that matters will go from bad to worse.

Yet, things cannot be always regulated satisfactorily. A South Sea Bubble is a South Sea Bubble, and excess is excess. Excessive land-values must be brought to a normal level, before normal conditions can be obtained. But once a normal level is established, it is up to civic order to make it stable. This might be a dream. Yet, it is a challenge to make this dream a future reality.

"All the same, it is a dream," is the short reply to this. We know it. And we accept it. But all those who carry this discouraging answer to the four corners of the city must know it is the planner's duty to make this dream come true.

It is a dream. And we have reason to suspect that this dream only seldom will become a reality. **It is so, because of the fact that only a few consider it their duty to bring into reality the dreaming of their community's welfare; whereas thousands dismiss such far-reaching endeavors with the remark, "It is just a dream."**

E.   LACK OF VISION

The foregoing was not meant to be a lamentation because of the general indolence in civic improvement. Our aim was to make it clear that organic decentralization of cities—even of the largest—is not an impossible task, **provided good-will supports such endeavors.** This is essential, for without good-will any striving is soon brought into a deadlock.

However, any permanent good-will presupposes a genuine conviction that the congested bodies of large cities cannot in the long run be kept physically adequate, much less fulfil their primary objectives of providing man with a physically and spiritually healthy place in which to live. Furthermore, any permanent good-will presupposes a genuine conviction that the necessary improvements are possible to accomplish. It goes without saying that lack of conviction in these respects cannot keep good-will permanently alive.

Even conviction in these respects does not always breed good-will, for, unfortunately, many are proud of their big, compact, and congested cities in which life pulses, masses crowd, and traffic speeds at breakneck pace. Blindfolded by false pride, they are unable to discern the dangerously detrimental disorder on all sides. Many harbor the egotistic belief that the suffering of human beings and the destruction of human values which is caused by this urban decline is no personal concern of theirs. Their pride in the great city is primarily based on its physical greatness. This is a false pride, for certainly, to concentrate great masses into congested confusion is no worthy feat, nor one requiring particular genius. It is just the trend of the time. **But to institute functional and livable order, amidst these ever-growing masses of people, would require intelligent leadership and would constitute a truly magnificent achievement.**

The most important quality of intelligent leadership, however, is **"instinctive vision" to discern the right road onward.** For mere leadership is of little meaning, unless there is instinctive vision to discern **where** to lead. But, because this kind of instinctive vision in civic matters has been unfortunately scarce, those with lack of vision have taken matters into their own hands. And in this spirit of lack of vision the urban ship has drifted without captain, compass, and helmsman. For sure, no undertaking could be successful in such circumstances.

Lack of vision has been the source of many blunders in planning. The roots of this deplorable situation can be traced—as we know—to the materialistic era of the nineteenth century. During this era, vision in planning matters amounted perhaps to little more than the surveyor's skill in handling the theodolite. Inexperience did not realize the dangers of congested growth, for this expansion was an untried phenomenon, and no one seemed to anticipate such conditions as the continuous growth of cities was eventually to reveal. Explosive growth without control replaced conducive vision, in which process man was a mere spectator— stupefied, or falsely proud.

Considering civic growth during the period now in question, it is significant to observe that in many cases the growing city did not emanate from a single town, but from several neighbor towns which were isolated one from another by spacious areas of free green land. In such cases, growth took place planlessly and haphazardly by filling the existing free areas, through which process the formerly isolated healthy towns were transformed into unhealthy parts of one and the same compact city. Ironically speaking, this uncontrolled growth was much of a **"disorderly concentration of orderly decentralization,"** in direct contrast to the present much desired **"orderly decentralization of disorderly concentration."** It was tragic indeed that those green areas which formerly protected the various small towns became intensely crowded as urban territories, creating such an integrated and compact mass of the big city that today's blighted areas and slums are the result. The so-called and much heralded "progress" from small towns into big cities has thus become the backward process from verdant protective lands into slums. This kind of progress was easy to achieve. But there was no reason for being proud of it.

So cities developed in those prosaic days of lack of vision. There was no dreaming. It was just a long dreamless sleep.

Past is past, however, and we do not help the present situation by criticizing the laxity of our forefathers, unless we do it for the sake of our own enlightenment. And as a matter of our own enlightenment we have mentioned this not too rare manifestation of lack of vision. Certainly, "not too rare manifestation," for we need only study the developments of almost every overgrown city, and we will find that almost all these developments have happened just in that same manner of lack of vision as above described; that is, from groups of individual town-communities into that compactness of the overgrown cities of today.

Supposing now that our forefathers, really, had the vision to understand the importance of protective zones as a means of preventing compact growth; and, consequently, that they had directed the cities development by preserving the original and natural tendency toward a system of individual neighboring town-communities. Well, in such case a good foundation would have been laid for the cities growth toward organic decentralization, and our problem were now much simpler and easier. And furthermore, supposing that we, **now,** would take our forefathers lack of vision as a healthy warning for ourselves, and that because of this we would understand the importance of these protective zones. Well, in such case we could find innumerable instances where this understanding could be excellently applied. To be sure, **there still are many cities and their neighbor townships where growth has not as yet developed so far that protective zones could not be successfully applied. It is only to be hoped that such an application really will take place; if so, the problem of our children then will be much simpler, and future generations will be grateful because of these protective zones of green land—which our "vision" has brought about.**

F. FREE AREAS AND DECENTRALIZATION

The most conspicuous characteristic of organic decentralization is the fact that the former urban compactness will be split by it into individual townships, separated one from another by protective zones of green land. In cases where this process of decentralization will be systematically and thoroughly carried out, these green areas of protection will become formed into a comprehensive green-belt system, embracing both the urban complex at large and the various community units individually as well. On these protective green belts, all ordinary building activities must be prohibited during times to come in order to safeguard permanent effects of protection, so essential in the case of organic decentralization. On the other hand, such activities as sports, games, outdoor recreation, and the like—which are by their respective natures related to these green lands—could be advantageously located here for the benefit of adjacent residential areas. Moreover, these green lands must be planned spaciously enough to enable an effective network of fast intercommunication to be established through them without disturbing the logical restfulness on those grounds designed for protection and recreation. It is obvious that this green-belt system will bring lasting effects insofar as the physical conditions in the city are concerned. Equally obvious are even the spiritual advantages of this green-belt development. For, thanks to this, the urban dweller is brought closer to the delights of nature, surely a blessing which cannot be overvalued.

It is an easy task to combine urban and rural advantages in a small town surrounded by country lands. In fact, this was a common thing in the past. Much has been written about the cultural life in the small towns of the times of our forefathers. Notwithstanding the limited size, the town was often the center of cultural activities—intellectual societies, artistic achievements, university life, science, literature, philosophy, and much of music. The town drifted along together with the surrounding country, which latter was used by the population as a play-ground for games and picnics. The countryside Inn was often the stage for philosophical discussions, literary assemblies, and artistic entertainment. Thus, while the hours passed, the debates tightened in the silent night during the slow stroll toward the town. It was the restful spirit of nature that elevated minds to deeper thought.

This is an idyllic picture from days gone by, which to a great extent has vanished and probably will seldom appear again in the same form, since history always brings new features to its colorful arena. Yet we still have the same opportunities as had our forefathers, for, in spite of the changed conditions, man is still the same with his faculties of thinking, of feeling, of enjoying, and of being influenced by his environment. Nature, too, is the same.

Hence organic decentralization is eager to bring man and nature to a closer interrelation, no matter how large the city may grow. To do this is in concert with the movement's primary objective, as in the creation of "healthy environment," nature's collaboration is not only important, but also indispensable.

In the gradual process from small towns to compact cities, a few spots of land were left free, and usually they were trimmed into parks. These parks, however, were relatively small, yet sufficient as long as the community was limited in its size and the surrounding nature was easy to reach. But as soon as the city began to expand itself, and the delights of nature became supplanted by those of the parks, it is quite obvious that in such changed circumstances these parks were bound to be insufficient in size. Yet eyes were not always opened to see this disadvantage, and things developed in a rather phlegmatic manner. In these respects, the park has a sad story to tell.

It is not difficult to understand why the park was out of place within the mediaeval town, because no reason for such a feature existed there. The town was compelled to extreme density on a small area, and the country about the town was free for everyone's enjoyment during the days of peace; whereas during enemy attacks nobody had time for the delights of nature, much less for such an unnecessary thing as a park. A park would have been a disadvantageous extravagance and, for certain, this thought must be accepted in the mediaeval case.

But what should not be accepted is the consequence of this thought with relation to the further development of the town, when the reasons for the extreme concentration ceased to exist. The park was still regarded as an extravagance, a luxury; and this conception of "luxury" was still more emphasized when the park was dressed into a formal trim for the pleasure of the ruler. The general urban lands, on the other hand, were reserved for practical purposes most efficiently. On the whole, only areas that were not suitable for building-grounds and streets were left free as green spots.

Accordingly, a number of small parks became scattered around in the city.

Meanwhile, as the expansion of the city went on, even large woodlands outside of the city limits, such as had been used by the population as public pleasure grounds, were protected, and the expansion of the city had to find its way around these. In this manner, these outside lands became inside features in the enlarged city; and so it happens that many an overgrown city has its large park: Paris has Bois de Boulogne; London has Hyde Park; Berlin has Tiergarten, and Manhattan is proud of its Central Park, to mention some.

All this was caused primarily because there happened to be suitable woodland for people to make use of during the hours of leisure, and not so much because of intentional efforts to bring nature into the city. This is obvious. For while the city grew, the planner considered only existing free areas and parks—more or less unintentionally gained —and did not try to improve conditions in the city by creating a deliberate system of green areas. In other words, he tried to save what was to be saved, but not to gain what still was to be gained while free lands about the city were available. For this reason, only a few of the cities have enough of free land within their boundaries.

But time changed, and habits of life were bound to change accordingly.

Now the urban dweller is longing for freedom and space, and for the delights of nature. The parks and green lands, however, are much too small when compared with the constant growth of the population. They are crowded, and life within and without them is restless and noisy. Mostly, these parks and green lands serve embellishing purposes only, or they are cut into pieces by a multitude of traffic lines.

Restful nature has vanished from its formerly close contact with the town.

In the following manner ran the course of things.

While the city spread itself, the distances to nature grew. As the distances grew, so grew even the urban dweller's longing for nature. As this longing grew, so grew even the traffic on the streets. Now the streets are crowded with those taking any possible opportunity of free time to leave the restless city and to enjoy nature. This, in turn, makes the city all the more restless.

Organic decentralization must now take the reins into its hands. When this movement progresses by breaking up the present compactness, the interrelation between urban and rural lands will undergo a corresponding change. The urban lands will spread themselves toward the surrounding rural districts as they form individual town communities. The rural lands, on their part, will spread themselves toward the heart of the city, filling in those areas vacated through the centrifugal urban movement. It becomes a double course, in two opposite directions, through which city and country are brought into a close contact one with another. Curiously enough, it becomes a circular course, too, for the result attained will be much the same as was the start; that is, **the individual town of the decentralized city becomes a small town surrounded by nature**—like the mediaeval town.

G. TRAFFIC AND DECENTRALIZATION

Traffic problems have pushed themselves into the brightest limelight, for today they are every planner's most grave concern in and about the growing congestion of the big cities. In cases where matters still are conducted along the old idea of concentration, the problems of traffic are again and again brought increasingly toward an inevitable dead-end of emergency solutions of one kind or another. Such is the situation, particularly where no comprehensive studies have been made of the city's development to come—and these cases, to be sure, are no scattered exceptions among cities of today.

The situation is different with organic decentralization, for organic decentralization—to be organic—presupposes comprehensive studies of, and suggestions toward, an orderly development of the city. As the aforementioned green-belt system is an essential result of these studies and suggestions, here then a good opportunity is opened for a methodical solution of all the traffic problems involved.

The scheming of a comprehensive network of intercommunication in conjunction with the green-belt system, already settles the traffic situation insofar as its location in the urban pattern is concerned. This is an important point to bear in mind when the general disposition of land-use and urban function is to be considered during the decentralization process. For, in this planning, the traffic problems are greatly decisive as to the respective locations and mutual relations of the various community centers. These latter problems—namely, those dealing with the various community centers—therefore, must be solved simultaneously with the problems of traffic, in order to make the intercommunicative arteries an integral part of the urban organization at large.

The embodiment of the fast intercommunicative arteries into the green-belt system is the fundamental solution of the traffic problem in the decentralized city; and, in agreement with this, all the other traffic considerations must be conceived and settled. There is not much reason at this moment for going into a detailed study of all the virtues and characteristics of urban communication in the light of modern means of traffic as applied to the decentralized community. As a general remark, it is sufficient to stress that the whole field calls for a thoroughgoing and unbiased readjustment; for, as has already been said somewhere, the old street-pattern is no good any more, and the street construction carried over from the horse-and-buggy days is not suitable for motor and rubber-tire. There are two points, however, which must be particularly mentioned in this connection. First, **we must accentuate the significance of flexibility in the** planning and construction of traffic ways, because the rapid development of traffic means might easily make subsequential changes and modifications urgent. And second, we must emphasize that the necessity for quietness is essential, and that this quietness must be achieved in the decentralized community in the face of the fact that speedy rushing must constantly go on.

Here we are confronted with two of the most basic problems of the modern community: "efficiency of traffic," and "quietness of living." In these two respects it must be observed that it is precisely the development of traffic means and the inclination to growing speed that have disturbed the formerly peaceful city life. Adequate readjustments in these points, therefore, are necessary. Yet these readjustments must happen in a manner that can offer these opposite poles —noisy rush, and quietness of living—the best opportunities of development in full accord with their respective natures. How to solve such a problem, avoiding half-baked compromises, is the concern of organic decentralization.

In order to proceed on a firm foundation, it might be wise to examine the principles of a rather appropriate traffic system—the blood circulation in the human body.

The heart is the center of the blood circulation system. From the heart the large traffic channels—the arteries—leave, carrying blood and needed substances to every part of the body. In the heart the veins end, functioning as transportation lines for blood and used substances. From the heart, the circulation goes to the lungs, and back again; then to the digestive system, and back again to the heart.

The aorta, the arteries, the great vein, and the vein system in general form the main circulation lines for the heavier load. The capillaries—the minute blood vessels between the terminations of arteries and veins—are for local functioning, carrying the divided and diminutive load into the very recesses of every organ, satisfying the needs of all.

257

The whole organization is minutely elaborate. But in its functioning it is logical and simple.

Logical and simple, too, are its principles.

First, because the load is carried directly to its destination without passing through other organs having little in common with this particular load. And second, because the dimensioning of the traffic channels is measured according to the load to be carried. Thanks to these two principles, confusion is prevented in the circulation.

It is obvious that these two principles of transportation are applicable to any circumstance of urban traffic. It is still more obvious that their application to the decentralized urban organism can offer a clear and easily adjustable traffic system of satisfactory efficiency, of whatever kind the traffic may be.

Applying, now, these two principles to the modern and decentralized city, one soon will find how obsolete the street-pattern from yesterday really is. For this reason, town-design of today cannot lean upon those dormant teachings in town-planning which still are seeking their material of instruction from the past. Town-design of today has not much in common with the various modes of street-net construction—regular or irregular—which during stylistic times have become crystallized into distinct systems. The street-pattern of today and tomorrow must emerge in close contact with the planning work, and its characteristics of design-pattern must spring from the planning work itself. Through this work—when organically carried out in accord with the two above mentioned traffic principles—one soon will make the encouraging discovery that the modern community can get along with fewer streets as compared with the old street-system of yesterday, notwithstanding the fact that the demand for efficiency of traffic has highly increased. Moreover, whereas formerly every street was constructed to carry traffic from everywhere to everywhere—as is particularly the case with that stereotyped gridiron pattern—the street-system of tomorrow is, in contrast, clearly discriminative in this respect.

The present street-system, naturally, must be laid out in accordance with existing traffic-means. With regard to this, the motor vehicle must be considered the main means of transportation; and insofar as can be predicted, motor power —or something similar—must be considered as a principal factor in planning for traffic, even with a long time period in mind.

However, the future might bring a radical change. It is wise, therefore, to look ahead upon things—just as does the huntsman, for ahead must he aim along the bird's flight. So, accordingly, must the planner apply foresight in his traffic lay-outs, because the problems of today are not the problems of tomorrow. Yet even the satisfactory solution of the problems of tomorrow might soon be found unfitting. Under such circumstances, why try to fix things on a temporary basis, and why not instead provide for the possibility of any future adjustments? For one thing is certain: new traffic-means demand new modes of road construction; and as the present time is a transition time even as regards traffic-means —and very much so concerning just these—it then is prudent to plan the circulatory roads so that their alteration to meet coming requirements will be an easy matter, whatever these requirements may be. Consequently, the more flexibly the road-system of today and of tomorrow is laid out, the easier can it be adjusted to satisfy future demands. This is the case particularly with fast traffic.

It is a hard fact—as has been amply experienced—that the rigid compactness of the city of yesterday cannot offer much flexibility in the alteration of existing obsolete streets to satisfy the demands of modern means of traffic. And where these demands are most urgent, great costs are involved for even alleviative improvements. Alas, how often aren't the costs prohibitive for improvements of real value?

Since these are the facts about the rigid street construction of yesterday, it then seems unwise to design new developments in an equally rigid manner to meet future demands—demands at which the present time can only guess. As regards this, it is rather amazing to observe how many of the most ardent advocates of the present machine-age are eager to superimpose extremely rigid schemes of traffic construction upon planning toward the future. By this we mean such suggestions as where highly mechanized and elaborate traffic systems are projected to form the skeleton of the "City of Tomorrow," or whatever the title may be, in such a settled way as to make any future alterations of consequence impossible. It seems to us that these very advocates themselves, in all their elation over the machine's triumphal progress, should take it for granted that tomorrow must be understood in different terms than today insofar as traffic-means are concerned; and that just they, therefore, should give leeway to their fellow-enthusiasts of tomorrow to fix their things in accordance with their own conditions. To superimpose this kind of rigidity **is not planning,** for, as we have learned, any planning presupposes flexibility.

In sharp contrast to this kind of rigid scheming of communicative arteries which cannot be changed to satisfy changed traffic conditions, the green-belt system can offer the needed flexibility. The green-belt system gives every opportunity to keep traffic efficiency permanently up-to-date; for here, any alteration in any direction at any time can be made within reasonable costs. It must be observed that within the green-belt system the bulk of road construction can happen on the natural ground level, and that such features as subways and elevated highways—those emergency products of concentrated confusion and lack of previous planning—can be obviated.

Speaking of future traffic problems, air-traffic should not be left unconsidered. Because, just here, an equation must be solved with too many unknown quantities to give anywhere near an exact answer; just here, consequently, flexibility of planning is most important to assure future satisfaction.

Long-distance air-traffic is already fairly well established, although it still is a combination of air and land means, insofar as the traveler is compelled to use land-traffic vehicles when going to and from the rather distant air-port. The question is whether or not this system will be satisfactory in the future when the aeroplane—or something of that kind—will be used for daily commuting more or less within the decentralized urban territory, if such be the demand in the future city. Evidently such an arrangement would not meet with future approval; for the present air-port, situated for obvious reasons in the outskirts of the city, cannot serve the daily air traffic of limited distance. This means that landing fields and parking areas—of whatever kind they may be in those future days—must be scattered along the broadened urban pattern wherever this seems necessary and appropriate. Because it does not seem possible that roofs, terraces, and the like—as has frequently been suggested for the future solution of the air traffic problem—could be either appropriate or sufficient for such purposes, our suggestion is that even needed areas for air-traffic purposes can be had within the green belt system.

Another point for close consideration is the previously indicated friction between efficiency of traffic and quietness of living. No doubt, to bring this friction to a satisfactory end is one of the major problems of organic decentralization; for, as said, in spite of the importance of efficient traffic, the bringing of quietness into the city is essential indeed. Surely, **city quietness is one of those good qualities that have been lost during the progress of things.**
Please, consider this:
Those who have visited Venice before motor boats were introduced there, know that the town was then silent with the slow, restful, and monotonously rhythmic clip-clapping

of many feet on the walks. No modern means of communication had trespassed its watery borders; no speeding of automobiles could agitate the loafing wanderer; no blowing of horns, ringing of bells, or clattering of motors could fill the air with noise. Rush and noise in Venice not so long ago were unknown.

Venice tells us the story of bygone days, because it comes to us that the silence of Venice was the silence of every town of earlier epochs; and the slow, restful, and monotonously rhythmic clip-clapping on the walks of Venice was characteristic of every town for thousands of years. In fact, it has been **always** so—with the exception of a few of the past decades.

Although silence is the tradition from the days of our forefathers and from much theretofore, this tradition has become confused and forgotten because of the gradual development from the formerly quiet conditions of the small towns to the terrific noise and restlessness of today's big city. The big city of today really is a noisy and restless product of human superficiality. Day and night, the constant rushing goes on; streets are crowded, traffic is nervous, ceaselessly moving hither and thither, always hindering others to move, always seeking to avoid hindrance by others.

Perpetuum mobile!

One has become accustomed to this; one regards it as a natural state of things inseparable from the functioning of the city; and one has the conception that things always have been so, always will be so, always **must** be so. But once in a while, when one takes the time to ponder over matters, one finds that noise and restlessness in the city by no means indicate positive vitality, but rather the lack of it. The truth of this is to be found just as easily as one can find that those who do the most and loudest of talking usually do the least of thinking. One feels that things have gone utterly stupid. And one asks himself, "Why must it be so?" Does the idea of the city necessarily suggest that noise and restlessness must exist in the very place built for man in which to live and work? Or, do not living and working already by their inmost nature presuppose quietude and restfulness?

Surely! For, just due to noise, restlessness, and that nervous rush, many of the finest strings of life in the city have been brought out of tune. And, just due to noise, restlessness, and that nervous rush, many of the evil qualities of human nature have been brought into the open.

Here, then, organic decentralization has an important mission to fulfil; for, in fact, quietude and restfulness of living must be considered the core of all the objectives of the decentralization movement. With regard to this, it was stated in the introduction that "the city's improvement and further development must be started with the problems of the homes and their environment," and that "in these very homes the seeds of satisfactory living and healthy environment must be planted, and must grow to transform the whole city's physical organization into a like spirit of satisfactory living and healthy environment."

It is obvious that such ends could not be attained unless, first of all, quietude and restfulness are secured. In order to secure these, we have founded the functional order of organic decentralization on premises that could eliminate the compulsory use of mechanical means of transportation in everyday work. Such an arrangement, it was said, is logical, it is practical, it is time saving, and it is human; above all, it offers the best possibilities of bringing quietude and restfulness into the residential districts of the various individual communities of the decentralized urban system.

Furthermore, an important objective of organic decentralization is to concentrate speedy traffic along separate arteries such as do not traverse or disturb residential areas and other grounds requiring silence. Due to the fact that protective belts of planted free areas are planned between the residential areas and the highways of speedy traffic—through this to isolate noise—it is evident that organic decentralization endeavors to undertake all possible steps to establish humanly livable conditions in the city.

H. SUMMARY

In the above we have analyzed organic decentralization. We have tried to view the process from all possible angles so as to present an all-sided picture of the situation. Before we leave the subject, however, let us undertake a short summary of the foregoing, emphasizing now the essential points only.

First:

When examining the "problems of today," it became evident that the status of town-building at the present time is of a kind such as mankind never before has experienced. Enormous has been the growth of many cities, and equally enormous has become the danger of threatening slums within these cities. Yet, because both growth and threat are of a rather recent date—namely, of a few decades only—there is not as yet enough of time perspective to let us grasp all the consequences of the situation.

Were we, in spite of this, to venture a prediction as to what might be the ultimate consequences in those cities where disorderly and compact growth has caused the spread of slums in the heart of the city, our prediction would not be an encouraging one. Really, our prediction would not be more encouraging than is our prediction in the case of a tree where decay in the inner core of the trunk spells a continuously spreading disintegration of the organism. Surely, the tree is doomed if nothing is done to prevent this. Equally certain it is that the disintegrating city is doomed, if nothing is done to save the situation.

Second:

Because the enormous growth of cities—and the equally enormous growth of slums within these cities—has never before been experienced, the right methods of curing this enormous slum disease have never before been experienced.

Consequently, we cannot take counsel with past experiences in town-planning in order to find the right methods to cure the present situation. We must find these right methods through the present situation itself. In other words, town-planning as hitherto conceived and practiced must from now on be considered "history of town-planning," and the new conception of town-planning must grow out of present conditions and their trend toward the future.

Third:

By a closer examination of the disease characteristics in the overgrown cities, we have found that the case is none for pills and drugs, but that a major operation is urgent. The objectives of this major operation, we have found, must be three-fold: first, to transfer activities from decayed areas to those locations which are functionally suitable for these activities; second, to rehabilitate those areas vacated by the foregoing action for such purposes as are best suited there; and third, to protect all values, old and new.

Furthermore, we have found that when this major operation is undertaken in accordance with the above three-fold program, and is running along a pre-established scheme, it results in **organic decentralization.**

Fourth:

It was found that the chief objections to this kind of a major operation, which aims to save the city from eventual disaster, are of economic and legal nature. **Indeed, it sounds almost paradoxical to harbor economic objections to economical rehabilitation of an economically disastrous situation. It sounds almost equally paradoxical to have justice object to such steps as endeavor to bring justice into an unjust situation.** Yet such is really the case on the economic and legal fronts when it comes to the changing of civic conditions from present disorder into future order. It is so because the prevailing economic and legal viewpoints are the results of a long-lasted concentration; and, consequently, there exists a prevailing tendency to look with prejudice and a lack of open-minded understanding upon those economic and legislative demands caused by decentralization.

Obviously, also, the economic and legislative problems call for further investigations. Our next step, therefore, must be to undertake these investigations in order to bring necessary enlightenment into the economic and legislative situations caused by organic decentralization. This we are going to do in the two chapters to follow—respectively, "Revaluation" and "Relegislation."

7. REVALUATION

SPEAKING about "Revaluation" in connection with urban problems, it must first of all be borne in mind that at present there is going on a vivid transition from the old to something new, and that this is true no matter which problems of life one considers—whether cultural problems, social problems, educational problems, art problems, problems of economic or legal nature, or problems in general. In order to keep pace with this transition, and to bring the general mode of thinking into harmony with the metamorphosing conditions, there must happen a corresponding adjustment of all those viewpoints—formulas, dogmas, doctrines, theories, standards, criterions, or what have we—which establish the various values of life, spiritual as well as material. In other words, **there must inevitably happen a general "revaluation of all values."**

In as vivid a transition process as that from urban concentration into organic decentralization, this matter of "revaluation" must permeate the whole structure of the process. All those standards that constitute the old mode of static town-planning must be revalued into standards which are in harmony with dynamic town-organization. All those standards that constitute the stylistic understanding of design must be revalued into standards which are in harmony with the organic understanding of design. And all those standards that constitute the economic structure of the rigid urban concentration must be revalued into standards of a new economic structure such as are in harmony with organic decentralization. In all these, and in many other instances, a decisive revaluation must take place. **And this fact the town-designer must steadily bear in mind.**

However, as we undertake, in the following, to analyze the said matter of revaluation, we shall confine our analysis to the economic problems, mainly. That is, this analysis is going to deal primarily with such value changes in urban properties as are caused by the decentralization movement, and with those problems connected with these value changes.

Value change in urban properties is a common manifestation. Such is the situation especially in disorderly circumstances where values are least stable: every haphazardly growing city has experienced ups and downs in this respect. When business is expanding to residential sections, values go up. When residences must yield to slums, values go down. When the tall building sucks all the tenants, values go up for one and down for the other. It is a constant revaluation, yet lacking any orderly system.

Organic decentralization must not consider this kind of injurious revaluation. The aim of organic decentralization must be to bring urban values into an orderly economic system so as to offer security to the people. It is true, of course, that this sort of organized revaluation is not always an agreeable procedure. In certain circumstances it must undertake even painful adjustments, for it must strive toward a logical control of logically established values, and therefore cannot accept blown-up and fictitious values such as derive from speculation or from other untoward affairs. Consequently, organized revaluation can accept only such values as are based on actual and downright estimation. Furthermore, organized revaluation must endeavor to keep values down on a normal level rather than to encourage raise. According to the city's primary idea, building-grounds constitute the needed areas for the manifold activities of the city, and, hence, the lower the price level of these grounds can be kept, the better can adequate conditions on a sound economic basis be arranged for everyone of the population. Speculation as a selfishly deranging intrigue, therefore, should not be allowed in an orderly community. This stands as a general statement. In order to introduce some "pep and vim" into civic activities, however, revaluation must be willing to accept a certain amount of speculation. Such a thought was already, in another connection, considered a good policy. But when speculation—contrary to the fundamental idea of the city—tries to go beyond a reasonable margin, revaluation must obstruct such inclinations.

Consider what frequently happens in the above respect. Increasing compactness has nurtured the idea that building-grounds are objects of trade—just as if they were some sort of bonds, securities, or ordinary merchandise. Properties are turned over from jobber to jobber, each one of them skimming his profit, thus adding to the price. Often it seems as if everyone were imbued with the big idea that any building lot would ultimately, by some sublime chance, be covered with a profitable skyscraper. Such a thought, indeed, can be fostered only by a lack of proper planning. Meanwhile an unwise bank policy—accustomed to look upon these things with similar spectacles of speculation—is eager to add still more encouragement to the game by lending easy money. In this manner, liabilities upon liabilities are heaped upon properties which in orderly circumstances could not possibly have a corresponding value. To make matters worse, that very disorder which caused the artificial rise will eventually exert its effect in the opposite direction. We all know how congestion reacts: it blights—just as cramping of an organism causes withering of life. Therefore, sooner or later, the high value is doomed to go down on much of the urban territory —often rapidly—whereas the liabilities remain valid.

So, things have been curbed and encumbered. And now, when the mess is at its worst, revaluation—through de-centralization—must enter in to bring order into the Augean Stables of both civic and private affairs.

In this general clearance, the process of revaluation should not proceed in a manner likely to violate the principle of ownership. For this reason the process must be slow—as it is bound to be by the very nature of organic decentralization —offering enough of time for value adjustments so as to make the result favorable to the property owners and the city as well. This is seen to be so much the more necessary when we consider the fact that, during the course of decentralization, revaluation deals not only with properties in their present state, but to a great extent with properties that are subject to change from one condition to another. It must be borne in mind that, because of decentralization, a rather radical transformation is taking place in some of the existing parts of the city. Many land areas which, while congested conditions have prevailed, have served a certain purpose— perhaps most intensely—might now, according to the decentralized scheme, become used for another purpose entirely— and, most likely, less intensely. This process, naturally, is apt to affect land-values with considerable change. Some values go down, because the new mode of building cities requires more openness and, therefore, restricts building volume on the property. Other values go up, because the new openness is apt to improve the surrounding conditions. Some values, again, must be written off because of created free areas, which presupposes that an equivalent compensation must be found somewhere on the enlarged urban grounds where new values have been established. The whole seems like a constant bubbling of valuation and revaluation, and it might seem to many as if the bubbling were apt to disturb, unfavorably, the economic status of the city. If properly organized, however, it rather will bring the formerly uncertain values to a normal stabilization.

It happens in the following manner:

Organic decentralization zones the enlarged urban territories for the various individual concentrations. It divides the territories of these concentrations between their various activities. It conditions these various activities according to the best ideals of modern town design as concerns air, light, space, privacy, quietude, humanness, and intercommunication. It establishes building lines, heights, and ordinances so as to safeguard a suitable openness in the grouping of buildings. Furthermore, it directs the three-dimensional design of the whole and of the details according to functional fitness, mass effect, and coherence. In other words, organic decentralization aims to systematize order throughout the whole organism—from which order land-values derive and according to which these values can be easily and precisely estimated. In fact, **but a simple mathematical equation is needed, where land-value is the sole unknown quantity.**

The above concerns primarily such land-areas as have been, definitely and in detail, planned for immediate use or subsequent use in a near future. Still other areas must be taken into account, the detailed planning of which depends on future demands. But, even in these cases, only slight possibility of value fluctuations can be expected, because the use of these lands as to function and intensity has already been more or less decided in the general decentralization layout. Also, even in these cases, the pernicious speculator has a rather meager pasture ground.

It is obvious that such a procedure as above described— if gradually carried out and economically adjusted—would bring values toward normal stabilization. Simultaneously, the procedure would direct the solution of land-value problems automatically along ethical methods, insofar as it would eliminate the possibility of obstructive speculation. On the other hand, it cannot be expected that the step from unstable values to normal ones, however gradual, could be accomplished without occasional economic losses, especially when considering the haphazard and often abnormal valuation prevailing at present.

Certainly, economic laws cannot be infringed.

Supposing, for example, that you had bought for speculative purposes a certain amount of stock at a "boom" price, and the boom had suddenly come to a definite end; do you think that your business in such circumstances could be maintained on an economically sane basis without writing off the loss? Scarcely. Well, in analogous circumstances, when urban values are at stake, it is equally important to write off the loss; for only by boldly facing such losses, individual or communal, can a normal state of things be achieved. On the other hand, if these losses are not boldly faced, and the abnormally high values are artificially maintained and superimposed upon the living conditions of the population, an increasingly abnormal state of things must be faced—ultimately with dire consequences. Therefore, before we can proceed in our discussion about these matters, it is of fundamental importance to accept the fact—even in practice—**that there are no other directives for urban property valuation than those directives governing sound economic valuation in general. Surely, the amount of potatoes decides the value of that land which produces those potatoes.**

A. STABILIZATION OF VALUES

Organized revaluation, already by its nature, must aim at stabilization of values. This stabilization, naturally, must happen parallel with the general organization process of the city. In other words, stabilization of values must proceed in accordance with the same fundamental principles that govern organic decentralization in general. In the latter respect, we have considered the fundamental principle of organic order, represented by its four satellites—"expression," "correlation," "flexibility," and "protection." So must we now examine the problems of stabilization from the angles of these four commandments.

Here, also, we have four distinct points to consider in connection with stabilization of values. First, we must have "healthy building units," meaning buildings of a good quality as to both physical construction and architectural form expression. Second, we must have a proper "correlation of building units," meaning proper co-operation in building design to achieve satisfactory form-coherence in the city. Third, we must have "flexibility," meaning such character of planning as can prevent the trespassing of the various activities upon one another's territories. And fourth, we must have such planning as can offer "protection" to all properties. All these four considerations we must have, if our aim is to arrive at a state of things in the city's development where value stabilization is guaranteed. In the following we will investigate these four points separately.

1. Healthy Building Units:

It is a clear fact that a decayed building is apt to spread decay. It is likewise a clear fact that a poorly built structure is subject to early deterioration and that it therefore has little to do with value stabilization. But it seems not to be as clear a fact that a building, however recently and substantially erected, if obsolete in both function and form, is a negative action in the stabilization process. Yet, it is.

Assuming that someone were to erect a new home with antiquated accommodations and with a multitude of trashy decorations suggesting a quasi-style of old origin—indeed, this were a downright step toward obsolescence. As things develop—particularly today, with increasing demand for openness, light, and air—such a "new-old" house would soon presage deterioration. To prove this fact is easy with examples from actual conditions. Sound reasoning proves this fact equally well, for **to introduce fallacies into honest endeavors is paradoxical and cannot lead to lasting effect.** This is fundamentally true, no matter whether these fallacies are of general nature, or of architectural.

Assuming then a reverse case, where some one who was animated by a supreme truth, proven by experience during thousands of years—i.e., that honest and straightforward simplicity is the most lasting form-quality—should undertake to erect his home accordingly. That would be a home of simple, inviting, and open design—so planned as to make it easily adjustable to new demands, and thus livable for a long time to come, whoever the future dweller might be. Evidently, this case would be a positive action toward stabilization.

Here we have two opposite cases—one looking backward in time, the other adjusted along the direction of progress. In the first case, the building unit is obsolete already by its very nature; whereas, in the second case, it is progressively vital. Accordingly, these two cases influence their respective neighborhoods—the former causing decline in its neighborhood, the latter adding to the neighborhood's physical strength. This is a statement of universal bearing. So, for instance, in nature, **any barren cell brings harm to the cellular tissue, whereas healthy cells forward healthy growth.**

It is true, of course, that any structure, however progressive at the time of its erection, must sooner or later fall into obsolescence as regards its useful qualities. This is an inescapable fact. Yet this fact has its relative side; for—to go back even to as distant a past as to the Mediaeval era—a large part of the buildings of that time have had resistance to deterioration up to our time, whereas a great quantity of rather recent work has already decayed into slums. The reason for this, as might be remembered, was found in the fact that the building forms of the mediaeval days emerged through honest search for expressiveness, and not through superficial imitation of obsolete forms—which most later work is. With regard to this, it must be borne in mind that as late a time as the latter part of the nineteenth century was the slum-breeding period par excellence. It was so because this particular time brought to the market all those incredible architectural fallacies which now cause the growth of countless slums. And, although we are fighting against these slums, nevertheless those fallacies still direct in many places the leading trend. Thus does the city suffer from the effects of inferior architectural design.

2. Correlation of Building Units:

If the neighborhood is decayed due to increasing disorder, the individual building in this neighborhood is doomed to decay accordingly. Even the most substantially constructed building is subject to decay in a decayed surrounding, just as a healthy tree is affected by surrounding sick trees. Alas, the annihilating contagiousness is more dangerous than that; for —as was already indicated in the above—a single deteriorated structure, if not in time removed, is apt to affect the quality of its neighborhood, just as a single decayed tooth can disturb the whole bodily system.

The above concerns physical values and their decline caused by surrounding disorder. Of course, these causes of decline on the physical side are obvious, and therefore generally understood. But the corresponding phenomena on the spiritual side are not as generally understood; namely, that haphazardly-combined buildings, however healthy in themselves, are subject to mutual destruction. Even in this respect the mediaeval town can be referred to; for the principle of correlation was, in the mediaeval case, just as effective in the creation of healthy form conditions as was that of expression. That is, in the mediaeval case, the resistance to dilapidation did not depend on the health of the individual buildings only, but equally much on the proper interrelation of these buildings into organic unity. If the mediaeval towns had not been constituted with their supreme sense for form-coherence, but only with buildings distributed at random, there would not, to be sure, be much left of these mediaeval towns, in spite of the expressively designed and substantially-built structures. Nature is a good adviser even in this respect, for—as we have learned—**vitality in a living organism does** not depend on the healthy cells only, but equally much on the organic pattern of the cellular tissue.

3. Flexibility of Planning:

It happens frequently that the restful atmosphere of residential areas is brought to an end, because the formerly quiet street has been made a traffic artery of high efficiency. Because of lack of foresight in planning, the existing traffic avenues are not sufficient to carry the ever-growing load, and so the practical planner sees fit to open new channels through the residential district. The home owners must face the sad eventualities, which not infrequently force them out of their homes. Disgusted by the short-sighted action of the practical planner, some of the home owners are ready to get rid of their homes—at any price, for any purpose, and to any person, without discrimination. This is apt to bring property values down, and the remaining home owners must swallow the stern consequences. Such a procedure is not the best road toward stabilization.

It happens frequently that factories expand themselves on territories designed for other purposes. In any city of industrial consequence, and of lack of order, such experiences are well-known facts. In case of industrial growth, the demands of industry will be first satisfied, of course; which, due to lack of another alternative, most likely means intrusion on residential areas. And as the factories oftentimes—because of some imperfect conception of decency—have taken the liberty of scattering about themselves open yards of miscellaneous material, disorderly cumulation of refuse, and such like, it is clear that the adjacent homes must suffer both materially and spiritually—eventually evolving into slums.

It happens frequently that business expands unrestrictedly, and apartment buildings and individual homes must yield. This expansion acts like an overflow, causing people to abandon their quarters. Conditions change, and the buildings are put to serve new, and for them strange, purposes. In the windows, where not long before neat curtains, flowers, and objects of various kinds revealed home life and privacy, now parade skirts, shoes, and sausages. Where yesterday the family members went in and out quietly and serenely, now shops advertise their wares and bright letters offer "Rooms for Rent" for the most indiscriminate use. Fine residences are vacated and filled again with who knows what and what not. Streets are satiated with business, yet not fitted for business. They are crowded with traffic, yet not appropriate for traffic. They are neither this nor that, yet everything; and the mess of "everything" goes on and confuses, street after street, block after block, loudly heralding disorder—and decay.

The above related three causes of intrusion of different natures—traffic, industry, and business—are only a few examples of many similar disturbances which are apt to keep values unstable. Yet the same reason is always causing trouble; namely, lack of flexible planning. This is to infringe the law of flexibility, which calls for planning such as in any circumstance could offer leeway for organic growth.

4. Protection of Values:

Supposing that the above-mentioned traffic-artery were not drawn through the residential district in question, but only along its border line. Supposing still that the factories were not expanded on the home areas themselves, but only directly adjoining these. Furthermore, supposing that business were not developed beyond its own boundaries, but only close to the apartments and homes. Notwithstanding such precautions, however, still the dangers for unstable conditions would exist. Still the direct contact with traffic industry, and business would impose a stern atmosphere upon those areas planned for living purposes. No doubt, this would bring undesirable circumstances to home atmospheres and consequently even to economic values. At first glance, such disadvantages would appear to affect primarily the directly attacked properties, and particularly these properties would be subject to depreciation of both value and atmosphere. It is not so, however, for once the value of these properties had gone down, even those properties next to them would be affected correspondingly. In this manner, the contagious germ of decay would continue its destruction.

In order to bring security into the situation, zones of protection—"no man's land" if you will—must be planned between areas of different functions and spirits. These zones of protection would not only halt the noxious trespassing commandingly—"Thus far shalt thou come, but no further" —but they would even isolate noise, restlessness, and many other negative qualities so characteristic of the nervous city of today.

In terms of protective no man's land, also, must planning be conceived, whatever relationship this protection may concern. These relationships are many and different. For example: interrelation between industry and business; interrelation between business and the various centers such as civic, cultural, and educational; interrelation between all these and the various residential groups of different nature and grade and housing different classes of people, and so on. These various groupings of activities must have enough land on which to expand. And their respective lands must be protected by planted zones. In this manner, the community's sane growth is made possible—and, thanks to the protective measures, property values are stabilized for times to come.

Assuming now that these various functions—traffic, residence, industry, and business—of the individual community-unit had been separated one from another by zones of protection, these community units would then have become organically decentralized. So to speak, they would exhibit a miniature picture of organic decentralization. Furthermore, assuming that the whole urban complex had been handled in the same manner with protective zones, the whole urban complex, then, would have gone through a systematic process of organic decentralization—**and all this for the mere sake of "value stabilization."** In other words, through our analytical examination of stabilization of property values we have arrived at exactly the same conclusion as we previously arrived at when studying town-building problems in the light of both urban rehabilitation and proper functioning. More than that. We have found that the protective measures of value stabilization go hand in hand with humanly livable conditions in the city.

Also, **though we may choose any angle from which to scrutinize civic problems, the satisfactory solutions in any field of civic activities point all the same toward organic decentralization. Such is the case even with the problems of value stabilization, as we have now learned. That is, organic decentralization in itself is a process which by its very nature is most effective in the stabilization of property values.**

B.   SOCIO-ECONOMIC ASPECTS

The above efforts to build a valid foundation for value stabilization have not as yet reached the bottom. It must be borne in mind that two main parties are engaged in the process of stabilization: "physical organization"—which was considered in the foregoing—and "social conditions." This latter is the city's personality, so to speak; and, as such, it embodies all the inclinations and caprices of the population during the intervening fluctuations of the social and economic life in the town-community. Consequently, planning of cities must be much a matter of psychological speculation —which, of course, on its part, is apt to introduce into the stabilization problem many inflections of uncertainty.

Self-evidently, a great many of these inflections are of economic nature; for, unless one is able to make a living in the city, one cannot exist there. To be able to do this pre-supposes that sufficient work is available, which means that stabilization of values is greatly dependent upon stabilization of work. This is true in any case, but particularly so in those urban communities which are predominantly of industrial character. The more steadily the various industries in these industrial communities operate, with equable numbers of workmen employed, the more stable is the economic status in these communities. Urban economic status, however, is greatly dependent on the economic situation of the country as a whole. This, again, is beyond the city's control, and therefore a prudent foresight is necessary which takes into account all possible fluctuations of a general economic nature.

In case work is uncertain, it seems unwise to have the workmen too much economically chained into the soil, for such a rigid system might easily cause undesirable conse-quences. Exceptions from this general statement can be many and different, that is true; but, however conditions may be, one thing is sure—flexibility in all circumstances is a wise rule to follow. Only that system which can offer the popula-tion—in particular that part of the population which is most likely to be affected by economic fluctuations—opportunities to establish their living conditions on a flexible basis, can protect, to a great extent at least, the general status in the city against the perilous results of economic fluctuations.

In this connection we cannot refrain from criticizing that unfortunate mode of home taxation which prevails. In-deed, this mode is illogical and unjust.

When one has a certain income a year, one's taxes are figured accordingly. And even if these taxes were compara-tively out of proportion—as they surely are in these days—one is able to pay them in one way or another. In case of income decrease, again, there is a corresponding decrease of the tax burden. In other words, the taxation remains always in a workable proportion to one's yearly economic status.

The situation is different with home taxation—for here

the yearly money must be paid, no matter whether there is income or not. Thus, when the times of depression enter— in which the blame is not with the home owner—thousands, nay tens and hundreds of thousands of homes become tax-delinquent, and the families driven out, and ruined. For sure, **one's home should be considered sacred, just as much as one's liberty, and faith.**

When speaking about homes, the problems of the "family" as a significant unit enter into our analysis in the housing of people.

Yet, what is a family?

Certainly it is not a constant quantity. It begins with the marriage of two; it might remain a matter of these two, or it might well grow in number (yet how many?); then it begins to branch out and diminish, till two are left over, or only one, for some time. As we see, this matter of family is an utterly changeable quantity. It calls, therefore, for flexibility of accommodation. Hence, trying to establish permanence of conditions with the family as a unit of standardized size is not a logical procedure—the less does it lead to stabilization.

Let us try an example:

Consider, for instance, the case of the Jones family. Let's assume that Jones and his wife are in humble economic circumstances, affording them but a little bit of a dwelling cramped between others with no possibility of enlargement. The situation is not so bad, provided the house and the garden are kept neatly in order and the family is continuously limited to these two. But, supposing the family is growing in number. In such a case, the situation might eventually become unbearable—particularly if further family growth were to be expected. Poor Jones would then be compelled to build or to buy a larger dwelling and to sell the old, probably with a loss. Having done this, supposing that our man Jones would some day lose his job and be offered another in a far-away community. In order to make things work, this would mean a new deal involving building or buying and selling, probably again with a new and additional loss.

This Jones story is but one of many. Perhaps it is more drastic than the average. Yet, it is telling, and we must accept its advice. This does not mean, however, that our argument is against home-ownership, for most certainly home-ownership is the best way of making a house into a home; provided, of course, that one can afford to own the house, to keep it, and to make use of it as a permanent home. In other words, home-ownership must make life delightful—not burdensome. With this presupposition, we will accept the home-ownership system in the solution of housing problems in the town-community. In fact, we are willing to accept any system, **on condition that it grows from actual habits of living, that it is used in the right proportion and spirit, and that it is instrumental in the solution of housing problems toward stabilization of values.**

Housing problems can be solved along many different lines, all of these having their advantages—nota bene, as said, they spring directly from respective conditions of life. As a balance against individual home-ownership, the apartment building with apartments for rent ought to be mentioned. This already is, in a certain way, a step toward a flexible solution of housing problems, since it offers the opportunity freely to select and re-select one's habitat. Another solution is the row-house-system which provides the individual apartment with an attached garden of private nature. In case this kind of a system is based on one ownership of land and building—as is the case with the apartment building system of housing—this would offer enough of flexibility to move in and out without the troubles of buying and selling. Many do prefer more privacy than this system could offer, yet with the freedom of moving in and out at one's pleasure. This again would mean a housing development with individual dwellings under one ownership of both land and houses. In case such a system is planned with dwellings of a great variety of size and number of rooms, it guarantees maximum flexibility.

Supposing now that our friend Jones—to return again to his restless case—were to rent the tiniest little dwelling in a housing development of the kind just described; his family of two were then excellently accommodated. Yet, if, because of family growth, he later on would stand in need of additional room space, it would be the simplest thing for the housing management to offer another more suitable dwelling and to transfer his furnishings there; and so, in less than no time, our man Jones would happily light his pipe in this new abode. Equally comfortably he would settle his affairs if obliged to take over a new job somewhere else—provided "somewhere else" had developed a similar housing scheme— and he would give his full benediction to the described system of housing. We, on our part, are inclined to do the same: because of the system's flexibility in offering suitable conditions to any family changes; because of the system's simplicity insofar as financial entanglements are concerned; and because of the system's possibility of reducing living costs, yet making living endurable.

Housing problems are primarily social problems, and as such they must be conceived and solved. Yet, because social conditions vary very much, depending on what countries and cities are considered, no rules can be settled as to which systems should be used and in what ratios they should be respectively employed.

Considering things at large, the situation at present seems to be as follows. In Europe the prevailing trend is the apartment building system of housing; in the United States, on the other hand, the individual house—privately owned— is the most favored way of housing, although even here the tendency is moving toward group-ownership in one form or another. However, it must be borne in mind that we are just now in the midst of a time of transition where new viewpoints and inclinations are in the making. Housing problems in particular are much dependent on these new viewpoints and inclinations; particularly they, then, must be so directed in present day planning work that any possibility is left open for future solution in accordance with future viewpoints and inclinations.

Accordingly, we do wisely in refraining from any positive advice—which might prove to be correct in certain instances, but incorrect in hundreds of others. If, notwithstanding this, we were to try the safest middle course, we would put it as follows: **the more privacy, quietness, and livability one can buy with least expense and least entanglements in economic troubles caused by changes in work and family conditions, the better the housing problems have been solved; and the more protected one's home and environment are against intrusion from without, the better the planning problems have been solved.**

This is not a novel thought. Yet it contains plenty of food for reflection; and the more those concerned do meditate upon this outlined thought, the better they can solve their problems, each one in his own community to fit the community's own specific conditions. This, we think, would suit everyone, no matter in what circumstances and in which country he happens to live. For, inside of the above presupposition, a large range of possibilities is concealed. These possibilities must be disclosed and then developed so as to achieve satisfactory conditions for everyone in the most flexible manner. It is up to everyone to discover and disclose the concealed according to his own best knowledge. And in this respect he must learn to know that no standardized systems could or should be blindly followed. He must, furthermore, learn to know that **"creative thinking" is the best and only real key to the secrets of good housing.**

Now, if we were to stake the road toward the most plausible solution of housing in accordance with the above-outlined thought, we would first of all recommend—as a basic idea for common concern and average use—the well-organized and substantially-built community unit of one-ownership of land: communal, corporate, co-operative, or private. In such a community unit—consisting of one or several super-blocks—the conveniences of modern life can be embodied, moderated, and modulated to suit everyone. In such a community unit, disturbances such as land-value fluctuations or speculation of any kind cannot exist. In such a community unit, the dangers of decay into slums are eliminated, provided proper planning has surrounded the development with protective belts of free-land. In such a community unit, a good form-unity can be had, provided its design is put into right hands, as it should be. Furthermore, in such a community unit, the balance between physical accommodation and living expenses can be made favorable to the dweller, provided the management is good.

Yet the most essential point in such a community unit is that its location has been selected in accordance with the general scheme of organic decentralization and its functional considerations, which presupposes that the daily contact between the home and the working place is made functionally satisfactory. This eliminates the constant rushing hither and thither, it makes living in the community unit quiet and human and, therefore, it has the possibilities of making homes of houses.

Although housing problems are the most important civic problems, insofar as healthy and livable atmosphere in the city is concerned, they have but seldom been carried out with enough care. Even when the efforts have been sincere, the methods of approach have not always been the best.

Please, observe this:

First: how often is a new housing development—slum

clearance for the most part, perhaps—protected against early decay caused by a decayed neighborhood? Second: how often is the housing location selected from the point of view of organic growth and functional relationship? Third: how often are land-values seriously considered so as to make the housing development economically sound? And because land-values are often out of proportion, then, as a matter of balance, another danger is pushed into the fore—"low-cost housing." It is a well known fact that this is bound to mean poorly constructed buildings, cheap building material, and costly maintenance. Moreover, it means short and unfavorable loans, making the interest rate comparatively high. And finally, it means early deterioration. Really, how could another result be expected, when a "poorly constructed building is erected in an unprotected neighborhood on an economically unsound basis!"

It is not difficult to understand why "low-cost housing" has come about. Its psychology is this: "What is the use of building substantially in conditions which are predestinated to early decay because of lack of protection; isn't it then wiser to build temporarily in temporary circumstances?" "Low-cost housing," also, is a child nursed by such planning as cannot offer protection.

We are not interested in unprotected "low-cost housing" on high-cost land with short-term loans, for to encourage this is much the same as to encourage slums. **Our concern must be to get substantially-built and protected "low-rent housing," because of low-cost land and long-term loans.** These are the presuppositions on which to establish economically advantageous housing. Through these presuppositions, slums can be prevented—and, consequently, the physical and spiritual stabilization of the community achieved. Yet these presuppositions for stabilization can be obtained only under the supposition that the community at large is undergoing the process of organic decentralization. For, as has been more than often stressed, **organic decentralization with its**

protective measures is the only way to, and warrant of, value-stabilization.

C. TECHNICAL APPROACH

Although organic decentralization is the only effective process in the bringing of order into the overgrown cities, much mistrust exists as to the possibility of actual rehabilitation along decentralization methods. Most of this mistrust is concentrated about the economic problems, which in fact are the nuclei on which decentralization hinges.

Our next step, therefore, must be to find a suitable mode of approach to these revaluation problems, in order to change the said mistrust into the conviction that organic decentralization is not a mere ghost, but a real body of flesh and blood, with a backbone of sound economy. It is furthermore important to make, **just of this mode of approach itself,** that very means by which to convince people of the possibilities of an actual realization of decentralization problems in a manner which can result in all-sided satisfaction. It might be true, perhaps, that the most direct way of reaching this goal would be to try the decentralization principles on actual town-building, so as to gather experience through practical realities rather than through theoretical generalities. However logical such a thought may sound, it must be borne in mind that in "practical realities" organic decentralization is a slow process and, therefore, a considerable time would be needed before the experience gained could constitute enough material to be convincing. Matters being so, it is necessary for the time being to lean upon illuminating reasoning. For such a purpose we will venture to build up a suggestive mode of approach, showing by this how a comprehensive lay-out can be dissected into its minute particles—which latter are easy to grasp, individually—and then by fitting these particles together into the comprehensive layout, make the whole easily understandable as a gradual process during a long period of time. This mode of approach, we think, would bring light into the situation. For it is the comprehensiveness of the decentralization process which fosters hesitation.

1. Tentative Scheme:

Organic decentralization was compared with a water spot which by the swift motion of the finger tip was splashed around the surface of the table, forming concentrated spots here and there. It was a quick action symbolizing the decentralized city of the future. Relatively quick would also be the action if some town-designer should work out a tentative lay-out of some particular overgrown city, demonstrating the city's possible future development toward organic decentralization. Yet, this relatively quick action, laid out on paper, would quite likely appear unconvincing to many, because of the comprehensiveness of the scheme—and because of their own lack of vision.

see
page
382

But, supposing the town-designer should make his layout intelligible—even to those lacking vision—by working out in a tentative manner a series of sequential charts, each one of them suggesting the actions to be taken during a certain short period—say, during one to five years—in order to show how the whole would evolve step by step from the existing confused compactness toward the proposed organic decentralization. With the aid of these charts it would not be difficult to explain the step-by-step value-changes and adjustments on the urban territory at large. Every year would show both value-decrease and increase. Every year would reveal the logical striving to constructive value-equilibrium so as to make value-decreases counterbalanced with value-increases. Supposing, furthermore, that a film were produced of this series of sequential charts, indicating in readable terms the gradual shifting and balancing of values, and then the film were unrolled at a slow tempo, thus to make the individual and collective value-shiftings appear in correct sequence, step by step. To grasp such a slowly-running symbolic decentralization would not require much vision, we believe. It would not be any more the much-feared dream-scheming of unattainable impossibilities. Rather, it would be just a step-by-step, year-after-year suggested execution of plainly practical and economically commonplace matters-of-fact. Yet, this step-by-step, year-after-year suggested execution of commonplace matters-of-fact, demanding no vision, would be directed according to a certain lay-out, studied in advance—which latter of course would presuppose vision.

In the above manner this broadly inclusive lay-out of organic decentralization would have been dissected into its particles—into rather easily discernible petty things such as usually belong to the yearly routine of civic improvements and corresponding budgetary considerations. The only difference—**and what a difference**—is that the petty things of yearly routine, as encountered in usual practice, are independent actions of immediate nature leading either nowhere or only a few steps forward; whereas the organically coherent petty things of a comprehensive lay-out would constitute a gradual evolution along a staked course toward a distinct goal. Things being so, it would seem that even the most inveterate short-sightedness could realize the difference between these two modes of approach.

As to this short-sightedness, we might add still another point. It concerns particularly those who do not believe that the actions of present day vision can cover the demands of coming events.

When we speak about a long-range tentative lay-out for the city's future development, we naturally mean a scheme which is flexible enough to allow necessary corrections as conditions change and new demands make themselves felt. Thus, when the building of the city actually proceeds in its course, those corrections in the sequential charts of the tentative lay-out of vision, which must be undertaken year after year, must be recorded even in the tentative lay-out itself so as to bring this lay-out of vision into agreement with the actual facts of reality. In this manner, as the years pass by and the decentralization process goes on, the city's actual development and the tentative lay-out of vision are brought more and more into harmony one with another—and ultimately into full accord. (Refer to Fig. 50.)

As we see, the matter of long-range planning is none of esoterics or prophecies, when reduced to its details.

Indeed, there are many things in life that the untrained mind cannot grasp because matters are presented in too large a scope before the idea of the details has been made evident. It is much the same as it would be to buy great quantities of some particular merchandise before it had been made clear whether or not this merchandise really could be useful in small quantities during a long period of time.

Or, let us take another illuminating parallel.

Supposing a child never had seen a cow, nor had heard about such an animal, and then someday a cow were introduced to him as prospective food; undoubtedly the child would shout, "No, that's too big for me to swallow." But if the master-butcher should invite the child to his butcher shop to attract him with displays of meat, sausages, and other delicious things, one wonders how many cows the child might then undertake to consume during his lifetime.

Now, the child's lifetime might be about as long as is the time needed for making organic decentralization, if not an accomplished fact, at least far advanced toward the goal. **It is up to the town-designer to be the enlightening master-butcher.**

However, the dissection of the large tentative lay-out is not for public enlightenment only. It is just as indispensable a part of the general conception as is the general conception itself. The town-designer's mode of approach, therefore, must run along these two lines: first, he must grasp the whole as an imaginative picture of future possibilities; and second, he must visualize the details of this picture as constructive realities. In other words: during the progress of organic decentralization, every individual property must be conceived as an economically healthy feature in an economically healthy living organism.

In this cautious and constructive manner the town-designer's double scheming—from the whole to the detail, and from the detail to the whole—is able to convince first himself of the soundness of his action, and then the public. This is important, for conviction gives strength inwardly. Outwardly it means authority. And only through the power of authority can the town-designer direct the city toward order.

2. Transference of Property Rights:

Speaking of conviction, there is still an additional question to be answered—a question of decisive nature. The question is this: can there be found a leading thought, according to which revaluation can be made advantageous to the land-owners individually, and to the city itself as well? It is obvious that unless an acceptable answer to this question can be had, the town-people could not be convinced of the economic soundness of the decentralization movement, nor could the town-designer obtain the necessary authority to make the movement work.

It is a matter of course that the efforts of decentralization must be concentrated primarily to correct the circumstances where property values have been depreciated because of decay from within or because of blighted neighborhoods. And because disorderly compactness in the city is the reason for such conditions, the correction must then happen by the breaking up of this compactness in one way or another. The most logical way—so it seems—is to undertake the necessary adjustments by shifting property rights from decayed locations to healthy ones. This suggests that **"transference of** property rights from one location to another" must be the leading thought in the city's rehabilitation process, economic and otherwise. For this purpose, a method must be found along which to carry out this transference—actually, technically, economically, and legally.

To illustrate the situation, may we consider the following example.

Let us assume that someone owns a piece of property which according to existing zoning regulations can be used, say, for apartment building purposes only. Let us still assume that the said property had lost, during the city's disarranged growth, much of the original suitability for its purpose—due to increasing noise, functional confusion, blight, low quality of the new invading population, and many other negative circumstances which, by their combined force, would point toward continuous decline. Now the value of the property in question is based: first, on the land-area itself which, because of the downward tendency of the neighborhood, is doomed continuously to depreciate; second, on its relative location in the general plan-pattern of the city, insofar as communicative connections and other circumstances of convenience are concerned, which qualities most likely have become less efficient thanks to the growing confusion; and third, on the existing structure on the site. The value of the existing structure, however, would be reduced year-by-year, till someday it would be necessary to erect a new one in order to have a reasonable revenue from the property in question.

Assuming now that when the time for the erection of a new structure had actually arrived, the community were in a position to offer several sites, on new areas which had been orderly planned and properly protected, from which the land-owner could at his pleasure choose one fully equivalent with his present property as to size, zoning regulations, communicative advantages, and other considerations of material nature. This already would constitute a full compensation, it would seem. With regard to appreciative values, on the other hand, the situation would be different. Because of the fact that the new property would be situated in an organized section of the city, qualities such as restfulness, air, light, comfort, and amenity would turn the balance of values much to the favor of the new property. In addition to this, the value of the new property, thanks to the protective measures of forward planning, would be stabilized for years to come. In other words, the new property offered by the community would be preferable from every point of view.

Now, we ask: wouldn't this be a fair offering from the community's point of view, and advantageous to the property owner?

Certainly!

Consequently, no ethical hesitations should exist to question why the present property under such circumstances could not be changed to another in accordance with the above idea of transference of property rights, or condemned —if such a step were necessary—by virtue of advanced civic legislation, and passed to the community after a certain length of time, convenient for both parties.

Transference of property rights such as described is nothing especially new. In fact, it is much the same as the common practice of trading old things for new ones, where the new is a gain to the new owner and the old useful to the trader. The described transference, however, might serve as an example of urban property-trading on which to build a system. Also, by means of an intelligent and well-organized system of the above kind, the key might be found to unlock the gates of decentralization.

We selected deliberately an example with a structure still good enough to be useful for some time to come, although located in a blighted environment. We did so in order to introduce the time dimension into the process of transference of property rights. The decentralization movement requires a considerable length of time, and during this time many buildings which at present are still in good condition are doomed to decay because of decayed environment. It is an easy matter to predict the fate of such buildings and, consequently, they might as well already now be embodied into the system of transference of property rights. This broadens the field of action. It offers more freedom in the planning work. Yet it prevents the immediate destruction of relatively good buildings.

However, transference of property rights does not concern individual properties only. To a great extent it concerns large blighted areas, slums, and other undesirable developments. We might in this respect refer again to a passage which was already cited in another connection from a report of the New York Master Plan. This passage is most indicative, and it reads as follows: "Recent trends in building-design and site-planning indicate that obsolescence of existing structures may proceed faster than has been the case to date, as people are rapidly becoming accustomed to thinking in terms of good large-scale developments. The process of rebuilding is therefore expected to take place not lot by lot as in the past, but whole blocks and groups of blocks at a time." This is perfectly logical, for as the decay into slums has run in terms of mass-production, so, likewise, must the rehabilitation of these slums run in a corresponding scale of mass-production. But the thing we are particularly interested in, as regards the rehabilitation of these large decayed areas, is that the rebuilding process must happen in accordance with decentralization principles. In other words, in the rehabilitation of those mentioned "blocks and groups of blocks," **the rebuilding must not necessarily happen on this same decayed location, but elsewhere in concert with the demands of decentralization.** This means a large-scale transference of property rights from the decayed areas to such new areas as are more suitable for the rebuilding development.

On the other hand, transference of property rights does not mean only a shifting from decayed areas to new ones. Due to the fact that the decentralization movement is a double one—a movement from decayed areas within the city into new developments about the city, and a counter-movement in order to rehabilitate the decayed areas within the city with new developments—transference of property rights, consequently, means also an inter-shifting of these rights in agreement with the predetermined organic pattern. On the whole, also, the transference of property rights works like a jig-saw puzzle, where the right location of the various sections must be found according to how they fit into the general picture.

The problems of transference of property rights are closely connected with those of land-value, as any shifting in the one brings about a corresponding shifting in the other.

As for this matter of land-value, we have earlier indicated, in passing, that land as such has no particular value: it is the use to which this land has been put and its relative location in the town pattern which constitute the value. It was likewise indicated that, because of a long-enduring concentration, the conception has been thoroughly ingrained in the general attitude of mind that "land" and "land-use" are inseparably one and the same thing; whereas now the growing tendency to decentralization must gradually bring about corresponding adjustments in this conception. For, when the actual decentralization takes place, simultaneously with this process transference of property rights must be effected by separating land-use from its former site and transferring it to a new site. Consequently, in the vocabulary of decentralization, the term "land-value" must be changed to "land-use-value" so as to make the term more expressive of its new meaning in contemporary civic development.

At what rate this change from the concentrated conception of "land-value" to that new decentralized conception of "land-use-value" will happen in actual practice, one cannot tell. But undoubtedly in this case things are bound to develop acceleratingly, even as they seem to do in many other phases of civic development. The above cited passage from the New York case which says, among other things, that ". . . people are rapidly becoming accustomed to thinking in terms of good large-scale developments," means presumably that people did not think so yesterday, that they begin to think so today, and that tomorrow they will consider it the most natural thing. Similarly, in the case of transference of property rights—and "land-use-values"—one might soon find that, although the matter might seem radical today, it might be accepted tomorrow, and after-tomorrow it might be a common practice.

Why shouldn't it be? For, once the matter has been made clear to the people, and those dwelling in decayed areas get the notion that there is an opportunity for them to have their decayed circumstances metamorphosed without economic sacrifice into flourishing environment, they would greet such an opportunity with general acceptance. What if there appeared unexpectedly an opportunity to have one's worn-out clothes changed into utterly new ones without additional cost? Indeed, there would develop a rush, for no one would like to miss such a glorious chance.

Yet, what's the difference?

D. LAND PROBLEMS

On the whole, transference of property rights means compensation with new property values in terms of urban land. Because of the fact, however, that a great part of those lands to be used for compensation are to be found on the enlarged urban territory, this means that the city should dispose of wide land areas in order to make the said transference practically and economically sound. Whether the city should own all those lands coming into question during the progress of decentralization, or whether it is sufficient for the city to control land prices, depends much on local conditions. However this may be, the land problems must be analyzed from these two points of view: "communal land ownership," and "communal control of land price."

1. Communal Land Ownership:

Looked at from the angle of practical management, the city is a comprehensive business enterprise, and therefore must be conducted according to sound business practice. Now, an important part of civic business practice is—or should be— the city's land policy. In this respect, speaking in metaphors, the city is a refinery of rural areas into urban lands. This is true particularly during a lively decentralization movement, for the farther outward the decentralization movement is stretched, the broader are those territories needed in this gradual change from rural areas into urban ones.

Now we ask, "Should the city own enough of those surrounding rural territories—the raw material to be refined— in order to make its business practice economically logical?" Well, should an industrial concern own enough of the sources of its raw material to make its manufacturing economically logical? In case the sources of raw material are close to the plant, we should say, "Yes." And so are things mostly arranged as far as this is possible. Consequently, in the city's case the answer must be affirmative; that is, the city should own sufficient rural land area about its urban developments, **and this is just as logical a procedure as that the brickmanufacturer should own enough clay about his mill to make brick-manufacturing economically sound.**

"Now," it might be asked, "if communal land-ownership is as clear as that, why then are not things carried out accordingly?" This is a fair question. It is not thought necessary to dig deep into civic history to understand why things with regard to communal land ownership have come down to us as a preconceived habit. During the days of compulsory concentration, communal land-ownership was of no vital consequence, as is easy to understand. Later on, when the town tended to expansion, the problem of land-ownership was raised to another plane. The logical action in these changed circumstances, naturally, should have been that the community had secured for itself those land areas needed for sound expansion. But as the speculator's minds—we suspect—were more alert than the sleepy minds of civic officials, things were handled as they were, and the results are as they are.

Although compulsory concentration was the chief historical reason for the negligence of communal land-ownership, other historical reasons, too, were effective—and these reasons were differently effective in different countries. The United States, for example, presents quite a specific situation of her own. Here, the restricting forces of compulsory concentration had less to do with the psychology of communal land-policy—but so much the more had the unrestricted freedom of the pioneering mind to do with it. In those exploring days, when the ruthless pioneer-land-speculator got the sanguine notion that at every new intersection of railroad lines a new town was bound to be born with much profit for the shrewd, he planted the seed in the soil from which the present unhappy real-estate-psychology has grown. From here originates likewise the backward idea that land-areas in and about the town are not for the sake of the town community itself, but for the smart man to make money with.

As to matters in general, it must be admitted with satisfaction that the past decades have witnessed attempts to correct previous negligences. In many a country, the idea of communal land-ownership has gained much ground. This surely is encouraging, for once the idea has become rooted as a general understanding of how these matters must be conducted, no doubt it will spread itself. The growing pressure of decentralization is all the more apt to foster such a trend.

2. Communal Control of Land Price:

If the city does not own sufficient land-areas, there is still the other alternative: communal control of land-price. Even as regards this, we seem to harbor the happy notion that our forefathers have fixed things for us. But the growing pressure of decentralization will gradually show that things cannot be taken as lightheartedly as that, and that we must take care of our own affairs ourselves. To that end, we must first of all learn to know how and according to what considerations urban land-prices must be decided.

Here we have a similar situation between rural and urban lands as was the case with communal land-ownership, for here, too, land refinement from rural lands into urban ones takes place. And, because land-areas are shifted in this manner from one category to another, the question is, "Which of these categories should be the basis for land valuation: the rural or the urban, the present or the future?"

Now, does the painter pay an art-price for his canvas or the sculptor for his marble block, just because the brush or the chisel eventually will increase the values of these respective materials? Surely not! The price of material—raw-material—must be fixed according to its own quality, and not according to what someone sometime might or might not produce out of this material by efforts and talents of his own. This is true in any circumstances where material is refined from one state to another. Rural land-areas about the city are no exceptions to this rule. The price level of rural lands, therefore, must be figured according to the suitability of these lands for rural purposes, and not according to what revenue some future building might or might not bring in.

"But"—someone might question—"doesn't the price level of building-ground depend much on the interrelation between demand and availability; and isn't this likely to be particularly the case in the growing cities where demand for building-grounds is constantly increasing, while access to suitable grounds does not always keep pace with this increase. Consequently, the greater the demand is, the higher are the prices apt to run." This reasoning is fully logical, and according to it have land-prices been established in and about the expanding cities. There is, however, this to be added: it must be borne in mind that our discussion does not concern civic expansion as generally understood, but merely organic decentralization. While the cities' expansion went on slowly, compactly, and evenly—as would thick porridge spread its coherent substance along the table surface—it was quite natural that land-prices were bound to rise accordingly. But organic decentralization does not use porridge as its fluid of illustration: it uses water, **for water splashes just as easily and rapidly as move modern means of transportation; and as easily and rapidly can new values be created, way behind the porridge line.** The porridge line, on the other hand, might easily be planned into free-lands of protection. And according to which standards should free-land be valued?

For sure, the caprices of an active decentralization are not so simple to forecast as are those land problems of compact growth. It is therefore a logical procedure that decentralization-land-prices be settled in accord with the thought that the present use of land must constitute the basis for valuation. And in accordance with this same thought must legislation be adjusted to assist and establish the city's control of land price.

E. ILLUMINATING EXAMPLE: CHICAGO

On the whole, we have finished our analysis of revaluation. It might now be illuminating to apply the results of this analysis to actual conditions, much in the same manner as we did previously when organic decentralization was the object of our study. Even now, as was the case then, we must begin with the remark **that the intention with the following is not to offer advice to those concerned in actual planning, but** merely to explain how essentials must be applied to planning work in any circumstance.

In the case of organic decentralization, New York was selected as the object of our examination, because it offered perhaps the most complex situation. Now we are going to try the problems of Chicago, not because Chicago is the next largest city in the United States, but because, as far as we know, it has of all cities the largest substandard area in the heart of its compact body. Therefore it stands in need of surgery, and of revaluation. Before going further, however, we see it necessary to make a few comments regarding earlier attempts to establish a suitable plan for Chicago. By this we mean, in the first place, the so-called Burnham Plan, laid out a few decades ago. Whether this plan still is valid or not makes no difference in our case, for we mention the said layout only because we wish to make it clear that the following application of planning essentials to the present conditions in Chicago is neither in opposition to the Burnham Plan, nor is it necessarily in accord with it. We have no reason for taking sides in the matter, because the two problems, Burnham's and ours, are two entirely different things. The Burnham Plan is an elaborate work of civic embellishment of the Haussmannian order. Our study is a mere example of how a certain planning method could be used in a particular case —as we look upon things. The Burnham Plan is a rather formal pattern of boulevards, plazas, and parks. Our study is only a direction of thought dealing with the problems of revaluation, with transference of property rights, and with the protection of values.

Generally speaking, this same applies likewise to all that planning work which has been accomplished within the limits of Greater Chicago, which work—as we happen to know —is in many respects creditable indeed.

At large, the situation in Chicago is as follows:
The magnificent park-belt bordering the shores of the

great Lake Michigan is the supreme pride of the city. This park-belt runs almost with an unbroken continuity throughout the whole Lake Front, beginning in the South from Jackson Park and vanishing in the North into the far distance, finally melting together with the wooded lands of the many and delightful northern suburbs. It really is impressive to drive along this tremendous development, with the vividly pulsing life on its driveways contrasting with the restful line of the Lake's emerald. Surely, it was a great achievement of unusual proportions to have conceived the scheme; still more so to have carried it out.

However, when comparing this Lake Front Development with the large areas of the city itself, one cannot refrain from wondering why the face was washed, while the heart remained dark and cruel. For, indeed, the city itself has been neglected.

While the shores were filled and planted, the Burnham Plan had but little influence upon the city itself. The Burnham Plan suggested a restful unity of building masses insofar as the three-dimensional treatment of the city is concerned. If this idea had been followed, at least as the leading thought —with the skyscrapers now and then entering in as rhythmic accords—much could have been added to the beautification of the city. As things are now, however, the forest of skyscrapers cuts its rich silhouette into the Western sky quite at random, and the whole reminds one much of a badly broken comb. During the nocturnal hours, to be fair, the effect is imposing, as the buildings themselves fade into the embracing darkness and thousands of lights glitter.

Beyond this forest of skyscrapers, a vast urban desert of factory grounds, railroad yards, and residential areas spreads itself. It is gloomy and depressive, and one wonders why it must be so and why it could not have been prevented.

Yet the result was inevitable, as things came to pass.

Long before Chicago became the great city of today, many factories were built in the outskirts of the city and along the river so as to have adequate means of water transportation. Parallel with this development, a great number of railroad companies grouped their track-yards and similar accommodations close by, offering their services to the growing industry and to the expanding city itself. So was the start; and accordingly things continued to develop. The factories and the railroads alike spread their plants and yards in ratio as the city grew. The more the city grew, the more the factory grounds and the railroad yards were changed from outside activities about the city into inside disturbances within the city. Thus things tightened—became compact and confused. There was no flexibility in the planning and no protection of what already existed. Matters were doomed to develop the way they have developed—and still seem to develop.

The growing compactness and confusion affected even the round-about residential districts, which now face an inevitable gradual deterioration. Now this substandard residential district embraces, alas, about forty to fifty square miles of urban territory, conservatively estimated. It might be true that this area in question is not as yet a thorough slum district; it might be even true that some slum clearance projects have already been developed here, and that others are under development, and still others are perhaps under consideration; but it is equally and inevitably true that this area in question is doomed eventually to become a desert of slums—for piecemeal patching will never work. Already it is the urban cancer center which threatens the whole city. A thorough-going surgery, therefore, is the **only** solution.

West and South of this district of urban desert, we find newer settlements that are still in a good condition. But, even here, occasional deterioration indicates the downward trend, and the neighbor slums, steadily approaching, threaten with their contagiousness. Unless conditions in these settlements are maintained in good order, and unless they are protected against dangers from without, surely the following generation will see it necessary to range these districts, too, among those to be put under surgical treatment.

Beyond the city's boundaries, Cook, Dupage, and Well counties open their lands, which, generally speaking, are still to a great extent virgin. They are eagerly waiting for the city's further expansion. We are eager, on our part, to know what this expansion eventually is going to mean. Perhaps it is going to mean the old story in a logical sequence and in the following manner: speculation causing rise of land-value, rise of land-value causing compactness, compactness causing confusion, confusion causing decline, and then, slums. So things really are doomed to go, unless in due time a dam is built to prevent the city's noxious flood from overflowing these lands also. Those who have followed the course of events—who know what has happened, why it has happened, and what will happen if matters continue to go as they have gone hitherto —are anxious to see what will be done to save these said country lands from a ruinous fate. They are anxious to see this, **for they know perfectly well that just these country lands are Chicago's only salvation.**

So much about the situation as it is at present.

Now that we are about to apply the principles of revaluation and the mode of transference of property rights to the situation in Chicago, the surgical instrument must first of all remove the perils caused by the afore-mentioned substandard desert in the heart of the city. In order to start right, however, it is of importance to review the development of the city's malady in the past. In this respect, we need not go farther back in the history of the city than to those days when Chicago's first slum clearance was proposed in the early seventies by the O'Leary cow. It was in that great fire of Chicago when much of the city was devastated, and after which much had to be rebuilt. Yet, however it was rebuilt, this is a cold fact: most of the structures which now exist on the substandard area were erected since that great fire, say, during the past sixty or seventy years. Moreover, this is another cold fact: almost all of the structures existing now on the said area must be replaced with new ones during, say, sixty or seventy years to come—to use an equally although unnecessarily long term toward the future. This means that a correspondingly extensive and entirely new urban development—insofar as territory and cubage of building masses are concerned—must be constructed during the period to come. Yet behold likewise this cold fact: this construction work will be good only to substitute for the dilapidated areas in question, and not as any provision for the rest of the population—least of all for Chicago's expected further growth.

These are the cold facts which the good Chicagoans cannot escape just by a shrug of shoulders. So that is that. But what we now are particularly concerned about is the question of how this reconstruction work will be approached. Will it be done phlegmatically as a matter of routine replacement, just as nonchalantly as one replaces old tires on his car with new ones? Or will the problem of rehabilitation be thoroughly investigated before the actual reconstruction work begins?

Supposing now that the substitution for the old structures of new ones should happen on the same decayed area, or on areas randomly selected as most conveniently had at the moment; supposing again that the rehabilitation work should go on in the usual compact manner without any organization according to functional considerations or preventive measures such as flexibility and protection, just as things have gone hitherto; supposing, furthermore, that the reconstruction work should be carried on in the same spiritless and gloomy fashion of mere walls and roofs for physical protection, as housing developments have so often been carried out thus far and as the discouraging practice seems still to go on; and finally, supposing that things should happen in this phlegmatic manner during the long period of sixty or seventy years to come: what would be the ultimate result of all this?

Well, what has been the result of the work done during the past sixty or seventy years, notwithstanding the fact that conditions in Chicago during the past sixty or seventy years, as regards compactness and confusion, were not nearly as bad as they are at present. Or—to take a parallel example—what would be the result if one were to erect a building by lining and piling rooms just casually and gradually without any consideration as to functional organization? Wouldn't the result be mere confusion, with the consequence that a thorough-going reconstruction of the whole according to an organic plan would become a compelling need? Indeed, any action, small or big, must be thought out before it is carried out; and the more comprehensive the action, the more consideration it demands. This surely is true in as comprehensive and gradual an organization as the city. Therefore, if we were to picture conditions in Chicago sixty or seventy years hence, with that promiscuous mode of rehabilitation above described, surely the picture would exhibit promiscuous results such as blighted areas and slums. So there we would be. Much money would have been spent, many slums would have been cleared, many housing projects would have been actualized, many buildings would have been erected—and yet each action would have amounted to much the same thing as to establish values on premises inevitably bound to bring early depreciation. What would have been gained by this? Simply, that sixty or seventy years hence one would stand just as one stands now: it would be urgently necessary to start over again, in spite of the work already done and the money spent. Yet, believe it or not, **the slum areas, then, would be much larger and more widely spread than they are now. And this is not just a loose guess, but the logic of inevitable processes in all creation.**

Surely, the past decades do not contradict this.

In those days when Chicago's famous cow got disgusted with the disorderly conditions of her home town, the population of the town was only one tenth of the present number.

Also, much has been built since then. If the Chicagoans of those days had taken advice implicit in the cow's significant action, and if they had thought things over—as the Chicagoans of today should have learned to do—the situation in present-day Chicago would be relatively good. But what is the difference between then and now as far as the citizens' obligation to keep their city in good order is concerned? The cow is gone, that is true, and nobody is inclined to play with fireworks in the same manner as did she. But as effective as fireworks is the public power to condemn inadequate living and working conditions in the city. It is only necessary to raise the border line of minimum requirements to a decent level, and then to condemn things below that level to be done away with.

Of course, everyone knows all this, and someday things must be settled accordingly, and on a large-scale, too. But before this can be done, it is important first to know how it should be done—for it cannot happen at random, as we have just learned, and as the good Chicagoans should have learned already long, long ago.

Now, if we were to fancy our own mode of approach to the Chicago case, we would refer to the previous investigations of organic decentralization and of revaluation as well, and then apply all the principles, rules, and essentials of these to the present conditions in Chicago. And we would approach our problem in the following manner.

In analyzing organic decentralization we learned that the movement must be based on a thoroughgoing research: research in this connection meaning "planning research" concerning the city's forward development, and not so much the usual research dealing with statistics and such like—which of course is also essential in any planning. Moreover, we learned that the movement must be free from such limitations as existing land-values and civic legislation. More than that, we learned that existing land-values and civic legislation themselves must be subject to research, and that both revaluation and relegislation must be logical results of this research.

Applying the above to the problems of Chicago, it is evident that a comprehensive and unified study of the areas of Chicago and its environs must be the first step to undertake. It is also evident that this study must be independent of those current civic affairs which must run their routine course on the basis of existing conditions—practical, physical, economic, and legal. It is likewise evident that limitations such as county boundaries and all the manifold regional stipulations should not hamper the freedom of this study. Furthermore, it is evident that this study should not be directed toward artificial beautification of the city and its environs by such means as have nothing in common with the city and its population. Rather, it must be directed so as to bring all the problems indigenously into organic solution in accordance with the best potentialities of the city. Therefore, the main objective must be an investigation of the best possibilities of organic decentralization as to "how" and "where" the various problems should be solved, respectively. In other words, the study in question must be a tentative and experimental planning with many and different ramifications, by means of which to find the most logical and likely solutions. From these solutions, the paramount results must constitute the material along which to direct the actual rebuilding of Chicago.

Supposing, now, that such a research work were already in process. In such case it would be up to the research institution itself to suggest the course of Chicago's rehabilitation.

But since this research work is not in process, at least—as far as we know—not in such a comprehensive and unified spirit of organic decentralization as has been above described, we might take a fancy to analyze Chicago's rehabilitation according to our own inclinations. For this reason, it would seem, we should first of all undertake the painstaking research work ourselves, before any positive suggestions could be made for the solution of the problems of Greater Chicago.

There is no need, however, for such a research work from our side, for we are **not** going to make any positive suggestions. Our problem is a mere explanation of certain thoughts, and therefore we can limit ourselves to a few such examples as might bring light into the nature of revaluation, not necessarily considering particularly Chicago, but cities in general. In order to simplify our task, we will confine ourselves to the substandard situation mentioned as existing in the heart of the city. And we will analyze the situation in the following manner.

Because things have, on the substandard area in question, during the passage of time become indiscriminately jumbled one into another, it is clear that this area needs to be subject to organic decentralization. Consequently, a great many of the present land-uses must undergo an organized change by means of a comprehensive transference of property rights.

On the whole, we have on this area four different **functional** values to consider: first, the river, which has lost all its charm as a river and which, in addition to this, is bringing considerable bewilderment to the street communication; second, the factories, which are ceaselessly bestowing their abundant blessings of smoke, dust, and grease upon the surrounding territories; third, the railroad system, which in the heart of the city cover incredibly broad areas of gloomy yards of tracks and more tracks; and fourth, the residential districts, which in many locations have become mingled with secondary and sundry business concentrations. Besides this, we have here three different **economic** values to consider: first, the present land-values which were already described as downbound; second, the future land-values which probably would continue their downbound course, provided adequate measures were not undertaken to prevent this; and third, the future rehabilitated land-values, provided forward planning should gradually metamorphose these decayed areas into flourishing areas of orderly neighborhood communities by transferring to these areas such property rights as are in harmony with the character of these communities. This latter point of transference of property rights "to" these areas, naturally, presupposes that property rights "from" here have already been transferred somewhere else in order to form there new communities.

Now, where should this "somewhere else" be?

To give an offhand answer to this question would presuppose that we had already undertaken the above described planning research—which we have not undertaken, of course —at least not as thoroughly as should be done. But if we were to try, in spite of this, a reasonable answer, we would be inclined—just as a mere illustration—to suggest certain land areas beyond the city limits, say, somewhere to the south.

As regards these areas, again, we have here four different **functional** values to consider: first, the possibility of having a fully modern waterway—connected with Lake Calumet perhaps; second, the possibility of having fully modern factory developments replacing those on the mentioned substandard area in the center, and concentrated at certain suitable points along the said waterway; third, the possibility of having here fully modern residential developments in good relation to the said industrial concentrations; and fourth, the possibility of having a green-belt system of free areas to protect these new developments in order to stabilize their respective values. In addition to this, we would have here likewise three different **economic** values to consider: first, the present land-values which are more or less of rural nature, depending of course on the selected location; second, the future uncertain land-values—which probably would be apt to go up due to unregulated expansion and then down due to growing disorder, provided such results had not been prevented by organic planning; and third, the future stabilized values, provided organic decentralization had been given the chance to direct things.

Assuming now that matters on these land-areas in the

center of the city and to the south as well had been gradually developed according to decentralization principles, the situation then, insofar as economic problems are concerned, would be about this.

To the south, the rural—or perhaps semi-rural—land-values would have been raised to urban ones; whereas, in the substandard district the depreciated land-values would have become rehabilitated. Also, there would be a land-value rise in both areas. There would also be in both areas a similar situation in the stabilization of these raised land-values. In the new industrial communities at the south, the stabilization of land-values would be a self-evident result, because organic planning with protective zones would have taken care of this automatically. Even on the rehabilitated areas this protective point would have proven to be true, for organic decentralization demands that even the individual neighborhood units must be separated one from another by means of protective measures of protective free land. This means that a park system would have to be planned here so as to divide the large areas of forty to fifty square miles into a number of segregated neighborhood units.

Also, in the long run—say, in sixty or seventy years, to stick to our time schedule—the outcome of the gradual reorganization of the areas concerned would exhibit, besides the mentioned economic points, the following situation.

At the south there would have been created new industrial communities in accordance with the best knowledge of contemporary town-design. Because these communities had been developed, relatively speaking, on new and virgin rural land, there would have been all the opportunity in the world to bring functional adequacy and three-dimensional order into the lay-outs. In other words, these communities could have been developed into model industrial garden communities of good order.

As regards the rehabilitated area in the heart of the city, on the other hand, one would have had a free hand to reorganize the present stereotyped and incessant gridiron lay-out into thoughtfully-planned communities. One would have been able to bring into this planning new ideas according to new demands and new ways of civic organization. Indeed, this would have offered the town-designer an excellent chance to convert the present substandard desert into an attractive development equivalent to the achievements along the Lake Front. By planning large sections of the river to become what a river with its river-banks really should be in the center of a well planned city, he could have brought just that much more delight into the scheme.

It is obvious of course that, if this above described large-scale transference of property rights from and to the oft-mentioned substandard area actually were carried out, there would be a corresponding shifting of the population. On one hand there would take place an emigration of people from this area, and on the other hand there would take place an immigration of people to this area. The emigration movement would free from the city's congestion a large number of people who, according to functional planning, should not have been living there and who now would find their living quarters in the new industrial garden communities and close to their working grounds. The immigration movement, on the other hand, would open possibilities of bringing to this area that type of people who would have functionally logical reasons for being close to the main business centers, but who due to the disorderly growth of the city had previously been compelled to find their living quarters somewhere else independently of functional relations. In this manner, as we see, these two movements would incline to bring into the city functional order. In the industrial garden-communities the satisfactory relationship between living quarters and industrial plants would eliminate much of the restless daily traveling and would therefore make these communities quiet and livable. The same would be the case in those new and many neighbor units in the central regions of the city. Undoubtedly such arrangements—if sometime carried out by forward far-sightedness—would prove to be of great future consequences to the people of Chicago.

In order to simplify our task as we analyzed the Chicago case, we confined ourselves to the substandard area in the heart of the city. Being a nucleus of the city's worries, this area as such is already a tremendous problem to solve. Yet tremendous or not, what does it matter, for sooner or later this problem must be solved in one way or another, in a direction that is right or wrong. Our aim has been only to sound a direction which according to our conviction is right. This is indeed an essential issue; for, in fact, we are inclined to believe that a right solution of this problem alone might prove to be the very solution of the whole urban complex of Greater Chicago. The clearance of as broad areas as are now in question, no doubt would put its stamp on the bulk of the city, and the rest would follow automatically in the wake.

Now we ask, "Is this problem too large a thing to handle?"

Surely not, provided the approach is right.

Let it so be that the clearance of the substandard desert seems too gigantic an undertaking: yet, in comparison with the work accomplished from the days of the illustrious cow to the present day, the undertaking really is nothing extraordinary. Let it so be that the undertaking calls for a tremendous amount of construction work and a vast number of transactions involving huge values: yet in comparison with the construction work done and the transactions carried out during the past sixty to seventy years, the undertaking is brought down to just commonplace routine work of months, years, and decades—which work, as said, must in any case go on in one form or another. Let it so be that the dimensions of the problem are too big fully to comprehend: yet the problem can be divided into sixty or seventy minor ones, easy to comprehend—or why not say into eighty as well, or a hundred, or even more if you please, for the number of years does not count in the long life of a city. Finally, let it so be that there still are hesitations as to the possibilities or impossibilities of carrying things through in accordance with decentralization principles: **yet to undertake a survey as to these possibilities or impossibilities is but a simple matter of intelligent decision.** Just in this simple matter of intelligent decision—**a very simple matter indeed**—the key to success is to be found in this Chicago case, even as it can be found in any circumstance where the road of progress must be prepared by human sensitiveness or intellect. Consider any walk of human life—social, economic, scientific, technical, commercial, or whatever it may be—**and you will find that the spirit of research is the driving motor of all that man has discovered, invented, and accomplished in terms of progress.**

We undertook this analytical examination of the Chicago case as a mere illuminating example of how revaluation and transference of property rights could be applied to urban rehabilitation in general. We do not mean by this that every city is in a similar situation to that of Chicago with its broad substandard area, and that exactly the same remedies should necessarily be applied elsewhere. We know perfectly well that there are great differences in this respect. There is a countless number of towns and cities, even relatively large ones, where the needed reconditioning can be achieved with less drastic methods. There are many towns and cities which need scarcely any reconditioning of consequence, and we could mention several such towns and cities. We could mention many of those delightful towns along the shores of New England. Going abroad, we could mention Stockholm with its many and long delightfully kept shores. We could mention Copenhagen with its many parks and lakes. However, we will limit ourselves to a single example—a rather conspicuous one, too, as far as concerns good order. We will take Münich, famous art city of art-loving King Ludwig I.

The urban body of München is just as healthy as it could be; its streets are neat and clean; its parks are large, delightful, and kept in remarkable order; and through all this the Isar River cuts its stream, reflecting parks and buildings in the watery mirror. The whole atmosphere of München breathes cleanliness, order, good taste, and much of art. Yet, in spite of all this, even München must be on its guard against compact growth which eventually might affect things just as compactness in the long run always affects. In other words, even München, in spite of its excellent order, must do its research planning in terms of organic decentralization. Through this research planning, undoubtedly, it soon will be made evident that certain sections here and there should be transferred somewhere else in order to bring more openness into the relatively compact body. It must be borne in mind that even München had its rapid growth during a period when concentration was largely of a compulsory nature and, therefore, sensible corrections here and there would rather help than bring harm. Moreover, even München has its satellite town developments, and these naturally must be directed toward an adequate functional relation to the whole in such a manner that they remain individual townships, surrounded by protective free areas.

Now, when all this is true in as orderly and healthy a city as München, it then shows all-the-more that every urban community of consequence, no matter whether conditions are bad or good, must consider its planning problems in terms of revaluation. **It must not be forgotten that the demand for openness, space, air, and light increases with time, and every town-community must keep pace with this increase.**

However, when the problems of a general "house-cleaning" in the spirit of organic revaluation are considered, this consideration hits primarily just that city which happens to be economically in bad shape, and the reaction is: "How could such a money-craving thing be even thought about when the city is on the verge of bankruptcy!" According to this reaction it happens frequently that planning-expenses, often already too limited, are cut down to the utmost—just because the economic situation is bad. **Isn't this just as intelligent a decision as to cut down the doctor's bills for the mere reason that someone is sick?**

Let's therefore ask a parallel question:

Why are so many business concerns in bad shape, while others seem to be prosperous and continue to do good business? Shouldn't just those business concerns which are in a bad shape seriously consider their situation in order to find out what should be done, and how it could be done best? Or should they stop thinking and say, "What's the use, nothing can be done anyhow."

Of course, they could quit.

But the city cannot quit. It must constantly go on, no matter what the conditions.

8.   RELEGISLATION

THE closing statement of the preceding chapter of revaluation maintained that cities are economically in bad shape because planning has been poor and insufficient. Civic administrations naturally must be blamed for their negligence in this respect. On the other hand, much of this negligence, we are sure, derives from the sad experience that sincere attempts at civic improvement are difficult to actualize and often virtually prohibitive, because of the existing civic legislation. This is true particularly in those cases where civic improvements are attempted in line with the ideals of decentralization. It must be borne in mind that the existing civic legislation is a child of concentration, and that it is nurtured accordingly, both as to its underlying philosophy and as to its ethical doctrines.

Far down in the Middle Ages, the groundwork was laid for the philosophy of rights and ethical standards in civic legislation. In some instances, this groundwork was laid to protect the interests of those having the power to enact protective ordinances for the benefit of themselves. In other instances, it was laid by the magistrates with the sincere aim of protecting the interests of the town people, generally and individually. But, however this groundwork was laid, it was laid with the assumption that concentration in the town was completely compulsory—a condition from which there was no escape, and should not be.

Later on, when the defensive reasons for the mediaeval concentration ceased to exist, concentration still remained compulsory during several centuries beyond the Middle

Ages, now merely for transportative reasons. Today, when conditions of life and means of transportation have turned the former compulsory concentration toward an indispensable decentralization, concentration is still in many respects compulsory, artificially so-maintained by means of existing legislation.

Because this existing legislation has its origin from those days when concentration was the only possible status in the town, the legislative ordinances consequently are bound to be obsolete for present-day urban conditions. It is true that, during the course of time, many more or less progressive amendments have been added to the old enactments in order to meet new demands. These amendments, at best, might offer new possibilities of planning, but they still breathe the spirit of concentration and, because of this, they are unable to support a logical progress of organic decentralization. In the long run, things cannot be managed along such a mode of emergency amendment. A thorough-going revision of the present civic legislation, therefore, must be undertaken, the sooner the better, so that the new—even in its spirit—will be a reflection of the new era of open, flexible, and organic planning. Surely, things have been ripe for a long time for such a revision.

This statement does not mean that nothing can be done in urban reconditioning along the lines of organic decentralization before the old legislation has been revised. On the contrary, every community of consequence must start without delay with its research work in order to learn how its planning problems should be directed. Such research work must not be restricted by any legislative command whatsoever; rather, this research work itself must be the authoritative adviser that conducts the process of relegislation. And from the results of this research work the new ordinances must emerge. The larger the number of communities which become engaged in this research work of planning, the clearer will the fundamental thoughts of re-legislation be discerned, and the stronger will be the united front demanding adequate changes.

In this understanding of legislation must relegislation proceed. That is, legislation should not be understood as restriction of rights, but as an enabling instrument in the development toward proper rights by means of proper planning. This must be the fundamental endeavor of civic legislation, just as it is the fundamental endeavor of organic decentralization.

However, it is not the ambitious aim of this analysis to wipe out obsolete legislative stipulations and to tell how the new legislation should be constituted. Its aim is to investigate matters as mere generalities, and those conclusions arrived at must be understood as open-minded suggestions such as might bring enlightenment into the subject. In fact, our analysis on this subject will be rather concise, for the legislative recommendations that we are going to present are only few. Yet they are of decisive importance in the case of organic decentralization.

In our preceding analysis of town-building problems in general and of organic decentralization in particular, we can discern certain fundamental thoughts according to which the new legislation should be established. In the following we will mention those points which, in our opinion, must constitute the basic directives for this relegislation process. We will mention them in such an order as they logically enter into the course of our reasoning.

First: Almost the opening remark in our introduction was to the effect that town-building is not the concern of towns and cities only, but of the whole country. This was found to be true because of the fact that orderly town-building furthers healthy physical life and cultural endeavors of the people at large, whereas disorderly town-building causes vice, crime, and mental delinquency of all kinds, which are contagious and spread themselves throughout the entire nation. Matters being so, it must be the legislative authorities' concern to enact such laws as will make it obligatory for town-communities to have their planning problems brought to such order that these communities are and remain healthy places in which to live, physically and spiritually.

As for this statement that "planning problems be brought to such an order that the communities are and remain healthy places in which to live," we have in our analysis arrived at the conviction that this kind of result in the growing and confused communities can be achieved by means of organic decentralization only. Consequently, it must be the duty of the legislative authorities to enact laws of obligatory planning such as can make organic decentralization possible.

Second: Decentralization, in itself, already means that additional land-areas are needed for an organic distribution of urban activities during the progress of decentralization. To make this organic distribution possible, presupposes that the legislative authorities must find a general formula according to which all those land-areas needed for organic decentralization can be brought under the jurisdiction of the central authorities of planning.

Third: Where additional land-areas are needed for the city's expansion, there speculation is soon alert. If speculation is given full freedom to manipulate, this will bring harm to the city's land-price-normalization, which later in the process of organic decentralization is one of its principal economic aims. Therefore, in order to prevent detrimental economic insecurity, the legislative authorities must undertake such measures as could bring land-price matters under the city's control.

Fourth: In cases where the city is unable to purchase certain land-areas, notwithstanding that these are necessary for the community's organic evolution, there is needed an adequate law of condemnation. It is obvious that the law of condemnation as it has been conceived under the rules of rigid concentration is not sufficient for decentralization purposes. It must, therefore, be the legislative authorities' concern to bring the law of condemnation up to the level of the demands of organic decentralization.

Fifth: Transference of property rights is an essential part of the processes of organic decentralization. In itself this transference, it was said, is nothing particularly new, for it is much the same as the commonly practiced trading of old things for new ones, where the new is a gain to the new owner, and the old useful to the trader. It is so, of course, in those cases where trading is a matter of mutual free will. But as soon as such trading must be compulsorily imposed as a necessary action of the city, there is needed an enabling law for such transference. This law is so much the more necessary because of the fact that transference of property-rights to a considerable degree means a corresponding transference of people from one location in the city to another. This latter point might prove to be the main stumbling-block for the legislative authorities, because such a compulsory shifting of people's habitats might easily be regarded as intrusion into private rights and against civil liberties.

Sixth: Organic decentralization calls for planning of protective belts of green land. This is to a great extent a matter of land purchase, of control of land price, and of land condemnation, and could therefore be covered by those legislative measures already mentioned. But this does not, as yet, cover the legalization of these lands for their protective purposes. In order to achieve such a result, these protective areas must be legally protected themselves, and this for a long time to come.

These are the six points where relegislation is needed to make organic decentralization workable. Once these points are intelligently settled, civic problems will have arrived at a plane where the dawn of a new era can be expected.

However, there is still a seventh point to be mentioned

—one of general nature. It concerns control of building design. In the introduction it was stated that "the city can be healthy—physically, spiritually and culturally—only when it is developed into a product of man's art in accordance with the basic principles of man's architecture." It must be the city's duty and privilege so to govern that its architectural formation is safeguarded in accordance with the above, and for this reason legislation must authorize the city accordingly.

Now, to make a short recapitulation, we have:
> first; obligatory planning:
> second; broadened jurisdiction:
> third; control of land price:
> fourth; broadened law of condemnation:
> fifth; legislation on transference:
> sixth; legislation on protective areas: and
> seventh; control of building design.

We will now investigate separately these seven points.

1. Obligatory Planning:

Obligatory planning is nothing strange, for it is just as logical a requirement as to make bookkeeping obligatory in business life. It is true enough that any town-community of consequence has its street-map; and yet, a sterile street-map is just as useless to the town-community as are all the books for bookkeeping if debits and credits are not recorded there. First, when those books record the status and development of business, and moreover, when these records show increasing gains and decreasing debts—bookkeeping mirrors good and healthy business. Similarly, first, when planning records the status and development of the town community, and moreover, when these records show that order is increasing and decay decreasing—planning mirrors healthy management.

Therefore, when we speak about obligatory planning to

make the community a healthy place in which to live, we do not mean the usual planning procedure of making mere maps. We do mean that legislation should so act that any town-community must place its planning affairs into hands that can make the town-community a physical, economic, and cultural success. This is not to impose upon the town-community something that it cannot afford. On the contrary, any town-community, if sincere in its efforts, cannot afford to be without this kind of planning standard, for that is the only real remedy which can bring physical and economic stabilization, so essential in any urban case.

It is, of course, obvious in any circumstance that obligatory planning must be made a continuous and dynamic process so as to prevent stagnation and obsolescence. Accordingly, the planning board concerned must be a permanent institution, and—as was indicated in connection with modern problems—this planning board must be independent of political and governmental shiftings, it must have the faculty of study and restudy, it must have the authority for planning and re-planning; so that, however conditions may change, the planning board is authorized to meet the changed conditions by corresponding action. In this work, the chance of any interfering influences from speculators, politicians, or any underground workers whatsoever, must be made remote by means of legislative authorization.

Furthermore, obligatory planning must not be understood to mean that through this the privilege and freedom of individual communities to ordain their own home affairs would be obstructed. Generally speaking, any legislation, however minutely dealing with people's activities, must not be so enacted as to limit the privilege and freedom of individuals, individual families, and individual associations in the development of their own interests and characteristics. On the contrary, these interests and characteristics must be encouraged by legislation, and protected by the same authority—provided of course that these activities are in accord with the good of the country at large. Similarly, the enactment of obligatory planning must not so happen that through this the interests and characteristics of the individual communities could not be freely developed by the communities themselves. The development of the individual communities in a spirit of "home rule" must be the life interest and the pride of these communities. This development, therefore, must grow from within. And obligatory planning must be so constituted that the development of the individual communities is encouraged to grow from within.

2. Broadened Jurisdiction.

Particularly in growing cities, the broadening of the areas of jurisdiction is essential. This broadening must happen to such an extent that an organic system of co-operation in the decentralized community can be achieved. What might be understood from the word "jurisdiction," insofar as the specific authority given to the central body of planning is concerned, is of secondary importance. After all, the authoritative stipulations are and must be more or less of local nature and therefore cannot be delineated by a general statement.

In order to illuminate the matter, we may take parallels from other walks of life where the situation is analogous. Consider, for example, the case of a university. A university is a complex of various departments which individually must have the freedom to operate in their respective fields in order to advance both science and education. Yet the whole organism of the institution has been schemed and must be developed and conducted by a central authority having the university at large under its jurisdiction. This is a logical procedure and hardly stands in need of further comment. In fact, how could any organization—whether educational, scientific, industrial or commercial—if developed into a number of ramifications, operate successfully without unified leadership and organized co-operation?

According to the above thought of leadership and co-operation must the city of decentralization be brought into organic order, and for this purpose the matter of broadened jurisdiction is essential. In many instances this fact has been accepted, and efforts have been made to change civic legislation accordingly. But, insofar as we are informed, the matter has as yet nowhere been brought into such a state as to be fully adequate to the demands of organic decentralization.

3. Control of Land Price.

Communal control of land price was discussed in the chapter on Revaluation. It was mentioned that, as a basic thought of appraisal, rural land areas around the expanding cities must be regarded as the raw-material which is to be refined into urban lands. We used analogies from other walks of life in order to make it clear what raw-material means, and according to which viewpoints price levels should be fixed. It is obvious that economic life in general would be obstructed to a considerable degree, if there did not exist a logical balance between the price-level of raw-material and the sales-value of merchandise. In this respect, generally speaking, legislation has no reason for intervening—with the exception of exceptional times such as, for instance, the present time of unrest and transition. In the field of town-building, the situation is different and often abnormal. Due to many facts, historical and psychological, land is not regarded as raw-material and appraised accordingly, but is rather held as an article of speculation. Such an attitude, we have learned, is not from yesterday, but has deep roots in the past. And because ingrown habits are difficult to overcome—particularly ingrown habits where one's speculative chances have to yield for the benefit of better living conditions for others—it is to be expected that the fight for land-price normalization will be hard and long-lasting. In view of the fact, however, that speculation has caused and still causes much of those urban disturbances which bring about deterioration and social delinquencies, it must be the legislative authorities' concern to constitute necessary adjustments in this respect. As to these necessary adjustments, it was maintained during our previous discussions, and we repeat it now, that the only sensible basis for land appraisal—once speculation has been distanced—is that "land-value" must be understood in the sense of "land-use-value," and that the present use must be the deciding factor. The city must be legally authorized to act accordingly.

4. Broadened Law of Condemnation.

The significant point with the law of condemnation is its sanctioning of the thought that common rights are superior to private rights. According to this, the law has functioned with varying grades of authority, through which certain planning improvements have been made possible. On the whole, such improvements have been local and, therefore—when the cities are facing improvements of as general and comprehensive a nature as are those of organic decentralization—the existing law of condemnation, even at best, is far from satisfactory and must be considerably broadened. Such a broadening, however, is likely to raise opposition based on that ethical thought which already far in the past has established the sanctity of private ownership. And, as this thought is one of the corner-stones of our civilization, it must be respected as a principle of ethical order. On the other hand, as said, the law of condemnation already at its present stage has accepted the superiority of common rights as an equal principle of ethical order. Once this has been accepted in certain circumstances and to a certain degree, may we then ask, "At what point is the ethical limit of the law of condemnation to be fixed?" The logical answer is, it seems, that the same ethical point of view which originally established the principle of condemnation as it stands at present, must be able to carry the same principle, within ethical limits, to the point of efficiency insofar as the good of the whole city and the welfare of its population are concerned.

5. Legislation on Transference.

The ethical backbone of the transference of property-rights from one property to another is, and must be, that the new property is at least equivalent to the old. This holds perfectly good in our case; for, when the matter of transference was discussed in connection with revaluation, it was clearly stressed that organic decentralization endeavors in each individual case—whether the case has to do with individual properties or groups of properties—to transfer property-rights from decayed and unprotected areas to new or rehabilitated ones in which protective measures have been established. In other words, any step undertaken by organic decentralization is to offer better values in the transference process. This is the fundamental idea of organic decentralization. And as long as things are conducted according to this fundamental idea, legislation should not have any scruples about joining the progressive movement of organic decentralization. Surely, **the fundamental maxim of organic decentralization, which is "improvement and protection of properties," and the fundamental maxim of legislation, which is "protection of people and their properties,"** go hand in hand.

However, as was mentioned, transference of property-rights means to a considerable degree a simultaneous transference of people from one location of the city to another. This point, it was said, might prove to be the main stumbling-block for the legislative authorities, because such a compulsory shifting of people's habitats might easily be regarded as intrusion into human rights and against civil liberties. Such a thought, we know, has often been expressed, particularly when the question has arisen of relocating a great number of people because of some town-planning alteration.

Now, if this kind of compulsory changing of habitat

really is intrusion into one's rights and liberties, then almost nothing could be done for civic improvement. It must be borne in mind that almost every civic improvement compels a number of people to change their living places in one way or another. In other words, the above kind of understanding of rights and liberties, if accepted, would cut almost to nothing those "rights and liberties" which could establish adequate living conditions for the bulk of the population in the growing cities. It is, therefore, a matter of common sense this kind of understanding is rather lack of understanding of the real meaning of those rights and liberties. For the sake of decentralization it is to be hoped that the legislative authorities will not exhibit such lack of understanding.

6. Legislation on Protective Areas.

Organic decentralization strives to dissolve the existing civic compactness into a system of individual townships surrounded by protective belts of green land. Consequently, the movement is not built on firm foundation unless these green lands really are protective for times to come. An essential point in organic decentralization, therefore, is that the said free lands of protection must be protected themselves by the authority of law. This means that, once a certain area has been designated to serve a protective purpose and has been legalized accordingly, no other authority then—not even in the future—should have the right to put this area to serve purposes such as are likely to minimize the area's protective efficiency.

In previous times, such legislative measures as now in question were not necessary. The olden towns were surrounded by free lands, by cultivated fields, vegetable gardens and the like; but due to the fact that there prevailed a relative standstill in the growth of these towns, protection was a self-evident result already because of this fact. When the relative standstill was first changed into intense growth, the time stood sadly in need of legislative measures of protection. Notwithstanding this need, however, such measures were entirely neglected, and because of this negligence, the growing cities are now increasingly threatened by expanding decay and slums—and there seems to be no protection.

Organic decentralization—when far-sightedly put into action—will bring about this protection by its methods of organic distribution of the existing compactness. On the other hand, organic decentralization itself must be protected by legislative measures in such a manner as has been described. And **because the purpose of these legislative measures is a "general property security" in town communities— which is in full agreement with the spirit of legislation—one has every reason to expect a favorable co-operation from the legislative authorities.**

7. Control of Building Design.

The necessity for control of building-design does not derive particularly from organic decentralization. It is of general concern. The building of towns, whether decentralized or concentrated, is basically a problem of architectural order, and must therefore be conducted in accordance with such principles as can result in satisfactory form relationship. As long as such a state of things cannot be achieved intuitively from within, corresponding legislative measures must be imposed from without.

The matter of intuitive sensing, and the lack of this sensing, have been earlier discussed rather thoroughly. There is no need, therefore, to repeat these cases now. It is sufficient, in this connection, to state the deplorable fact that, generally speaking, architectural design in our days has very much shown signs of non-intuitive insensitiveness insofar as expressiveness of form and coherence of forms are concerned. This means that such measures must be undertaken as could safeguard adequate design qualities in the city. This is nothing new, however, for the necessity of protective measures in the above respect has been recognized almost everywhere, and steps have been taken accordingly. But, due to the fact that these steps have been taken along two different directions of thought, it is of weight to confront these two directions in order to discover their respective weaknesses and virtues.

First we have the granting of licenses for architectural practice where the license is some sort of a trade-certificate and where architecture is considered primarily from the point of view of a building-trade, with adequate construction and workmanship so as to take good care of people's havings and savings. This kind of license system, from the point of view of a building trade—and of a business practice perhaps —might be essential or might not be—we harbor no opinion. But from the points of view of good building-design and good correlation of buildings into order and unity, this kind of license system is of little value, if of any. Any good and conscientious workman in the sacred vineyard of architecture is and remains good and conscientious whether he has been licensed or not; whereas, those who because of lack of ability and concern are likely to bring about architectural mischief, when licensed, are actually turned loose to make of this mischief an uncontrolled danger to the city's architectural formation under the wings of this very licensing law itself. Indeed, a routine examination of one hour or two in order to obtain a license cannot metamorphose skill and character of mind. Obviously then, if this kind of a license system is the sole means of preventing architectural disorder, it is one rather to harm than to help. It is to harm, because it conveys the thought that things have been satisfactorily solved and, consequently, those solutions of design control that are more effective have become overlooked.

The idea of effective control of building design has arrived from the conviction that adequate form-coherence is impossible to achieve unless every building-design is controlled as to its fitness to site and environment. Of course, such a control should be, a priori, the leading desire of every architect's own ambition, but inasmuch as this is not always the case, a comprehensive control method is indispensable. For such a comprehensive control method there is needed a controlling board which will pass adequate building designs, and refuse to pass those which are not adequate. This controlling board, **by the mere fact of its existence,** would be apt to create among the designing architects respect for formunity, forcing them to take this very fact into account during the design work. Naturally, much of the success or failure of this kind of controlling method would depend on the qualifications of the controlling boards themselves. As for our case of organic decentralization, this matter has already been taken care of—theoretically at least—for, when speaking about obligatory planning we stated that "legislation should so act that any town-community must place its planning affairs into such hands as can make the community a physical, economical, and cultural success." **This means, in other words, that the controlling board must consist of minds imbued with those principles that are fundamental in the building of towns.**

Of course, at this point we discern a murmur of scepticism, for always when one speaks about the indispensable qualifications of such a controlling board as described, the sceptic is ready to interfere with his negative argument—always the same. "This kind of controlling board is impossible to have, "says he," for politics and intrigues always creep in, and the result is apt to be the reverse of what is wanted." If this be granted, well, what's the use of trying anything worth while, then, for surely politicians and intriguers lurk behind almost every bush.

Such a mode of general control of building design as described above might seem to many a rather drastic procedure. This impression, we are told, might be so much the stronger when the "drastic" procedure takes place in such circumstances as are considered imperialistic or otherwise conservative. Such an impression, however, is based on misinformation; for the design control in question has always sprung from a sincere concern in town-building matters, and not from systems of government. In order to make this point clear, we might mention an example which is thoroughly illustrative, we think—and which the writer of this knows best. It is the design control situation in as remote a place as Helsinki, the capital of Finland.

Besides the usual control of building-code requirements and construction standards, the law in Helsinki requires that not only must any building design be legally authorized for execution, but even any exterior design change of existing buildings within the city proper—such as, for example, the changing of doorways into windows or vice versa, when facing public street or plaza—must undergo the same controlling process. This kind of "rigid" control system may be considered a violation of rights, liberties, and other such ideas; but if considered so, there is an evident misconception about words and ideas. It must be borne in mind that Finland is and has been one of the most liberal countries in the world, and, although this said mode of design control has been in force already for more than a century, there never has existed a sentiment that individual rights have been violated. On the contrary, this mode of design control has been and is regarded as just as natural a thing as to have police officers posted at street corners to see that order prevails on the streets.

Any police department has the right and duty to see that order prevails on the streets. Shouldn't then any town-building department have the right and duty to see that there prevails along the same streets **architectural order** as well? Certainly they must have this right and duty. To make this right and duty legally authoritative, is the last of our seven recommendations for the legislative authorities to consider.

The above list of legislative measures does not cover the whole field of enactments that are necessary for making organic decentralization possible. It is only an outline of those essentials on the basis of which all the other legislative measures must be studied and decided. Again as to these, there is no reason now for going deeper into the subject, for there are innumerable ways of settling matters within the framework of our seven recommendations.

Another problem, essential indeed, is to have these seven recommendations officially sanctioned. In order to achieve this, much open-mindedness must be demanded from those having the matter in their hands, many preconceived ideas must be abandoned, and progressive viewpoints must take their place. We are, of course, aware of the fact that the progress of relegislation in the manner above outlined, is likely to be hindered by the opposition of many traditional viewpoints, not only of constitutional nature, but also so deeply grown into the general opinion as to make necessary amendments difficult, if not impossible. On the other hand, we are also aware of the fact that the present transition time is accomplishing a miracle in the opening of eyes and minds to see and understand things from other angles than heretofore during the period of conservative petrification of ideas and opinions. Surely, things which were impossible yesterday, seem plausible today—and tomorrow they will be the most natural matter. In our case, those things involved are already a priori the most natural matter, as we have tried to explain, point by point. With this in view, one's attitude must not be too pessimistic. On the contrary, **when one is facing problems that are vital for the welfare of the whole nation, one must adjust his will accordingly and decidedly in an optimistic direction. For, where a strong will is present, there is hope for success.** Someday, therefore, we might have an adequate civic legislation.

This might happen, or might not. If it does not happen, and the attitude of the legislative authorities is not favorable toward our case, it is not—as we have learned—because of technical, economic, or ethical reasons. **It is because of lack of good will.** In other words, civic relegislation, whether it will be actualized or not, is in the last analysis entirely a matter of mind.

9. URBAN POPULATION

WHETHER or not there is going to be an adequate civic legislation, depends on the attitude of mind of the legislative authorities. So we have just learned. This attitude of mind, however, is likely to be, to a great extent at least, a reflection of a corresponding attitude of mind of the urban population. For, if there is a general and urgent demand for legislative changes on the part of the urban population, no doubt legislative authorities are likely to act accordingly, influenced as they must be by this general and urgent demand. On the other hand, a widespread indolence in civic matters on the part of the urban population is apt to foster legislative indolence in a corresponding degree. This is true not only in legislative cases, but generally as well. Obviously then the attitude of mind of the populations of towns and cities is an important factor on which the solution of town-building problems largely hinges. It is therefore important to investigate the relationship between urban population at large and town-building problems in general. This we will do in the following discussion.

To consider the attitude of the urban population in connection with town-building problems, is just as natural a thing as to consider the characteristics of a family when designing a home for that family. For, after all, the characteristics of the family must be reflected in the design of the home, if the design pretends to be honest and expressive. Analogically, urban population is that community-family whose characteristics must be transposed into corresponding characteristics of the town's physical order of steel and glass and brick and stone. This kind of relationship between town-population and town-formation was made evident in the mediaeval case. In fact, such a relationship can be found in any circumstance, no matter whether this finding is encouraging or discouraging. Surely, any town and city is a reliable script in which to read about public alertness and indifference.

When speaking about public alertness and indifference in town-building matters, we would have at present a rather dark story to tell—if we were satisfied with things as they appear on the surface and should tell our story accordingly. But we are not satisfied with mere surface appearance. We know that no matter if the water surface lies calm like a mirror, it can be easily stirred up into much movement and bubbling of life. Similarly, it may be true that sleepy indolence prevails about towns and cities because town-building matters have been mere prosaic proceedings and there has been nothing to be excited about. But as soon as some extraordinary and convincing actions have been undertaken, there might be excitement, approval, and perhaps positive interest. From this point of view of a **"change from slumbering potentialities into alert co-operation," we must examine the relationship between the urban population and those town-improvements which result in better living.**

First of all, it must be admitted freely and frankly that, generally speaking, public interest in town-building matters is none of encouragement. The cause of this may be manifold. There may be a rather general satisfaction with present-day town conditions, because people have become used to living in disorderly circumstances and do not therefore demand better. There may be a lack of that imaginative sensitiveness necessary to have a true picture of better living conditions as compared with conditions as they are now in slums and decayed areas. Even if the imaginative sensitiveness were alive enough to picture better conditions, there may be a lack of conviction that those promised and planned improvements really can make good out of bad. Moreover, there may be a lack of actual examples of improvement such as might bring enlightenment to the public, and, through this, conviction and active interest. And finally, there may be the simple reason that those who have had civic improvements in their hands are not those who should have had civic improvements in their hands. All these mentioned causes lead in the same direction, where the answer to the question of public indifference in town-building matters is the logically perfect answer that something must be done by the planners for the enlightenment of the population, before the population is going to do something for the planners. **Surely, no piece of art can be admired before this piece of art has been created, or at least outlined.**

Therefore, now that we are going to investigate the human aspect in town-building, we are going to do it from three different angles, as suggested above. First, we are going to analyze the general attitude of town-population toward town-building matters—and we will find that here prevails a dull indifference. Second, we are going to investigate educational possibilities of raising public understanding and interest—and we will find that in the cities of today there is a scarcity of constructive form-atmosphere wherewith to offer enlightenment and inspiration. And third, we are going to study the situation among town-designers—and we will find, even here, a discouraging scarcity.

A.   INDIFFERENCE OF POPULATION

Fully to understand the general attitude toward town-building—and toward cultural interests in general for that matter—it must first of all be borne in mind that the present generations are not direct descendants from those days when great things were achieved in the province of creative art and when living in the atmosphere of art creation kept art appreciation alive, but that there exists a broad gap of materialistic platitude between those days and the present time. What happened during this broad gap of materialistic platitude, particularly insofar as creation and appreciation of art is concerned, has been rather lengthily described in the chapter "Decline of the City." There it was told that a gradual decline of art creation and its appreciation took place, and that this was true to such an extent that "the general taste degenerated ultimately to a parvenue taste of a kind which the world never has seen before, and which—we are sure, and certainly hope—never can be surpassed." The lowest ebb of this decline was reached during the closing years of the nineteenth century—during the "Gay Nineties"—and, as was stated in the said chapter, "we are just now living in the midst of the consequences of this lowest ebb."

The chief cause of this taste degeneration, we found, was the growing industrial mass-production of all kind of vulgarly ornate stuff, which, to a large extent, consisted of the most tasteless nonsense that the human brain and the machine were able to bring about. Alas, this mass-production still goes on. On the other hand, it must be noted with great satisfaction that our age witnesses a considerable improvement in this respect; for at last the fundamental fact has been recognized that industrial production should not imitate those design characteristics which belong to hand made processes, but must have design characteristics of its own. As this new understanding of "industrial design" is growing rapidly and spreads its influence over ever new fields of life, in town and country, it can be predicted with a fair amount of conviction that our age is heading toward a general taste improvement, at least insofar as future living accommodations and physical form-atmosphere are concerned. But in other areas of life we are not so sure in this respect. Consider, for example, all that pernicious stuff which is daily served to people through radio, screen, and all kinds of books and magazines, and you cannot be optimistic with regard to a general cultural deepening. That often expressed presumption that people want this sort of service and that they must get what they want, is just as intelligent reasoning as to say that towns and cities are made ugly and discordant because people want ugliness and discord about themselves. Nay, such procedure is mere inexcusable mongering, which totally disregards the fact that its actions bring young and old out of tune with those issues that are essential in the progress of culture. **For, as harmony and concord in any stringed-instrument depend first of all on a proper tuning of its strings, so are there certain strings in the human soul which must be properly tuned into accord with cultural issues, if man's aim is to be worth his case under the sun.** A reverse procedure, such as above mentioned, fosters reverse results, and should not be allowed. It is not, however, the idea of this analysis to preach social reforms—for our interest is the physical city —but, for the sake of a sound development of this physical city, it is to be hoped that those concerned with social problems would take matters into their hands by using their judgement and influence in the discrimination between good and bad spiritual nourishment.

But, however all these and many other influences may affect people's disposition toward cultural problems, and whenever things are going to turn to the better—if, after all, they are going to turn to the better—the fact remains that at the present state of things there prevails on the part of the urban population a rather general indifference in town-building matters.

Always, when we have been confronted with the blank wall of indifference in town-building matters, we have referred to public enlightenment, believing that this might do the trick. Generally speaking, it does, we are sure. But, even here, the oft-discussed tendency to speculation seems to be a difficult obstacle to overcome.

When this matter of speculation was previously the subject of our scrutiny, it was found that there are two kinds of speculation in the city—constructive and destructive. The former kind of speculation, it was said, is apt to support, promote, and encourage urban development in the spirit of the city's primary purpose, which is to provide suitable living and working conditions for the population. Consequently, in the case of this kind of a speculative attitude, enlightenment is not particularly pressing.

In the case of destructive speculation, on the other hand, enlightenment is very pressing, but perhaps less effective. For when someone has a cold, speculative mind which seeks every opportunity for material gain, his speculative ego conducts his actions, notwithstanding the fact that he understands the benefits of a properly organized community where the well-being of the population is the prime issue. After all, the value of his pocket-book is superior to the well-being of others, and in such a case enlightenment to him is much the same as spectacles are for the blind. This is true, particularly, when the speculator suspects that his own material interests might become unfavorably involved, if he should undertake this or that for the common good. The result of such a state of mind might easily be that the community's economic order cannot be maintained, especially in those cases where much opportunity for speculation can be scented and many are eager to dominate the situation by methodical tactics.

With a predicament like this in view, one must learn to esteem the blessings of proper organization such as organic decentralization can offer. For, thanks to a proper organization of this kind, noxious speculation can be eliminated to a considerable degree. As we know, organic decentralization aims at systematized order of land-use throughout the whole urban organism, from which very order land-values derive, and according to which these values can be easily and precisely estimated. As organic decentralization, furthermore, aims at the stabilization of these thus-normalized values for times to come, there is scarcely anything else left for the speculator than to maintain these normal values by safe-guarding orderly conditions about them. Once the speculator has been made conscious of the fact that civic order pays, this very civic order will become the object of his speculation, and we will be on the safe side, at least insofar as speculation is concerned.

However, there are still many obstacles to overcome before we are positively on the safe side, for much of the attitude of the population seems still to be indifferent to civic improvement. This is the situation particularly in the case of organic decentralization because the movement is slow and requires a long period of time before any result of consequence begins to appear.

Those engaged in planning matters often place the blame for indifference on the citizens, maintaining that lack of interest on the part of the citizens prevails because comprehensive civic improvements cannot be carried out quickly and with immediate results. Because such improvements require a considerable period of time, and because people, generally speaking, are slow to become interested in slow developments which seem of little direct personal benefit, they have no great interest in comprehensive planning.

This reasoning might be partly true, particularly in the city's case. But when it comes to "generally speaking," we decline to accept such reasoning. Many examples could be mentioned to contradict this.

It takes a great number of years to grow a tree from a tiny plant, yet people in general take a keen interest in this kind of planting, the real results of which they oftentimes might not see with their living eyes. There is considerable interest on the part of older citizens in the development of educational institutions for the benefit of the young, although the time has past when they themselves can derive direct and personal avail from that interest. Then, last but not least, every mother and father knows that only after several decades can the new-born baby assume its share of social responsibility, and yet from the day of the child's birth they are eager to commence his or her education toward such an end. For sure, the education of the child is an instinctively natural matter, and therefore the parents do not hesitate to plan this education toward a future good and useful citizenship.

When such an instinctively natural long-term endeavor is evident in those households into which children are born—and these households constitute the bulk of the population—there should be no lack of interest in such measures as could grant these very children—the citizens of tomorrow—healthy environments in which to live in their days of manhood and womanhood.

These examples render it evident that people in general are not as egocentric as the aforementioned statement about people's indifference would have us believe, and that this assumption of egoism—conscious or subconscious—is not the chief cause of indifference in civic development. No, there must be deeper reasons for this indifference. The planter of the tiny specimen which is going to grow to a lofty tree would not be interested in its planting, unless he were sure that the tiny specimen really will grow to a lofty tree. The person interested in educational matters for growing generations would lose his interest if he believed that the schools were not beneficiary to the growing generations. The parents would be indifferent in their children's long-range development unless they were convinced that this were the only positive means for the breeding of good citizenship. In other words, **we are not confronted with the question of interest versus indifference, but with the question of belief versus disbelief.**

Similarly, civic improvement is not confronted so much with lack of interest, but rather with disbelief that the proposed improvement really could be carried out and be worth one's while. If the citizens, the educators, and the parents as well were convinced that efforts in civic improvement really would result in such improvement as could bring about healthy environment for their offspring, surely their indifference in town-building matters would turn into an efficient interest.

Indeed, steps must be taken to transform disbelief into certainty. And inasmuch as town-planning has been encouraging disbelief by its manifestly inadequate measures, it is time for town-design to show the citizens a positive direction by a positive action. By positive action we mean qualified town-building that will be proper educational material.

B. SCARCITY OF EDUCATIONAL MATERIAL

Meanwhile, we might try to find proper educational material in earlier town-building work. It goes without saying that this material must be of a quality good enough to convey to people the spirit of genuine town-building **at its best.** And because we have previously accentuated the genuineness of the mediaeval case, we will now examine the relationship between town-population and town-building work during the days of the Middle Ages.

The struggle for daily livelihood from which the mediaeval town emerged has long since ceased to exist. Trade and shipping, selling and buying, gains and losses, all that in those days was most important—to many perhaps the only important things—have gone forever. All that once filled the buildings with men and merchandise, that caused the streets to ring with clamor and clatter, is gone and forgotten. Only the forms of the town which once housed the past life, still remain.

What do these forms say of the aims of the population?

Well, when we earlier examined the mediaeval town as to its pattern, its characteristics, and its architectural atmosphere, we came to the conclusion that there must have existed an intimate although perhaps subconscious understanding between the people of the town and those who built the town. We still house this opinion, for one must bear in mind that the town was an indigenous expression of life itself, belonging to everyone in the town, and creating a genuine atmosphere for everyone in which to live, and in which to breathe this very atmosphere of one's own life. Therefore, the forms of the town, in spirit, belonged to everyone in the town—**just as much as the forms of folk-art belong to the people who created it, and who live with it, and who feel that life is not fully worth living without it.**

Certainly, the forms of the mediaeval towns, at best, disclose how those times approached their town-building problems. If the mediaeval town was a creation of art, as it generally was, one then feels **that the town people had the wisdom and ambition to put the design work into the hands of the best of men in the field of art.** The town, with its layout, its buildings, its objects of displayed art, and whatever features there may have been—be it only the simplest sign at the street-corner—grew from the spirit of the time as an organic pattern in an organically conceived ensemble—creative, expressive, and symbolizing the **best** of its time. The architects of those days were the designers of these towns; and these architects—those "idealists" and "artists"—were kept in high esteem.

Nothing now remains of the mediaeval business, politics, and fighting. But the form-values of the mediaeval town still remain vivid reminders of the work of the "idealists" and "artists." **Their work is now valued as the tools of culture, inspiring new tools for new cultures—centuries after the mediaeval life died and was forgotten.**

If life pulsed in the days of the Gothic, it is surely pulsing today. But the pulse beat is now faster and stronger. Just as they were then, people are now concerned about trade and shipping, about selling and buying, about gains and losses.

Even more men and merchandise fill the buildings, and even more the streets are crammed with rush and roaring. But gone are the days when sensitivity to form was vital in creation, and vital in correlating forms into organic pattern. Since then, the bane of imitation has swept over lands and towns, leaving heavy cumulations of ornamental nonsense.

The present fast tempo of the people of today will some day cease to exist and give way to new tempos of new peoples. But the heavy cumulations of ornamental nonsense remain— and we wonder what the future will think of the cultural endeavors of their forefathers.

Our chief concern, however, should not be the thoughts and feelings of the peoples of the future, but rather we must ask ourselves, "How does this nonsensical stuff of ornamentation affect ourselves and our children?" We must bear in mind that we and our children alike are doomed to dwell in the atmosphere of this nonsensical stuff and suck its influence day-after-day and year-after-year. **Surely this influence cannot be culturally healthy—if art after all exercises influence upon the human mind.**

Such is the situation to a large extent in present day cities. It was different in those mediaeval days.

The mediaeval town-dwellers—and the town-builders alike—wherever they turned their eyes in the town, they were met by a form-language genuinely their own. Such was the case already from their earliest childhood, and therefore they learned intuitively to sense the rhythm and order of this form-language just as intimately as they learned to understand the rhythm and sound of their own tongue when mother spoke to them. In the city of today, we find entirely another state of things. In the city of today, the city dwellers—and the civic designers alike—wherever they turn their eyes, they are met by an alien form-language—sterile and lacking meaning. Already from their earliest childhood, and together with their mother milk, they have imbibed the bane of sterility and meaningless form. This early infection, and the lifelong

existence in the atmosphere of this sterility and meaningless-
ness, has blindfolded their eyes and stupefied their minds so
as to make them unable to discriminate between right and
wrong in the realm of form. Surely, such an environment
could not nourish a congenial relationship between man and
form, and the consequences were bound to appear. One
should not be surprised, therefore, that there is lack of interest in town-building matters on the part of the population.
Nor should one be surprised that there is lack of understanding of proper town-design on the planner's side. The conclusion then is that, **because of the scarcity of adequate educational material, the cities of today, generally speaking, have
not been able to offer enlightenment in town-building.**

C.   SCARCITY OF TOWN-DESIGNERS

Enlightenment in town-building has two sides: first, to understand the necessity of orderly town-communities; and second,
to understand how to accomplish these orderly town-communities. The former concerns the population at large; the latter is the problem of the design profession. Yet both must be
in a reciprocal contact, where the population must be educated to appreciate the advantages of orderly town-communities, and where the design profession must bring about
orderly town-communities to strengthen this appreciation.

No doubt everyone realizes, without much talking and
gesticulating, all the advantages of an orderly-built city and
understands that such an achievement brings contentment
and glory. But as long as this order still remains a far-away
dreamland being only lectured and harangued about, it does
not convince—the less does it inspire to concrete action.
When first the lecturing and haranguing is translated into the
convincing language of brick and stone, when organic coherence has been at least to some extent materialized in actual
execution, and when the blessing consequences of these ac-

tions begin to appear, then understanding might first become conviction, and conviction on its part might turn into a positive support of action. This is the right sequence. And the only one.

Accordingly, we will now turn our attention from the population of cities to the professional designers of these cities—primarily to the architects—to demand from them positive action. However, when we speak about architects in this connection, we do not mean such architects as know by heart all the dimensions and characteristics of Greek columns and Gothic buttresses, and who can produce, correctly and elegantly, imitations in any style—classical, mediaeval, or otherwise. After all, this kind of stylistic production is no positive action in the art of town-building, for it infringes the principle of expression which demands genuine form-expression, and by no means imitation. Moreover, when we speak about architects in connection with town-building, we do not mean architects for the sake of a mere title. We mean those who have an architectural mind such as can conceive architecture as an organic and social art-form. We mean those who can conceive architecture in a broad scope, beginning from the organism of a single room and ending with the comprehensive labyrinth of a large city. And we mean those who have the vision to conceive the gradual development of an extensive lay-out, organically, rhythmically, and expressively —no matter whether they are architects by profession or not.

"Well," some might say, "this all sounds good and fine, but such minds are scarce and cannot be so easily had." We grant this, and the reason for it is utterly logical. It is because of the long-lasted stylistic domination in architecture during which there was no demand for architects in town-building otherwise than in a decorative sense. The practical town-planner took care of the rest. **But as soon as there will be a demand for architects to design cities in organic sense, there will appear even those town-designers whose minds fit into our above description.** In fact, there is such a demand already today. Tomorrow there will be much more. And the needed town-designers will soon be at hand.

But the architect is not needed for town-design purposes only; he is needed for the designing of every building in town and city. Therefore, it really is the architect's problem to enlighten the public by means of his work. He has in his hands the real means and methods to make his ideas understood and appreciated—provided of course that he uses these in a constructive spirit.

Mere words do not help. It must happen by positive work. The architect may spread his ideas through speech and propaganda: but he is able to convince only by showing through his work that he is sincere about his speech and propaganda. The architect may speak against the ugly building: but as long as he designs the ugly building himself, his speech will lose its effect. The architect may advocate a proper correlation of buildings: but as long as he forgets the proper correlation himself, nobody will listen to his advocation. The architect may preach about the beauty of the city: but as long as he brings discord to the city himself, his words will be cast to the four winds. The architect certainly must perform his words through his work. Otherwise the saying will hold true, even in the architect's case—that those trying to improve others, frequently forget to improve themselves.

On the other hand, it is easy to claim that the architect must do so or so in a perfect manner. In practice, matters do not run as smoothly as they do in theory, for the architect's work is frequently met by all kind of obstacles, often impossible to surmount. In this respect we do not consider such difficulties as derive from client's demands, often of speculative nature and in disagreement with the organic demands of the environment. For, in those cases, the architect must have enough of a moral backbone to refuse co-operation along such lines; otherwise he is personally to be blamed for his non-ethical behavior. We are now considering such difficulties where the architect is—often helplessly—lost in the whirl of the existing lack of order, in which he, notwithstanding his sincere efforts, cannot accomplish desired results.

Now, the claim is that the architect must design his building in coherence with the neighborhood. But supposing that this neighborhood already has been bungled into such a mess that a decent solution is impossible. Such conditions do exist sometimes—we are told. Well, what is the poor architect going to do in such circumstances? Yet let it even be that the neighborhood really is favorable, offering the best opportunities of a decent solution. Even then, there might be dangers lurking somewhere—for how can the architect be sure of what the next neighbor's designer is going to do?

Really, we are facing the discouraging fact that, unless the whole architectural profession, solidly, supports those principles that must guide the art of town-building, the present disorderly situation in the cities is bound to remain. An individual architect might be able to govern the building, but the city's development is in the hands of the architects corporately and, consequently, it is up to the architects to maintain form-order in the cities with their combined influence. **The more generally they understand their duty in this respect by exhibiting their understanding and aims through concrete action, the stronger grows the public confidence in the architectural profession** and, reciprocally, **the stronger this confidence is, the more influence will the architects gain in the art of building towns.**

When the architects join themselves corporately in this spirit, they will become the leaders of the city's development toward better order. With the support of the strengthened confidence they then are able to control even the activities of those undesirable parasites who profess their pernicious activities under the shadows of architecture, spreading poor taste in the city and about the country. In this manner—provided the architects really do take their profession sincerely and act according to this sincerity—**it could and it might hap-**

pen that the profession of architecture would become the supreme educator of the people: toward better physical living, toward better spiritual living, toward better standards of taste, and toward deeper cultural aims.

All this might seem to express too optimistic a point of view. For—says the sceptic—one never can reach such a state of things.

We are far from being optimistic. On the contrary, we have just now made the frank and discouraging statement that nothing can be done, unless the architects corporately, join in the action. This statement, behold, can be taken just as easily for a desperate cry of distress, as it can for a jubilant halloo of optimism. This does not, however, mean that we should be sitting with our legs on the table in a "nothing doing" spirit. No, we are fighters! We must fight with all available means! To that end we must find where and how to fight.

And so, we arrive at the point.

Seriousness among architects—architects considered as a body—shows that those principles that have been responsible in the creation of a good body of architects, are correct; and that the fundamentals of architectural education are true. In other words, the soil from which true architecture and town-design must get their nourishment, is the architectural school. Hence we turn our attention from the architect to the architectural school, demanding there an investigation whether things stand right or wrong from the standpoint of town-design; **and if wrong, we advise a decisive turn to the right.**

EPILOGUE:

TOWN-DESIGN

EPILOGUE: TOWN-DESIGN

HAVING brought our investigations to a conclusion, it now remains to undertake, on the basis of these investigations, a closer study of the inner nature of town-design. In this study we have to consider two different phases: first, we have to consider town-design in general; and second, we have to consider town-design as applied to existing conditions. The former phase applies to both Part One and Part Two of our investigations; the latter phase applies particularly to Part Two where contemporary civic problems have been analyzed and studied to find their logical solution, organic decentralization.

Considering town-design in general, the subject has already been introductorily dealt with, and in this connection a few fundamental principles were mentioned. These principles were found to be of universal bearing, as revealed during our excursion into the realm of organic life in nature. The most influential of these principles is the universal principle of organic order: the "mother" principle including all the others; in fact, the fundamental principle of architecture in all creation.

Town-design, also, is fundamentally an architectural problem. Here, architecture of man is manifested in its most comprehensive form under the guidance of the said principle of organic order. According to this principle, men of olden times erected their towns by instinctively sensing the existence of the principle and of its commanding impetus. The truth of this came clearly into light during our examination of the organic growth of the towns in the past. Particularly the mediaeval town was found, during our preliminary analysis, to be an enlightening example in this respect.

As regards the second point—the application of town-design to existing conditions—it must be borne in mind that the solution of this problem, particularly that of organic decentralization, is not as yet greatly experienced. Consequently, our preceding analysis regarding this phase of town-design was not a statement of generally accepted facts, but an endeavor toward positive suggestions such as were found indispensible for satisfactory civic organization and fully in accord with fundamental principles. From these positive suggestions we are now going to draw our conclusions as to how town-design should be adjusted to meet the demands of today, particularly the demands of organic decentralization. Indeed, this is just as important a problem to be properly solved, as are the civic problems themselves.

A. TOWN-DESIGN IN GENERAL

The distinction between town-design and town-planning—as understood throughout our analysis—was stated in the introduction. It was said that although they both embrace the same field of action they are based on different principles and entirely on different spirits. Town-planning has gradually become surrounded by an aureola of insipidity due to the degrading effect of superficial practice. In our analysis, therefore, at least as far as the three-dimensional conception of the physical city is concerned, the word "planning" has been avoided in all cases where misunderstanding could have arisen. It is a word which implies a vapid dryness, just the same as does a stereotyped street map laid out on paper as a mere utilitarian pattern of intercommunication. Therefore, to avoid misunderstanding, the word "design" was preferred. It implies that civic organization must spring from wells deeper than the utilitarian purpose only.

To establish a clear distinction between "planning" and "design" was our first concern. This distinction was particularly essential in our case, for during the course of our investigations we have had much reason for confronting these two modes of procedure—planning versus design. This could scarcely have been possible unless we had been able, in each individual case, to define which is mere superficial planning and which is appropriate design.

The above does not mean, however, that we are eager to consider the said distinction generally important. On the contrary, outside of our case we are willing to accept the appellation "planning" for common use—in spite of the fact that it has been much misused.

It is evident that in these two cases—planning and design —the primary characteristics are bound to be different, and often of opposite nature. The same, then, must hold true even concerning those working along these two different lines —the "planner" and the "designer," respectively. Being ourselves concerned particularly with design, it is logical from our point of view to ask two questions: first, we must ask which are the primary characteristics of town-design; and second, we must ask which are the primary qualifications of the town-designer? To seek an answer to these questions is not mere curiosity. It is essential. Indeed, **it is essential to understand the quality of the work to be done, to find the person qualified to do this work, and then to entrust him with its execution.**

However, before we set out to attempt an answer to these questions, we must first, so to speak, paint a background against which to reflect these questions and their answers. In other words, we must first examine the characteristics of town-planning, and the qualifications of the town-planner.

1. Misconception about Town-Planning:

In the course of our discussions we have occasionally touched the weak strings of town-planning. On everyone of these occasions the point has been this: unless town-planning is animated with the ideals of town-design and professed in its spirit of dynamic vigilance, it is deceptive. It is deceptive because it assumes a virtue which it does not possess, the virtue of bringing order into the city, which order it is unable to accomplish. This is similar to selling merchandise under a false label.

True enough, there are many phases of town-planning: there are such phases as are of a positive value; there are such phases as perhaps are harmless to the city; and there are such phases as can be put down as merely negative. These negative phases are merely deceptive assumptions which only play at planning. Yet, since these deceptive assumptions are rather frequent, it is necessary to bring such instances to light.

First:

Frequently it happens that planning officials, having gathered a great quantity of material pertaining to the city's past, are seemingly exhausted because of this work, and end by doing nothing more about it with the exception perhaps of effecting a few improvements of local nature. Yet the immense material collected has created the widespread impression among the town people that the city's planning affairs are running satisfactorily. However strange such a misconception may seem, we are by no means relating an exceptional situation. On the contrary, this kind of camouflaged planning happens with a frequence almost amounting to regularity—even in large cities—and many prominent examples could be cited to prove this. Obviously, whether intentionally or not, this is deception, for it lulls the population into a false content that planning matters are in safe hands.

The mere gathering of statistical material is not planning, it is only the first step on which planning must be based. Not to use this material for constructive planning, but only to pigeonhole it, is much the same as to fill one's store-rooms with food, and food, and more food, and then to starve while the food lies there putrefying.

Second:

Oftentimes the town-planner has produced elaborate street maps, zoning regulations, pamphlets, pretty renderings of this and that, and such like. Once all this has been put on paper, properly and nicely, everyone seems to be satisfied, and that's the end of that story.

Now, what does all this mean? Simply that the city has now a "definite plan," which in view of constantly changing conditions was bound to be obsolete even before it was off the drafting board. Now that very plan hangs there in the City Hall perhaps—with much water-color, coats-of-arms, cartouches, and decorative lettering. One needs but little of imagination to forecast the city's fate under this kind of a procedure. Actual facts support this forecast, for there are plenty of telling examples from which to learn of the perilous character of this kind of planning. It is true, of course, that there might be a few more or less effective improvements made according to this plan—improvements which, at best, might not hinder a future organic solution. But as a counterbalance to these possibilities of improvement, a great many thoughtless commitments have been made of a sort to make other and more essential improvements impossible. These thoughtless commitments—being generalized under the general heading of "zoning," and made by the lump without any organic considerations whatsoever—will constitute the worst obstacles to any future organization. It is all too easy, and indeed short-sightedly irresponsible, to grant land-use rights in such a generalized manner. For, remember this: once done, such blunders are hard and costly to rectify later on. Those parts of the city which have become saddled with this kind of legalized blunder are doomed to suffer for years to come. It so happens that such regions as stand most in need of intelligent treatment are the ones usually ruined in this manner.

But, what about the rest of the city? Well, usually the rest of the city is left to its own devices, and ultimately—as frequently happens—the whole incident of planning falls into dim oblivion. All—except for the irreparable blunders. The making of sterile maps like these described, is definitely harmful. It creates an illusion of planning, yet it is nothing more than routine map-making. It is the best of sleeping medicines, for it puts the officials and the population alike into a contented slumber of confidence in the proper care of their city. Through this slumber of confidence, real planning is postponed. Or entirely forgotten.

Third:

The practical planner is concerned particularly with traffic problems. Accordingly, he builds roads and arteries wherever he finds a likely opportunity, regardless of the detrimental effects of his action upon the neighborhood. Anyone having the slightest idea of proper town-building knows how detrimental such actions can be, and we learned of their effects during our analysis of the stabilization problems. Of course, it often happens that the planner is seemingly compelled to take such steps of traffic improvement, simply because previous thoughtless planning has brought the situation to such an impasse that the matter of improvement is an action of virtual emergency. This might serve as some sort of an excuse. But no excuse is satisfactory. First, because the planner is heaping disorder upon previous disorder, and is therefore to be all-the-more blamed for not having undertaken an all-sided study of the situation before he took the harmful steps. Second, because the excuse is too transparent to be even vaguely convincing. Nay, oftentimes the mentioned procedure of traffic improvement has become a phlegmatic routine where the planner has only one concern in his mind; and that is, traffic. Accordingly, the more this traffic grows, the more this phlegmatic routine accelerates toward conditions which make planning seem a comic paradox.

Curiously enough, this kind of approach to planning problems is commonly believed to be planning. Still more curious is the fact that this procedure originates with planning boards and civic officials. Surely, this is not planning. It is only a tardy effort to correct something which should have been planned in the beginning—and which now is corrected by utterly dangerous methods.

Fourth:

Let us not forget that much revered "civic embellishment." In general, this means some stylistic cosmetics for certain parts of the city. In most instances it is only an echo of what we have previously characterized as the Formal Continuance, a movement which, as can be remembered, was an inheritance from the Renaissance days, but which in the course of time has declined into a meaningless decorative shadow of its former grandiose self. This kind of treatment is to dress the city in borrowed theatrical effects. Civic embellishment in such terms has little in common with the indigenous development of the city toward architectural order —toward beauty if you will—by means that really express the characteristics of the place and the people. Civic embellishment in such terms has little in common with the vital problems of living and working in the city.

Even small towns are often ambitious to decorate their "civic center" by means of imported and imitative forms. And, about this center, business districts and slums cluster in dirty heterogeneity. This is not planning. Nor is it design. It is like hanging false diamonds around a dirty neck.

Enough now of illustrations about planning misconceptions. The reason for these misconceptions is the superficial attitude toward the city and toward its vital problems. Although those concerned are often regarded as reputed authorities in planning matters, their superficial efforts have failed to bring necessary order into the city. Their work, we repeat, is deceptive.

We wish not to be misunderstood. We are not discussing things by the lump; on the contrary, we discriminate between good and bad. In the field of planning there has been done a great deal of work with good and constructive points. There have been and are sincere endeavors, not only to produce plans, but even steadily to see that these plans are followed, and that they are kept dynamically up-to-date with changing conditions. We admit this willingly. Yet we are not always in sympathy with these endeavors. We cannot sympathize with them when the aim is too concentrated on practical matters-of-fact, and when a mere two-dimensional plan indicates a lay-out of streets and a stereotyped land-use only. Such a mode of planning, we think, cannot accomplish a satisfactory three-dimensional form-relation. It rather makes impossible the spiritual expression of the community's cultural aims. More than many examples could be mentioned where the practical planning in two dimensions has been most excellent from a technical point of view. Yet, look at the tangled third dimension.

Isn't this logical? How could one expect to have a good building done by conceiving only a two-dimensional plan of rooms, and letting the rest grow by chance? Surely, the building must be three-dimensionally conceived from the very start.

Three-dimensionally, likewise, must town-design be conceived from the very start, even if planning work proceeds two-dimensionally on paper. This two-dimensional procedure on paper of three-dimensional matters in space, calls for spatial imagination; and, thanks to this spatial imagination, "city-plans" are made to represent "civic design"—just as much as building plans are made to represent building design. So it must be, for two-dimensional "planning," as such, is inadequate unless it is an integral part of "design" which has been three-dimensionally conceived.

Also, here we have two tendencies to compare: the half-measure of two-dimensional planning which considers primarily practical technicalities; and the complete three-dimensional design, which considers, besides practical technicalities, even spiritual problems so as to achieve a satisfactory architectural atmosphere in the city. The former is the matter-of-fact understanding of planning which calls for the practical mind. The latter is the architectural understanding of design, which calls for the creative mind.

With the above reasoning we have painted the background against which to reflect the characteristics of town-design and the qualifications of the town-designer. On this background we discern town-planning as an inadequate half-measure, and the town-planner as a distinctly practical mind.

2. The Practical Moment:

Now, what is "practical"? Is is something lasting; or temporary? That is, are the practical steps of today necessarily practical in the future? Not necessarily, particularly when viewing things in the light of constantly changing conditions like those of the dynamic city. Consequently, in planning matters, the practical point is not a static thing, and might just as easily in the course of time turn to the reverse. So it really does, as experience shows; and this fact tells precisely why the purely practical mind is ill-suited to the job of planning in terms of organic evolution toward the future. Rather, the possessor of such a mind is excellently fitted as an executive of expedient matters of today.

This is not only obvious, but self-explanatory as well.

Usually the practical mind inclines toward consideration of problems from the standpoint of existing needs. But as soon as he is confronted with the task of a comprehensive organization of manifold and constantly changing problems which are to be actualized over a long period of time—as are the problems of a growing city—he is out of his depth. He amasses practicalities upon practicalities with little feeling of organic and logical interrelations. Impractical confusion is the likely result of such a procedure. This is not a mere theory, for it holds good in every instance where an unimaginative mind deals with problems calling for vision. And it can be proved by thousands of examples.

Let's try one of these:

We all agree to the fact that the railroad engineer is a practical man, for he can make his tracks and track systems work perfectly; and he deserves much credit for this. But insofar as foresight in long-term planning is concerned, he is not, generally speaking, equally fortunate. His interest is concentrated about the problems of today mainly, and accordingly he makes his lay-outs. When more tracks are needed he adds the necessary number of them. When traffic thereby increases, he keeps adding and adding, often expanding his schemes over areas intended for other purposes. The results of this mode of piecemeal adding bespeaks the real nature of the railroad engineer's practicality. However practical his step-by-step procedure may be considered from the point of view of railroad operation, it is far from practical from the point of view of general town-planning. Alas, look at the cities with broad areas made unpleasant and inadequate for any but the lowest use, simply because track-lines and track-systems have been planked down without any other consideration than to secure the greatest possible practical functioning of the passing moment. If these cases were merely sporadic, there would be no reason for being concerned. But as they constitute a danger of disorder where almost every large city is the victim, they must be recorded as significant signs of lack of planning. Yet the most significant point in all this is the fact that each move contributing to this disorder emanated from a mind which was predominantly practical.

The cited example shows, as any similar example would show, that purely practical actions in civic development doom the city to eventual impracticality and consequent disorder, unless the process is guided by a mind broad enough to visualize the problem in organic integrity. With reference to this, let us take the liberty—with Sir Raymond Unwin's own consent—to quote some remarks made by him during a discussion about just these matters. Said Sir Raymond: "It is not advisable for the town-designer to load his brain and memory with detailed knowledge of all kinds of practical technicalities; this only would prevent him from seeing the major problems in the light of organic unity. Dealing with the sewer system, for example, the only thing he needs to know is that water runs downhill, the rest he can give the technical specialist to figure out. But so much the more must he know how to design cities—of which design the sewer system is a derivative. To be able to design cities, however, he must have vision."

Taking now the essence of the aforesaid, we discover there two points of fundamental significance.

Firstly, Sir Raymond's remarks indicate that too much delving into the practical details of town-building matters prevents one from seeing the essentials in their integrity— prevents one from seeing the forest because of the trees. Now, the builder, for example, deals in terms of nails, screws, brick, stone, steel, lumber, and thousands of such minor items and their price levels. Constantly occupying his mind with practical details of material and construction, he has but little chance, generally speaking, to develop his mind along the other side of the building problem—the spiritual. It is always so: overemphasis of any aspect makes toward unbalance in the development of the whole. Accordingly, the builder but rarely visualizes the structure as an organic integrity where proportions, rhythm, and expressiveness of form, culturally speaking, play a decisive role. The builder may have been dealing with "building trade" for decades, but **only in cases where he has genuinely inclined toward complete consideration of the building has he been dealing with the "art of building."**

Isn't this a significant situation in the art of building? Yet, how much more significant is a similar situation in the art of town-building? For here, and just here, the senses must be alert to discern the meaning of proportion, rhythm, and expressiveness of form—long before the concrete results take shape.

Secondly, Sir Raymond's reasoning informs us that two kinds of faculties are needed in the building of cities: the designing faculty, and the practical executive faculty. Sir Raymond, with his admittedly limited understanding of sewer construction, would soon be lost without the technical man's knowledge. And the technical man could not know where to put his conduits without Sir Raymond's advice. Consequently, they must both be correctly related to the work.

This all is based on logical selection, and therefore it has bearing in any walk of life.

The author must know how to write books, the printer must know how to print these books—and not vice versa. The sculptor must know how to give form to his sculptures, the bronze caster must know how to convey these forms into bronze—and not vice versa. The relationship in architecture is just the same. The architect must first of all know how to design a building, the builder's part being the practical and technical execution of the building—and not vice versa. Yet both are necessary in this co-operation. The architect were but a bloodless ghost with all his schemed masses and proportions, unless the practical builder stands by him infusing into these schemes material reality. Similarly—to return to our main subject—the town-designer were but a hopeless dreamer of dream-towns, unless he has the practical man's technical help.

Consequently, where the practical man has here so far been rather coldly criticized, this criticism was meant only in cases where he oversteps the boundaries of his real province of action. Properly connected with the action he must be treated with all the respect he deserves. With this in mind, the town-designer must wholeheartedly shake the hand of his indispensable associate, with whom he must collaborate.

3. Design and Execution:

The real reason for misconception about town-planning, as we see, is the fact that the men entrusted with the twofold process—design and execution—have not been rightly related to the work. The practical mind, the excellent executive, set himself up as the designer. The creative mind, on the other hand, has deserted his duties.

Now, who is to be blamed for this backward situation? Certainly not the practical mind, for he has done what he could do within his limitations. The blame lies with the creative mind, for he is at fault because he did not stick to his duties in the designing of towns. He deserted the field of town-design and preferred the easier job of imitative ornamental prodigality. As we have learned in our previous examination, and in everyday bitter experience, this retrogression reached its lowest depths in the dark decades of the nineteenth century when the designer—the architect, to be exact—mistook the art of imitative decoration as his civic duty, and, leaving the task of town-design to the surveyor, he strewed all the ornaments of past times about the town.

The surveyor was a practical man. He cut hills and valleys with straight streets, the straighter the better. He laid out his gridiron schemes with correct corners and exact lot-lines. Indeed, he did a precise job; and people thought he was "planning." The engineer, on his part, constructed pavements, bridges, and harbors; the gardener planted parks, squares, and boulevards; and people thought they, too, were "planning."

So things went on. So they are still going on.

For the sake of our towns and cities, and in the name of logic, it is high time to reverse things. The practical mind must be relieved from tasks that are beyond him, and the creative mind must return to his duties. The former with his experience along the practical line makes a perfect fit as the executive in the building of cities; and the creative mind

—the architect—well, what does he know **now** about the designing of cities? Is he any more creative in this respect? Hasn't he already forgotten his most precious art-form, an art-form which in bygone days was so full of vitality?

For our encouragement we can say that the creative mind is already beginning to take up his duties. When we previously discussed the Informal Revival—the movement originated by Camillo Sitte—we learned about attempts to revive town-design in terms of architectural order. We learned that these attempts developed into a vital movement spreading over many countries. The movement has since then continued to grow stronger roots by spreading its influence all the more. It has attracted architects in many places, and much experience has been gained along its principles. Although the architects in other places are still too sleepy to see what is going on and why it must go on, there is no doubt that the revival of town-design in architectural terms is constantly gaining broader fields, and growing in strength.

True enough, the movement has been slow. It was bound to be so, and we all know why. The movement has been slow due to the fact that the architects but seldom have gotten an adequate education in town-design. The architectural schools, generally speaking, are still to a large degree lingering over the notion of architecture as an art-form whose predominant interest is in the style of the individual building. Style has thus been raised to the governing position in architectural design, and this seems to hold true no matter whether it be the imitation of historical styles, or that puzzling problem of the so called "modern" ones.

4.   The Educational Moment:

Let's now turn our attention to educational methods in order to find out where and how corrections must be undertaken. Surely, by so doing we will get to the roots of our troubles.

We need not dig deep into the prevailing methods of architectural education to find evidence that style imitation has long been fostered and encouraged. All the past styles have been brought to the classrooms, and from the classrooms to architectural practice. These styles have been tried, revamped, remodeled, and "put together" in every conceivable and inconceivable manner, till—as was said somewhere in the foregoing—the last drop of expressiveness has been squeezed out of these once so expressive styles.

In this eclectic spirit, architectural education has been conducted generation after generation.

However, the eyes are now opened, and a new era in architectural education is dawning. After centuries of dependence on Greek forms, the old truth has gradually become understood even by our time, that the Greek form was only for the Greeks, and not for us or any other civilization. Accordingly, our age begins to realize the fact that **the highest standard that architecture ever can reach is "true expression of the best of existing life."** From this realization will the new era even in architectural education emerge, and gradually the curricula of the schools will be changed to suit the changed situation.

Meanwhile, there is a growing consciousness among educational circles that even town-design belongs to the realm of architecture and, consequently, instruction in town-design is introduced into the schools. Only a slight glance at current changes in the curricula shows clearly that things are on the right track. Yet, not entirely so, for particularly confusing is that mistaken divorce of two interrelated subjects, "Architecture" and "Town-Design." Architecture—that is, the building as such—is considered the nucleus of architectural education, and its study is required of every student. The study of town-design—so far, however, mostly city-planning —is made optional. Surely, such a discrimination is unworthy in a valid education, for the primary aim of architectural education must be to convey to every student under-

standing of the fundamentals of his art-form at large, including even town-design, regardless of the student's inclination in
his future practice—be it designing of cities, housing communities, buildings, or just chairs, tables and the like. **The
doctor in his practice may specialize in the treatment of ears,
eyes, or something else, but most certainly he must be familiar
with the whole human body and all the manifold functions
of its organism.** Otherwise he is a charlatan.

The understanding of principles covering the whole
realm of architecture must be the leading thought in the educational methods, and accordingly must every student be
guided in his studies. Therefore the problem of education
toward town-design is not solved by merely including "town-
planning" in the curricula as a subject per se and only for a
few to study. It must be solved by infusing the spirit of
"town-design" into every problem, and for everyone. It must
be understood that any building in city, town, or country
must be an integral part of its environment, physical and
spiritual as well, and as such it must be studied and designed.
It must be understood that the designing of self-sufficient
buildings—buildings independent of their surroundings—
should happen neither in architectural practice, nor in the
classrooms of architectural schools. In this spirit must education be understood, and **in concert with this spirit must the
thought be conveyed to every student**—and this is most essential—**that town-design is not just something for a few, but
something that no architect should dare to slight.**

Let's explain our point in the following manner:
To design a school building, for example, without having in mind a specific site, region, and social background, is
to design a school building whose forms are predestined to
become sterile and inexpressive. There is no such a thing as
a school building in itself—or any other building in itself for
that matter. Any school building has its social background
and educational purpose which must come into expression

in the forms of the building itself. Any school building has its precise location and environment whence its formation must emerge and into which it must be correlated physically and spiritually as well. Any school building has its outside traffic requirements of manifold natures, leading to and from the building, serving various kinds of people and purposes, and adequate for various traffic means. For this reason, the problem is not the mere designing of the school building as such, but even the essential problem of site selection from a great many different points of view, practical and spiritual, so as to be able to design the whole into a comprehensive organism. **When the design problem is approached in this manner, the spirit of town-building is automatically infused into the design and, conversely, the school building becomes an integral part of its environment and of the plan-pattern of that community concerned.**

What is true concerning the design of the school building, is true concerning any architectural design in general, whether it be the design of an individual building, a group of buildings, or the whole community. We live in a collective society and its environment. From this we develop as individuals, and into this we must adjust ourselves as members of that society. Analogically must architectural design develop from the society of architectural forms and from their environment—the city, the town, and the village. Any building, individually, must express this society of architectural forms and their environment. And any building must be adjusted—physically and spiritually—into this society of forms and their environment—into the city, the town, the village.

It must be borne in mind that architecture in its inmost spirit is a social art-form insofar as social organization, social trends, and social fluctuations must come into expression in the community's architectural formation. In other words: we live in and amidst architecture, and this architecture must express how we live.

In this spirit must architectural design be understood and, consequently, in this spirit must architectural education convey understanding of architecture to every student. **The student must be so educated that he understands this social side of his art-form, and learns to express by means of architectural language how we live today in our cities, towns, villages, and in the country—and not how someone lived hundreds or thousands of years ago elsewhere.** The student must be so educated that the designing of a self-sufficient building without actual site, spiritual environment, and social background is to him an absurdity which can result only in unreal and spiritless "composition." Once he has imbibed this, he has within him the principles of building-design and town-design—and design in general as well. If the principles of building-design and town-design—and design in general as well—do not flow in the blood of his veins, **his education has failed to equip him as a reliable workman in the architectural development of his community. And the school which failed in this respect is, on its part, responsible for the architectural disorder in our cities, towns, villages, and in the country.**

No doubt, with the above we have probed to the deepest roots of town-design. We have arrived at those sources where minds must be formed to carry out the important task of bringing physical order into our towns and cities. How this order is going to be accomplished, depends largely on the quality of these sources.

B. APPLIED TOWN-DESIGN

All town-design, whether regarded from the standpoint of education or practical town-building, must be based on those fundamental principles which we have endeavored to formulate. The mode of applying this town-design under **actual conditions,** on the other hand, depends much on the characteristics of these conditions. The mediaeval approach in designing of towns, consequently, was bound to be different from what our approach must be today. Two characteristics made town-design in the Middle Ages a natural process: first, the slow growth of the town; and second, the unfailing form-sensitiveness of the mediaeval era. Contrasting with these, the present trend to speedy growth, and the comparatively low form-sensitiveness in our days, make designing of cities a process where incessant caution, control, and research is essential. The mediaeval procedure in town-design was like a slow plodding along a narrow path, slow enough to watch stones and steps close by. Today the motion is so fast that the attention must be glued far ahead along the line of that motion. Mediaeval town-design was much the same as to design a horse-drawn carriage where nothing particularly novel was to be expected and design could proceed easily in continuation of past experiences. To direct the course of cities' growth today is much the same as to outline the automobile's subsequent development toward something yet unknown, where ever-changing new demands and ever-occurring new inventions require the designer's attention, and where his eyes must be turned toward the future in constant research.

We drew the comparison between the Middle Ages and our time in order to stress the difference in the approach to town-design as it appears in the extreme. In actual fact we need not go so far into the past as the mediaeval time to discern enough difference in this respect to be fully conclusive. The gap between the old and the new modes of town-design has grown broader step-by-step. It has grown broader, particularly, parallel with the step-by-step development of traffic means. The railroad was the first step; the electric streetcar was the second step; and now the introduction of the motor vehicle makes the gap between old and new modes of town-design virtually so broad as to make an entirely new basis necessary.

In spite of this fact, there seems still to be, in many quarters, much dependance on the old mode of town-planning, and the teaching of this old mode goes on in that stereotyped routine manner. This fact has caused grave disturbances—and, because of this, the city's dynamic growth has strayed. It is true enough that much investigation goes on, but mostly this goes on in terms of concentration. And whenever one manages to work one's mind toward a bold decentralization, one falters and hesitates. It seems as if one were afraid to cross that River Rubicon.

As Caesar crossed the Rubicon, he discerned beyond its banks his real problems to come. So must the town-designer of today stretch far beyond the boundaries of present possibilities, for his real work lies way out there in the future. **The character of his action, therefore, is that of the "pioneer," and the means and methods of his work are those of "research."**

When we speak about research, however, we do not mean mere digging through statistical material pertaining to the city's past. This kind of research does not belong to the realm of actual design, it merely is that material from which actual design must grow. We mean now—as we have meant always when this matter has been considered—"planning research" dealing solely with the city's organization henceforth. Such work aims to outline the city's future by producing a number of tentative schemes, through which to survey all the various possibilities of future organization and growth. This is the kind of progressive planning research from which future realities can and must emerge.

Any industrial organization of consequence has, besides its production plant, a research institution which is responsible for keeping the quality of production up-to-date with new discoveries and new needs. This research institution is the pioneer of production, and, as such, it must be in close contact with the evolution of science; it must endeavor to discover new means and new methods; and it must try to turn impossibilities into possibilities. These new possibilities, when production is ripe for their application, will from time to time be turned over to the plant. This keeps production vital. Without this, production would soon fall into constant repetition—into obsolescence.

A research institution is essential to any organization expecting continuous growth. And if there is anything that at present must be prepared for continuous growth, it is the city of today. In the city's case, therefore, research must be the pioneer of design. This kind of pioneering-planning-research must stretch the feelers of prehension far beyond existing conditions; it must find new ways and means to forward far-sighted design toward better order in the city; and it must open-mindedly discern future possibilities in present impossibilities. In this manner the new possibilities, when the city is ripe for their application, will from time to time be graduated from the research stage to the actuality of final design. By this kind of procedure, the city's physical development will keep pace with the progress of life. On the other hand, in case this kind of a research-toward-design process is ignored, the city is doomed to continue its road toward increasing compactness and disorder.

It is clear that the city must have its own research institution which must be in constant action and in which its present and future planning matters must originate. This means that the approach to urban physical organization must be a twofold procedure: "tentative planning" as a matter of research, and "actual planning" as a matter of current demand. This is, as said, the same procedure followed in any industrial organization. Moreover, just as in any industrial organization the governing minds of the two departments, research and production, must be appropriately chosen—in the research work because of scientific inclination, in the production work because of practical experience—so must the city's choice of men contribute toward adequate working organization—**in the research work of tentative planning because of**

open-minded vision, and **in actual planning because of practical adaptability to the products of vision.**

Research in science is much a matter of vision. Thanks to this vision, countless discoveries have been made, often surpassing even the boldest imagination.

Similarly, town-design must be much a matter of vision, for it must span a long bridge toward that unknown future. The designer must visualize his city as it might develop over a tentatively estimated period of time. This period of time constitutes the designer's field of action, within which his imagination must evolve the tentative lay-out, intended to show the most appropriate direction of the city's development toward the future.

In order to avoid misunderstanding in the above respect, however, it must be said in passing that we are not referring to any high-flying city conceptions like those set-termed, super-mechanized, and highly theoretical schemes titled "City of the Future," "City of Tomorrow," or otherwise. We cannot but feel that these schemes are too rigid, sterilizing by their rigidity the foundation of all future planning, for planning dreams must allow ample leeway even for the future dreamer.

Planning toward the future must run in terms of flexibility. The more flexibility the designer infuses into his planning toward the future, the greater are the opportunities for the future designer to co-ordinate design to life. This kind of a flexible procedure is most essential, for if flexibility after all is accepted as a fundamental law governing all circumstances of today's planning, there is so much the more reason for applying flexibility to schemes that span over into tomorrow's planning.

Therefore, when we speak about the city's gradual growth into a "dream scheme" such as the town-designer sees it grow within a tentatively estimated period of time, we do not mean that the city's "actual" growth is necessarily going to take exactly the same form as that dream scheme of the designer's vision. But we do mean that while the town-designer proceeds with his tentative dream scheme by taking into consideration all the potentialities concealed in his problem, he must do it in such a flexible manner that, while the city "actually" grows, this growth can be adjusted in a correspondingly flexible manner to meet the changing conditions, and yet be so directed by means of that very dream scheme as to secure continuously organic and physically healthy conditions in the city during the whole growth. In other words—metaphorically speaking—**the town-designer must stake out the course along which the urban ship can proceed without running into the concealed dangers of compactness, disorder, and decay.**

The outlining of the future dream scheme, however, is only the first step in the process of research design. The next step must be to dissect this dream scheme into a number of sub-schemes showing the city's step-by-step development during corresponding time intervals. This matter of dissection has been earlier mentioned, for when discussing the technical approach to decentralization in the chapter "Revaluation," it was said that the town-designer's problem was to make his lay-out intelligible "by working out in a tentative manner a series of sequential charts," and that by such an approach "this broadly inclusive lay-out of organic decentralization will be dissected into its particles: into rather easily discernible petty things, such as usually belong to the yearly routine of civic improvements and corresponding budgetary considerations." Furthermore, it was mentioned in this same connection, that such a dissection of the dream scheme "is just as indispensable a part of the general conception as is the general conception itself."

Now supposing, for example, that according to a certain city's potentialities of growth it would take fifty years, tentatively estimating—the number of years being a mere symbol —to arrive approximately at that status of civic development as set by the dream scheme. It would then be, relatively

see
page
384

speaking, a simple matter to calculate the city's approximate plan-pattern after forty years of development. Again, from this forty years plan-pattern it would be equally simple to calculate the city's approximate plan-pattern after thirty years of development. And so on. In accordance with this kind of a calculus, the research design would go on step-by-step backward in time, approaching gradually—and perhaps with reduced time-intervals—the existing realities. Likewise, this step-by-step, backward in time, research design must happen in a flexible manner as a matter of suggestive thought. The more such a scheming approaches existing conditions, the more real the suggestive thought must be. And when the scheming coincides with the very present time, this backward-in-time-scheming will be changed into town-design of actual conditions. From then on, the design work will run forward in time, parallel and in close co-operation with actual town-building.

The imaginative research design, as we see, moves in a direction opposite to that taken by actual design. **We have also a two-fold movement with opposite orientation: first, we have town-design from the future toward the present; and second, we have town-design from the present toward the future. Both are indispensable. That is: although the course has been staked out for the ship to go, the ship still needs a captain to steer along the staked course.**

Indeed, in this spirit of continuous and two-fold vigilance—continuous and two-fold "bookkeeping," if you please —must town-design, as applied to present and future conditions, go on.

Finally:

There is one more thing to be said about this matter of town-design before we close our investigations:

When we look at paintings or sculptures, when we listen to music or read books, we like to know in each individual case who is the creator behind the work. Again, when we visit olden towns—classical, mediaeval, or otherwise—we say, "This is century so, or so." In other words: **in the former case we discern a certain mind behind the work; in the latter case we sense the spirit of the time.**

Consequently, when we speak about town-design, we must conceive the driving power behind this design in collective understanding. It is true, of course, that the general pattern of the basic lay-out is likely to be the work of a leading mind—and such is frequently the case. But the more this general pattern evolves and branches out into its various ramifications, the more planning results will bear the marks of collective collaboration of many aims and inclinations. Eventually, the more things become interwoven, the more the city's formation becomes the mirror of the aims and inclinations of the town people themselves. Also: "Show me your city, and I will tell you what are the cultural aims of its population."

So was the opening statement at the very beginning of our analysis. So will be, likewise, our closing statement at this very end. To this statement there is only to be added that, due to the fact that the cities of today show an increasing tendency to disorder and decay, **and as the fundamental cause of this disorder and decay is the prevailing indifference among the population, it is of prime importance that the matter be thoroughly examined and explained.**

This we have endeavored to do—on our part.

SOURCES OF ILLUSTRATIONS

DIAGRAMS

Figures 49 and 50

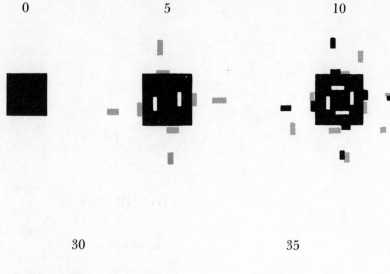

FIG. 49. DIAGRAM ON ORGANIC DECENTRALIZATION

Assumptions: The concentrated city is compactly built. Fifty percent of the city is decayed and must be rehabilitated in accordance with a preconceived decentralization pattern. This process takes fifty years—the number of years being a mere symbol—during which period of time the city's size will be doubled. This decentralization process is divided into ten five-year programs, as the above diagram indicates.

The gray spots represent those new values which are created during each of the five year periods, and which become protected for times to come.

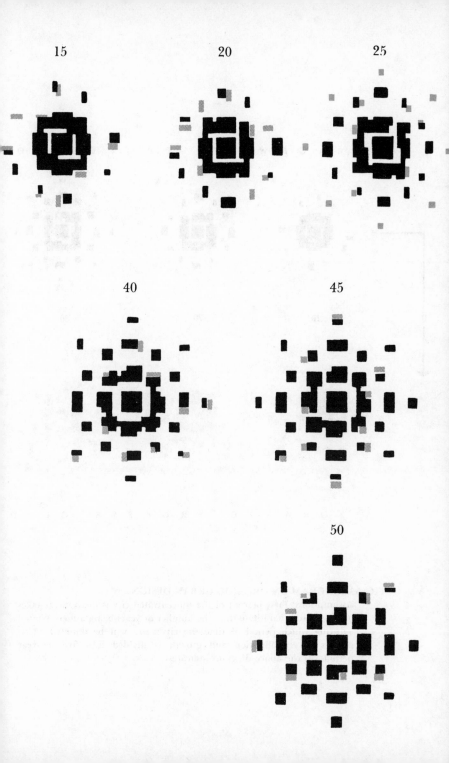

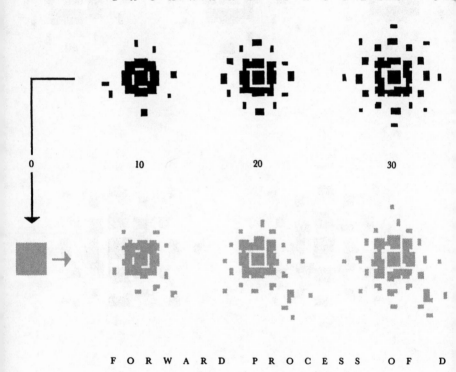

FIG. 50. DIAGRAM ON ORGANIC URBAN DESIGN

Assumptions: Fifty percent of the concentrated city is decayed. It takes fifty years to rehabilitate this—the number of years being a mere symbol —during which period of time the city's size will be doubled. This process of rehabilitation and growth is divided into five ten-year periods, as the above diagram indicates.

DESIGN RESEARCH

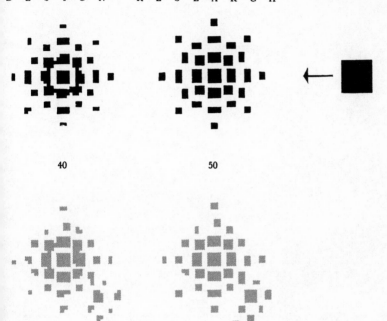

40   50

IGN READJUSTMENT

THE M.I.T. PAPERBACK SERIES